Praise for
Step into the Metaverse

"Mark has created a comprehensive introduction covering the history, the current state and a look into the future of the metaverse. This book is a fantastic dive straight down the rabbit hole whilst wearing a jet pack, and you'll come out the other side fully able to work out what it means for you, and your company or organisation."

> —**Paul Hamilton**, Ogilvy Managing Director Growth & Innovation and
> Founder of metaverse design agency vTogether

"I've been obsessed with the Metaverse since I first read Snow Crash many years ago. I've written thousands of words on the Metaverse, work in the industry, built VR experiences, and write a weekly newsletter covering the topic.... and yet I learned so much from Mark's book. There were still whole aspects of the Metaverse I hadn't considered. Even if you think you're educated on the topic, pick up the book. You'll come away from it filled with new things to research and explore, new connections you hadn't made in your mind yet."

> —**Daniel Sisson**, Writer, consultant, and XR developer

"Van Rijmenam provides an extremely thorough explanation of the many facets of the metaverse. If you're just starting to learn about the concept or you are already well-versed in some of its pieces but want to see the 10,000-foot gestalt, this book will be illuminating."

> —**Rabindra Ratan**, Associate Professor and researcher of metaverse
> technologies (i.e., avatars, online game4s, VR) since 2005

"A comprehensive and candid coverage of the opportunities and challenges posed by the metaverse and Web 3. A must read for entrepreneurs and business leaders."

> —**Avinash Kaushik**, Founder & CEO,
> Waka Metaverse Suite

"*Step into the Metaverse* is a timely book as Web3 unfolds into a third dimension that promises new ways to interact, collaborate, and engage with other individuals, products, services, entertainment and more."

—**Raghu Bala**, CEO, NetObjex

"[Mark van Rijmenam's] illuminating book on the beginnings of the metaverse is a light in the darkness for the curious and the bold."

—**Matthew Brewbaker**, CEO of VEU Inc./Enterverse

"Van Rijmenam takes us on a journey through the state of the art in the metaverse, exploring both the myriad opportunities presented by this evolution of cyberspace, as well as threats to its potential, including a lack of standardisation and regulation. This nuanced exploration of the fledgling industry is a must-read for anyone interested in the space, demonstrating The Digital Speaker's deep knowledge as one of its first inhabitants."

—**Sam Johnston**, investor and CEO at Acumino

"In *Step into the Metaverse*, Mark van Rijmenam takes a comprehensive view of the converging forces that will fuse and someday become a future paradigm for human growth, prosperity and existence. That is, unless we f* it up."

—**John Gaeta**, Creator, Inventor, Executive

"A comprehensive tour of vital contemporary metaverse discussions!"

—**Neil Trevett**, President, The Khronos Group

"Van Rijmenam provides an extensive exploration of the metaverse. He surfaces timely questions of ethics and sovereignty. At this moment, while our next digital reality is still being constructed, this discussion is critical."

—**Tiffany Xingyu Wang**, President & Co-Founder, Oasis Consortium

"Dr. Mark van Rijmenam does a masterful job sharing a promising vision of the nascent metaverse while also being pragmatic about the challenges and gaps in existing solutions."

—**Alec Lazarescu**, Founder, VerseTech Metaverse

"The next chapter of human existence is being formed right now, and as you 'step into the metaverse' you'll fully understand the power of the convergence of technology, consumer trends, brands and reinvention of personal self expression."

—**Justin W. Hochberg**, CEO & Founder, Virtual Brand Group

Step into the Metaverse

How the Immersive Internet Will Unlock a Trillion-Dollar Social Economy

Mark van Rijmenam

WILEY

Published by John Wiley & Sons, Inc., Hoboken, New Jersey.
Published simultaneously in Canada.

978-1-119-88757-7
978-1-119-88758-4 (ebk.)
978-1-119-88759-1 (ebk.)

Limit of Liability/Disclaimer of Warranty: The publisher and the author make no representations or warranties with respect to the accuracy or completeness of the contents of this work and specifically disclaim all warranties, including without limitation warranties of fitness for a particular purpose. No warranty may be created or extended by sales or promotional materials. The advice and strategies contained herein may not be suitable for every situation. This work is sold with the understanding that the publisher is not engaged in rendering legal, accounting, or other professional services. If professional assistance is required, the services of a competent professional person should be sought. Neither the publisher nor the author shall be liable for damages arising herefrom. The fact that an organization or Website is referred to in this work as a citation and/or a potential source of further information does not mean that the author or the publisher endorses the information the organization or Website may provide or recommendations it may make. Further, readers should be aware the internet Websites listed in this work may have changed or disappeared between when this work was written and when it is read.

For general information on our other products and services or for technical support, please contact our Customer Care Department within the United States at (800) 762-2974, outside the United States at (317) 572-3993 or fax (317) 572-4002.

Wiley also publishes its books in a variety of electronic formats. Some content that appears in print may not be available in electronic formats. For more information about Wiley products, visit our web site at www.wiley.com.

Library of Congress Control Number: 2022934259

If you believe you've found a mistake in this book, please bring it to our attention by emailing our Reader Support team at wileysupport@wiley.com with the subject line "Possible Book Errata Submission."

Cover image: © Getty Images/akinbostanci
Cover design: Wiley

To all creators and creatives
of the open metaverse

Contents

About the Author   ix

Foreword   x

Preface   xii

2032   xiv

Introduction   xxiii

Chapter 1:   The Future Is Immersive   1

From Web 1.0 to Web 3.0   1

From AR to VR to XR   8

What Can the Metaverse Become?   12

Six Characteristics of the Metaverse   17

     Interoperability   18

     Decentralization   20

     Persistency   22

     Spatiality   24

     Community-Driven   25

     Self-Sovereignty   26

     An Open Metaverse Means Freedom   30

An Endless Blue Ocean   31

Chapter 2:   Creating an Open Metaverse   35
Open vs. Closed   35
The Hybrid Web   41
An Open Economic System   44

Chapter 3:   Be Who You Want to Be   47
The Rise of the Avatars   47
Digital Fashion   55
iCommerce   62
A Cambrian Explosion of Identity   65

Chapter 4:   Be Where You Want to Be   67
Virtual Worlds   67
Gaming in the Metaverse   74
Sports in the Metaverse   77
Media and Entertainment in the Metaverse   80
Education in the Metaverse   83
Power to the Creators   86

Chapter 5:   Unbounded Creativity for Brands   89
Beyond flash   89
The Power of an Immersive Community   92
   Endless New Touchpoints   94
   Continuous and Real-Time Insights   95
   Increased Sustainability   96
   Virtual World Considerations   97
The Era of Experience Marketing   98
Creativity, Community, and Co-Creation   102

Chapter 6:   Exponential Enterprise Connectivity   107
A Changing World   107
The Future of Immersive Work   110
   The Metaverse Job Market   114
   How to Get Started   117
Digital Twins   117
The Role of Governments   125

Chapter 7:   The Creator Economy   129
A Vibrant Metaverse Economy   129
Why Tokens Matter   133

Challenges of NFTs   138
Digital Real Estate   143
Economic Mechanisms   146
From DeFi to MetaFi   150

Chapter 8:   Digitalism in the Metaverse   155
Technology Is Neutral   155
Dangers of the Metaverse   156
    The Datafication of Everything   157
    Privacy Is an Illusion   158
    Abuse, Harassment, and Illegal Content   159
    Imposter Avatars   160
    Data Security   161
    Increased Inequality   162
    Bad Bots Controlling the Web   162
    Increased Polarization   163
    Biased AI   164
    Health Issues   165
Verification, Education, and Regulation   165
    Verification   166
    Education   168
    Regulation   169
Surveillance or Empowerment   171

Chapter 9:   The Future of the Metaverse   175
BCI: The Future of Immersive Experiences   175
A Renaissance of Art, Creativity, and Innovation   178

Epilogue   183
Acknowledgments   186
References   189
Index   215

About the Author

Dr. Mark van Rijmenam is The Digital Speaker. He is a future tech strategist who thinks about how emerging technologies change organizations, society and the metaverse. Dr. Mark van Rijmenam is an international keynote speaker, 4x author and entrepreneur. He is the founder of Datafloq, and he hosts the *Between Two Bots* podcast with Dan Turchin, covering the cultural, technological, and ethical implications of artificial intelligence, technology and the metaverse. He holds a PhD in Management from the University of Technology Sydney. His research was on how organizations should deal with big data analytics, blockchain and AI.

The Digital Speaker is available for in-person keynotes as well as holographic presentations, and Van Rijmenam's avatar delivers talks in virtual reality. He is a recognized speaker by the Professional Speaker Association Australia, and he is a member of the Global Speakers Federation. He is the publisher of the '$f(x) = e^{\wedge}x$' newsletter, read by thousands of executives, on the future of work and the organization of tomorrow. The Digital Speaker has spoken in 20 countries across the globe and collectively inspired over 100,000 managers, directors, and C-level executives.

Foreword

Science-fiction stories such as *Snow Crash* or *Ready Player One* have described the metaverse as a virtual world of unlimited potential for entertainment and value extraction. In the metaverse depicted in these books, a centralized entity controls the metaverse, including all data, digital assets, and the people entering it. This is a dystopian future that by no means is impossible to happen in the real world, given that we have already built a centralized, closed, proprietary, and extractive internet. The current Web is governed by shareholder supremacy instead of user centricity, and we all have become addicted to "free" access to these platforms.

The downside of all these "free" services has been the degradation of privacy and the lack of control over our own data and identity. That is why I started Outlier Ventures in 2014, because I felt the need for a different story. It is a story where end users can regain control over their digital lives, driven by the convergence of technologies such as blockchain, crypto, artificial intelligence, and mixed reality, among others. Over the years, we have invested in dozens of companies that are building Web 3.0 technologies across all three key layers of Web 3.0 innovation: infrastructure, middleware, and applications.

Web 3.0 technology will enable a decentralized, permissionless, open digital economy centered around the user and identity and data portability. It will allow us to create a fairer, more inclusive internet. It is vital that we embrace this paradigm shift toward decentralization, especially now that we are at the dawn of the metaverse, or the next iteration of the internet.

If Web 2.0 and the social Web enabled data harvesting at a large scale, imagine what can happen in an immersive digital environment. The possibilities to collect and analyze our data will grow exponentially, enabling corporate or state surveillance at unprecedented levels. That is why we need an open metaverse, owned and controlled by users instead of a select group of tech elites.

When I first heard about *Step into the Metaverse*, I appreciated the vision of Mark van Rijmenam to write a blueprint for an open metaverse. The metaverse will unlock an entirely new economy, where the lines begin to blur between the physical and digital worlds, or our virtual lives and physical lives. Looking at the metaverse from an economic perspective raises important questions about how inclusive it is and who can participate in the digital economy and who cannot. Van Rijmenam does an excellent job discussing how we can ensure an open metaverse economy, where interoperability of digital assets, a self-sovereign identity, and cryptocurrencies play a vital role.

Web 3.0 technologies are vital for an open metaverse, and the companies we are supporting at Outlier Ventures are all contributing to this. In an open metaverse, everyone can finally contribute to and benefit from the first truly universal and permissionless economy humankind has ever known. In *Step into the Metaverse,* Mark van Rijmenam succinctly explains how we can build this immersive internet that can deliver magical digital experiences while incorporating a fully open economic system, enabling the interoperability of digital assets and changing our society from one of value extraction to one focused on value creation.

—Jamie Burke
Founder & CEO
Outlier Ventures

Preface

On October 28, 2021, the digital world stopped when Mark Zuckerberg announced that he was pivoting Facebook from a social network to the metaverse—the future of the internet. At the same time, he claimed the next iteration of internet and rebranded Facebook to Meta. Although Zuckerberg said all the right things—we need an open, interoperable* metaverse powered by the users—few believe him. In fact, there was a Forrester survey that showed 75 percent of the 700 respondents not trusting Zuckerberg with building the metaverse.[1] Research by WSJ showed that of the 1,058 US internet users interviewed, 72 percent do not trust Facebook much/at all. This matches my own simple survey on LinkedIn, where 78 percent of the 469 people indicated that they do not trust Zuckerberg with building the next iteration of the internet.[2] Time will tell how successful he will be, but if users and content creators can choose between a world owned and controlled by one person or a world owned and controlled by those creating it, I think I know the answer.

---

*Interoperability is a crucial aspect, and I will discuss it in-depth. It basically means that you can take your data and digital assets from one platform to another, something that is not possible today.

In the past months, I have gone down the rabbit hole of the metaverse. As part of my research for the book, I have spoken with almost 100 creators and creatives all involved in building the metaverse and another 133 completed a long survey about the metaverse. They are the pioneers of this new internet, and they are all building an open, decentralized, inclusive, and interoperable metaverse.

I hope you will enjoy this journey as much as I did uncovering this magical world where we are only bound by our own creativity. In this book, I will share my vision for the metaverse, what it can become, and how it will change our identity as well as how we play, socialize, shop, and work. If we manage to develop an open metaverse, the trillions of dollars generated will be shared with all creators and creatives. But beware, there are dangers lurking on the road ahead that we need to think carefully about to avoid making the same mistakes as we did when building Web 2.0 or the social internet. I realize that every chapter of this book can be an entire book by itself as there is so much happening when it comes to the metaverse, and the world is constantly changing. However, I tried to keep it brief while covering as much as possible. I will start with offering a glimpse of what the future might look like when the metaverse is here, in 2032. Enjoy!

2032

Ae, one of the latest AI virtual assistants, and Daryl, a young intelligent man from a small village in the south, stood in holographic form on the other side of Laya's large oak desk. Behind them, a virtual presentation sat floating in the air.

"Good morning, Prime Minister," Ae's neutral soothing voice announced. Laya's chief of security always had reservations about using Ae, but the software worked well, and with the founding of the M.C.P, the Ministerial Cyber Police, Laya disregarded his old-school aversion to new tech.

"Can we just get this over with? Today's the first day I'll see my family in months," Laya told them, AR glasses resting on the bridge of her nose. Ae and Daryl exchanged a knowing look and got to work.

Daryl began his spiel in his usual tone, updating the Prime Minister on three key programs, New Skills, Cultural Protection Program, and Blockchain Plus. Daryl started with *New Skills*, an initiative added onto Universal Basic Income with the idea to support and encourage redundant workers to retrain and transition into future-proof jobs. After, Daryl covered the *Cultural Protection Program*, a program created to reassure the older citizen, a group who've witnessed so much change within such a short amount of time.

Ae took over for the third. With an uncanny-valley smile, she stepped forward and changed the presentation to display the latest on Laya's education reforms, and an update on the Treasury's *Blockchain Plus* program.

They discussed the most pressing issues for another hour and, at the stroke of nine, Laya bid a "good morning" to her assistants, and with a touch of her glasses, she was alone. It was the first day in two months she'd put aside to spend with her family and she'd be damned if anything was going to keep her from it.

Laya stood up and walked over to her Communication Wall. There, she removed a sleek lightweight metal-coated headset and walked to the middle of the room where a 6×6 box had been outlined on the floor. On the far side of the box, a comfortable but sturdy-looking safety chair sat. Most VR zones had one considering how tiring VR could be. Laya stood in the middle of the outlined box, put her gear on, switched on the smart lidar system that captured her movements, and issued a command.

The screen illuminated, and suddenly she was standing in a digital twin of her office. It was almost exactly the same in every way, down to the panic button under her desk and even the pile of coats hanging in the corner. The only difference was a data screen with live economic projections and headlines floating above her desk.

Using her default avatar, Laya walked over to a digital wardrobe. The glowing doors opened automatically, spiraling away into nothingness. She cycled through a few outfits and avatar choices, before settling on a light tan suit. It had an air of casualness, ideal for family and any unannounced digital paparazzi.

With another slightly different wave, she raised a group of tabs. Swiping through a few, she stopped on People. There at the top of the list, a contact labeled "Terry XOXO" sat. Having pressed the name, Laya selected the "Travel to" option.

Laya's vision turned black for a moment, spare a small ball, roughly the size of a basketball, spinning in front of her, slowly filling with color. The moment the ball was fully colored, Laya found herself in front of an endless row of squash courts, all styled in various fashions. She still hadn't quite gotten used to how instant everything was, when only a couple of years ago lag was pretty much expected no matter where you went in the metaverse.

To her front was the back of her husband's digital twin. He was intensely watching a match of hyper-squash between two avatars. One of which looked like a salmon, the other George W. Bush. The avatars smashed a golden ball back and forth, dashing and jumping in ways only possible in the digital realm.

"Terry," Laya called, almost retracting at her own unfamiliar loving tone. She hadn't heard her own voice sound so sweet in what felt like an eternity. She moved closer toward him, her real smile projected onto her digital twin.

Terry turned, excited to see his absent wife. They hugged, virtually, their feedback sensors warming as they did.

"What happened to brunch?"

"Nothing, I was just watching some hyper-squash while I waited," Terry explained. "I'm already there."

* * *

Terry was wearing his AR glasses, enabling him to enjoy his wife's holographic presence and his food at the same time. From Laya's perspective, she was sitting in Al Pancho's digital twin and looking at the digital twin of her husband.

Al Pancho's was one of many holo-restaurants that now called the mall their home. These establishments were designed with both the physical and digital guest in mind, letting friends, family, and lovers share meals while sitting in restaurants separated by hundreds of miles. Laya ate a brunch prepared by her kitchen staff, Terry from Al Pancho's.

Once they'd finished, Laya waved her holographic hand over a physical card machine, held by a waiter wearing a pair of Al Pancho–branded AR glasses, who then handed Terry a physical receipt.

Terry pushed his face towards Laya, "Thank you for brunch, honey." He was putting on that cute voice he does sometimes. "Although I do wish you could've been here in person."

"I know. I do too, but we'll see each other tonight. I promise."

"It's fine. When I see you in person, we're always haunted by your security anyway," Terry added with a raise of his eyebrows and his voice slightly deflated.

Terry walked out into the mall, Laya's hologram automatically tethered to his movements. As they strolled, various adverts, both physical and digital, subtly changed. The words *Laya*, *Terry*, and *husband and wife* seemed to repeat across a few of them. To Laya's annoyance, one particularly aggressive ad for menopause supplements popped up in Laya's path, floating about 3 feet off the ground.

Terry knew she hated those adverts, so he reached out and grabbed the advert and then tossed it across the mall like a frisbee.

"Oh, look," Terry added, changing the subject quickly. "D'Argento is having a sale. How about that necklace we saw last time?"

Laya started smiling again. She connected her holographic hand to Terry's digital hand, and together they strolled into D'Argento, an upmarket jewelry store for both the physical and digital jewelry lover.

The inside resembled a classic turn-of-the-century jewelry shop. The glass display cases of various shapes and sizes were full of beautifully crafted items of aesthetic pleasure. Above and besides the physical pieces, digital jewelry floated and glowed. Signs stating *NFT certified* and *Unique Digital Items* were proudly displayed in AR fashion.

Together, they perused the selection, eventually agreeing on the same necklace they'd flirted with a few times before. Terry paid this time, swiping the palm of his hand across the card machine. Once the payment was confirmed, the necklace appeared in Laya's digital inventory.

After she equipped the necklace, they stood there for a moment admiring their buy in a virtual mirror, giggling and whispering sweet nothings like they did when they were younger. In the midst of Terry telling Laya how beautiful she looked, a red flash appeared in the corner of Laya's vision—the word *Ae* on the screen. She had to take it. For a brief moment, Laya had forgotten about her age, about her job. "Yes, Ae? I asked not to be interrupted."

"Ahh, duty never takes a day off, Prime Minister," Ae quipped as she strolled into Laya's vision.

"And apparently you never listen to your programming."

Ae narrowed her eyes at Laya but kept the conversation focused. The *Cultural Protection Program* had just landed a celebrity spokesman, pleasant news to Laya's ears, plus it was almost time to go to Mia's school for her show. Mia was Laya's 15-year-old and eldest child.

Laya thanked and dismissed Ae. She turned to her husband with a sad look in her eye. She was so grateful for Terry. Many other men wouldn't support a spouse with a job like this. But Terry, Terry got it. She wondered how she would've coped 20 years ago before the metaverse helped them steal days like this every now and then. Before we had virtual AI assistants to do the paperwork.

They said their goodbyes and promised to see each other, in person, for dinner that evening.

With that, Laya brought up the central directory and opened a door to The Imperial College of Arts' new metaverse performance space.

* * *

It was always the sound first. As Laya stepped through the door the noise of a full hall poured over her. A wave of conversation, laughs, and cries from excited kids and teens reverberated through her headset. She adjusted the volume on the right side of the headset and looked around the large, darkened hall.

A stage sat at the far end, brightly illuminated by invisible lights. She looked up and noticed the hall just faded off into blackness, never actually coming to a ceiling, just an endless void.

Ms. Hutchkings, the school's principal, had turned up to personally guide Laya through the crowd of mixed avatars. Digital twins, some sporting tuxedos, others shorts and T-shirts, lined the hall. Some more outlandish avatars were also dotted about, including what looked like a Ninja Turtle, or at least some type of giant walking reptile.

They found their way to the designated viewing area, and within minutes, the hall fell silent. A row of masked faces appeared center stage. The show had begun. Students began showcasing content they created in their Content Creation Module, a module added to the national curriculum as part of Laya's 5-Step Modernization Program.

About 30 minutes in, Mia's digital twin came on dressed in a tutu. Mia had tweaked the color scheme and appeared black and white, almost film Noir-esque.

She stood center stage and took a ballet pose, as she softly moved, a black bar appeared at the bottom of Laya's vision. *Bach - Air on the G String, Suite No. 3, BWV 1068* gently scrolled across in a small white font. The haunting sound of a stringed orchestra rose through Laya's ears as her daughter gracefully began moving with the music. As she moved, her fingers would leave brush strokes behind them, hanging in the air.

Mia danced beautifully, the changing colors flowing out from her hands as she did. Dark blues, a deep green, violet, gold, blacks, whites—a palette of colors drifted out from her hands staining the air. At the piece's crescendo, Mia struck a pose in front of the picture she'd just birthed. From a thousand seemingly random lines and colors, a vision of Vincent van Gogh's *The Starry Night* had formed.

Mia bowed to the audience. Cheers and whistles swelled from the crowd, with the occasional digital firework being let off too. Laya jumped up in excitement, waving like a madwoman to her daughter on stage who, thanks to a family setting on the avatar filter, could see her mother and gave an excited handwave back.

Laya had missed this. She'd missed being around when her kids did incredible things. With a smile on her face, a single tear slowly rolled down Laya's real cheek, catching in the reservoir where her headset meets her face.

Laya kept cheering for her daughter, but eventually, the crowd settled, and the next student came on.

Laya moved out of the viewing area, and having beckoned a door, she went backstage. Unable to see her daughter in the crowd of frantic students and teachers, Laya pulled open her menu—a rather simple trick achieved by winking your right eye—and invited Mia to a private chat. As Mia accepted, their avatars were compelled together and the surrounding sights and sounds darkened.

"I'm so proud of you, sweetie," Laya told her daughter. The pair chatted for a while about the show, the song, the whole thing. They'd obviously missed each other and were in dire need of some mother-daughter time.

Right in the middle of their celebrations, the red flashing light appeared once more. It's Ae again. Hiding her annoyance in front of her daughter, she apologized and answered. "Does this need to go through me, or can Daryl handle it?"

Ae explained how Sweden had just announced the same education reforms that Laya was working on. They'd just secured a contract with one of the tech-goliaths to supply all Swedish schools with the latest headsets and lidar systems and even build the Swedish government a metaverse embassy, something all governments were beginning to do.

Mia stood there watching her mother speak with an invisible person, Mia's enthusiasm slowly fading as she remembered why her mom's job annoyed her so much. Laya looked at her daughter knowingly. She gestured her hand and muted Ae, midway through a breakdown on the details of the Swedish deal.

"I'm so sorry darling. You did so well today. I'm super proud. I'll see you at home later."

They exchanged loving emojis, and Mia disappeared back into the crowd. Laya unmuted her mic. "Save the details for later, Ae. Can you locate my other one? Zack should be finishing school soon." Within moments, Ae had a position.

"He's in the Pondbox," Ae reported, her tone preempting Laya's disappointment.

* * *

Pondbox was a newer region of the metaverse. She had told Zack, her 12-year-old son, not to go there as the whole area was Non-GAC Protected. GAC was Government Anti-Cheat software.

The region had hundreds of new experimental game types, content, and NFTs, but it lacked any guidelines or rules. It reminded Laya of the internet in the early 2000s, when she used to scroll sites like FunnyJunk and the earliest version of YouTube. And just like the internet back then, there was a boatload of bots and catfish phishing for passwords and a whole lot of unrestricted adult content. It was not exactly a place a parent wants their 12-year-old to hang out.

Ae had tracked Zack down to a password-protected shoot-'em-up concept a rouge programmer had dreamt up. Using her Ministerial Digital ID, Laya went straight past the password-protected door. On the other side, she saw Zack and Mia talking. The words, "Can't you just lend me yours?" rang out just as Laya stepped through.

They all turned to face each other, Zack and Laya looking equally confused. Mia's expression, on the other hand, didn't alter and had a certain, almost, uncanny quality to it.

Zack hated it when his mom checked in on him. "Mom," he explained. "You don't need to check up on me." Zack turned back to Mia. "Now, stop bugging me. Ask Mom." He then turned his back to them, taking the stance of a soldier in the midst of an invisible battle.

Laya knew something was up. She reached out her left hand, freezing both avatars, and lifted her right to the panic button on her headset, opening a direct line to the M.C.P. and an emergency exit to her right.

Back in the real world, in a nondescript building halfway across the country, a well-rehearsed parade began. A team of programmers and coders donned headsets and wrist-mounted devices. The gentle sound of a low humming interrupted by the occasional murmuring bounced off the dimly lit blue wall. The sign "M.C.P - Ministerial Cyber Police" shone dustless in the well-ventilated room.

Dragging Zack's avatar, Laya stepped through the emergency exit. As the door closed behind them, multiple M.C.P agents appeared around the fake Mia. Laya and Zack were now in a digital twin of their own back garden, permanently set to a mid-summer's afternoon. Laya unfroze Zack and guided him to sit in his real-world safety chair.

"Zack...," Laya started softly, "You know that wasn't your sister, right?"

Zack was confused at first, but his expression quickly changed into one of shame and embarrassment. Through tears, Zack confessed to his digital mom that he was going to lend Mia their home password. "She said she'd lost it," he reasoned.

Laya comforted her son as best she could, but no words could replace a real hug. She felt a sudden sadness wash over her as she so desperately wanted to comfort her son.

"I'll be home soon. I love you."

* * *

Determined to get home, Laya replaced her headset with a pair of AR glasses and marched out of her office door. As she did, the red light flashed again. "This better be important."

"Always, Prime Minister." Ae's normal neutral voice was now cheery. "A UN published report just announced the 2024 Supply Chain Resilience project a resounding success. Smart Contracts and a UN-backed Central

Digital Currency are now firmly established." Ae's uncanny smile peaking slightly in the corner as she gave the news. "The WWF also published a report earlier this afternoon claiming the metaverse reduced traffic pollution," Ae quickly added.

An hour later, Laya's driver pulled into her family home's tree-lined driveway. While her government-issued autonomous 4×4 could drive itself, this was one time Laya listened to her security and stuck with a human driver.

"We're here, Prime Minister," a tired voice announced from the front of the car.

Laya sat there for a moment, taking shelter from the bracing wind and looking in through her kitchen window. As she sat in the cold and dark, she was warmed by the sight of her smiling family. Well, her smiling Zack and Terry, with Mia just sitting on the kitchen side, scrolling what Laya assumed was an AR social feed. Laya took it all in, soaking in this rare moment of peace.

Laya burst through the door, loudly announcing her presence to the household. Excited, Zack and Mia came running from the kitchen and embraced their mother.

"We haven't seen you in so long," Mia told her mother through dewy eyes.

"It was only a few hours ago."

"Mom...," Mia pulled back slightly to look at her mother in the face. "We haven't seen you in 64 days. I've been counting."

As the evening went on, Laya basked in the physical company of her family. Sitting around the same table for the first time in months, they regaled each other with stories from school and work. Midway through their meal and halfway through one of Terry's anecdotes, that flashing red light appeared in Laya's eyes. Her family knew what that meant, and a saddened silence descended on the table. Terry, trying to hide his disappointment, stood to hug his wife.

"If they need you, go. We love you."

Laya raised her hand to her glasses but hesitated. Instead of answering, she removed them. Her family looked confused. Happy, but confused, as Laya calmly put her glasses down on the dining room table. "If it's important, they'll send someone."

Introduction

On November 13 and 14, 2020, American rapper, singer, and songwriter Lil Nas X, also known as Montero Lamar Hill, appeared on the virtual stage on Roblox, the global gaming platform especially popular among children. As a first for Roblox, the concert attracted an incredible 33 million attendees, enjoying a unique performance inside the virtual world.[3] For Lil Nas X, who is often regarded as a trailblazer, the virtual concert provided a unique opportunity to connect with millions of his fans when physical shows were not possible due to the pandemic. While in-person concerts are capped by the capacity of the stadium and the laws of physics, anything is possible at a virtual show to wow fans, and they can offer a magical experience. Lil Nas X debuted his new single *Holiday* during the concert, and by all measures, the virtual show was a massive success. It generated a lot of publicity for both Roblox and the rapper, launching a new entertainment format for Roblox and generating almost $10 million in virtual merchandize such as digital costumes, accessories, and avatar skins, which users could purchase using the in-game currency Robux.[4]

Lil Nas X appeared as a larger-than-life digital twin and transported users to four different themed worlds, from the Wild West to a Wintery snow-filled world. Roblox's users regarded the unique experience well. Though some children would have wanted to watch the show alongside their friends, it was impossible to bring together all 33 million attendees on one server due to the current hardware constraints. Above all, it would have been utterly chaotic. Hence, players saw only around 50 other attendees watching the live performance, making it feel a bit empty. Apart from the occasional glitches expected from such a novel experience, the concert was a blazing success.

Less than a year later, in October 2021, Decentraland organized not just one concert but an entire, four-day metaverse festival with 80 different artists.[5] Decentraland is a fully decentralized 3D virtual world controlled by a decentralized autonomous organization (DAO) where users can build their own unique digital experience and interact with others. The biggest drawcards for the virtual festival were Deadmau5, a Canadian electronic music producer and DJ, and Paris Hilton. Roblox and Lil Nas X targeted its young players, while the Metaverse Festival was focused more on the tech-savvy crypto community. Users could purchase digital merchandise using the in-game's crypto MANA, such as digital wearables for their avatars,[6] and all attendees received a nonfungible token (NFT)* in their wallet as a *Proof of Attendance*.[7]

When you started reading this book, you might have wondered why does a business book on the metaverse start with a fictional story and discussing two virtual events? Am I in the right place? Well, yes...you certainly are. The two concerts, and the many other concerts that have taken place in games such as Fortnite,† show that the lines of the real and

---

*We will discuss nonfungible tokens in-depth, but to give you a head start, *nonfungible* means that these tokens, which are (digital) representations of (digital) assets similar to how casino chips represent money, are nontradeable. This then means that one nonfungible token cannot be exchanged for another nonfungible token because they do not hold the same value. Casino chips or dollar bills are fungible; a one-dollar chip or one-dollar bill can be exchanged for another one-dollar chip or one-dollar bill, and you still have exactly the same thing. A Pokémon Go card is nonfungible, because one card can be more valuable than another and exchanging it means you will have something different with a different value.

†For those unfamiliar with Fortnite, it is an online video game developed by Epic Games and released in 2017. It is a so-called *Battle Royale Game*, where players fight each other to become the last player standing. It offers different game modes that enable users to not only fight each other but also watch concerts, build an island, or socialize.

virtual worlds are starting to become intertwined experiences working in tandem. The fictional story shows what the metaverse can become, and it won't be long before we live in such a future. In its most basic form, the metaverse is where the physical and the digital worlds converge into a *phygital* experience, augmenting both the virtual and the physical worlds. As we will discover, the metaverse will radically change our society and offer experiences that until recently would have seemed magical. The first glimpses of the metaverse can already be experienced, and people around the world are living, experiencing, and exploring it. In the coming decade, the metaverse will come alive, and it won't be too long before unique hybrid experiences will become a (virtual) reality.

Welcome to the Metaverse

The rise of these massive interactive live events (MILEs) is a first indication of where the internet is heading and the opportunities that come with the next iteration of the World Wide Web. Who would have thought a few years ago that 33 million people could attend a concert at the same time? All could experience it from the best possible vantage point and sharing that experience with friends who are scattered across the globe, creating collective memories in times when physical connections were not possible. Online entertainment and socializing in virtual gaming environments are very normal for Generation Z (those born between mid-to-late 1990s and 2010) and especially Generation Alpha (those born after 2010), even before the pandemic hit.

Already, Generation Alpha, the first generation to be born entirely in the 21st century, will have a completely different perspective on the (digital) world than previous generations. These kids are born in an age when the iPad was introduced, Facebook became the dominant social network, and massive multiplayer online games (also known as MMOs) attract millions of players. You might be familiar with the 2011 video of a one-year-old baby easily navigating an iPad but struggling with a paper magazine because she couldn't pinch and zoom. To her, the magazine was broken.[8] Although Gen Alpha is, of course, also very familiar with physical artifacts such as children's books or coloring books, the fact that these children can so easily navigate the digital realm from an early age is an indication what we can expect as their brains are wired for the digital world from the start.

Ten years later, the baby has grown up in a world where the internet is everywhere, always available at the push of a button, and online interactions are as normal as physical interactions. She looks at the world from a completely different perspective than Millennials, let alone the Baby Boomers who currently run the world. As such, she feels very comfortable immersing herself in a virtual world with endless possibilities and opportunities, despite all the problems that come with that, as we will see later in the book. To her, the metaverse has always been here, and the more advanced our (digital) technologies will become and the more the physical and the digital merge, the better she will be able to navigate this so-called phygital world.

One of the amazing new experiences that the metaverse has brought already is these massive interactive live events. To Generation Alpha, these MILEs offer substantial benefits over real-world concerts. First, they are easy to attend. Children do not need to ask for permission from their parents because they don't have to go anywhere. They can attend from the comfort of their home. Second, they can appear at the concert in their favorite outfit or character, using the avatar as an extension of their real-world personality, creating the ability for the ultimate self-expression. If your child feels like going to the concert like a unicorn, they can, and it probably doesn't cost the world to be a unicorn either. Next, their friends from around the world will also be at the concert. Note here that Generation Alpha has friends from all over the world from the start. They have made close friendships with people they might have never met in real life and probably never will meet physically. To them, globalization is not something that is bad, but an opportunity to meet new people and learn more cultures, albeit completely virtually. Finally, they will have front-row seats at the concert, even if they happen to be late for the show. In fact, they can stand next to their favorite singer while he or she is performing, taking a screenshot of the experience and sharing it with their friends who could not be there. Once the concert is over, your children are already home in time for dinner. The best thing is that next week, they can go to another concert, without paying $100 for an entry ticket that allows them to see their favorite artist from afar in the physical world. For many children, the virtual concerts offer as good an experience or even a better experience than traditional physical concerts.

The metaverse will provide benefits like these interactive concerts and many more as portrayed in the fictional start that will be hard to ignore for both consumers and organizations. The metaverse offers a new way of doing business, connecting with customers, and collaborating with colleagues. As we will see, those companies who have already stepped into the metaverse are already benefiting from it, creating increased brand loyalty, optimizing product design and creation processes, becoming more sustainable, and generally increasing their bottom line. Similar to those companies who were first to adopt the internet when it appeared in the 1990s and those companies who were first to venture onto social media when it appeared in the late 2000s, those companies who have already entered the metaverse will reap the benefits from this new trillion-dollar social economy that will be created this decade.

However, as we will also see, it is not business as usual in the metaverse. Yes, the immersive internet is another channel that you need to master as an organization, but it is a channel that requires your full attention. It will require significant up-front investments, trial and error, and strong connections with your community. After all, designing a series of nonfungible token (NFT) collectibles related to your brand or creating an immersive digital version of your headquarters for your customers to explore during the pandemic is a lot more capital- and resource-intensive than creating a social media campaign. In addition, "datafying" processes and embedding operating equipment with sensors to create digital twins (virtual representations of physical processes or assets) that will provide valuable insights to constantly monitor a remote production facility and continuously improve its output is easier said than done. Finally, moving from Zoom or Teams to a virtual reality meeting room where employees from around the world can come together, collaborate, and spend potentially even more time in the virtual world requires a significant change in employee behavior. As we know, building the technology is the "easy" part, while changing user or employee behavior is a different ballgame.

Of course, for the metaverse-natives (Generation Alpha and, to a lesser extent, Generation Z), embracing the metaverse is easy. The challenge lies with the older generations who are not accustomed to an omnipresent immersive internet and persuading them that embracing virtual and augmented reality offers new opportunities, including amazing experiences.

This book aims to help you understand the metaverse, what it is, how it will work, how you can benefit from it, and how we should build it. Of course, no book on the metaverse is complete without referencing its origin. The metaverse is a term coined by novelist Neal Stephenson in his famous 1992 novel *Snow Crash* (Bantam Books, 1992). The novel defines the metaverse as a place where people use virtual reality headsets to interact in a digital game-like world. The novel has enjoyed cult status, especially among Silicon Valley entrepreneurs, and HBO is turning the book into a series. The same applies to the book *Ready Player One* (Crown Publishing Group, 2011) by Ernest Cline, which was turned into a movie by Steven Spielberg in 2018, where the protagonist depicts the metaverse as a "virtual universe where people go [..] for all the things they can do, but stay for all the things they can be."[9] Both sci-fi books see the metaverse as a digital universe that we interact with using virtual reality. This falls short of the actual metaverse that is being constructed at this moment, where virtual reality is only one channel to interact with the metaverse. In addition, both authors depict the metaverse as commercially owned and as a way to help people escape the dystopian reality of the future world. While this is certainly a possibility for our own future, we do have a chance to prevent a dystopian future where a small elite controls the metaverse and our planet is distraught by climate change. It will be a long and challenging fight—those in power generally are very reluctant to relinquish it to the community—but one we cannot afford to lose. If anything, the dystopian future as described by Stephenson and Cline is not something to look forward to, so we should ensure we build an open, decentralized, and community-driven metaverse and fix the mistakes of Web 2.0.

With this book, I aim to give you the tools to create an open metaverse so that we avoid ending up in a worse version of today. I hope it will help you navigate the immersive internet, and, more importantly, it will discuss how we can build a metaverse that is open, inclusive, decentralized, and not controlled by Big Tech.* After all, we should avoid making the same mistakes as we did when building Web 2.0.

When Sir Tim Berners-Lee invented the Web, he envisioned it to be decentralized and open, with data to be controlled by the user, but we ended up with silos controlled by Big Tech.[10] Now that we are entering the next phase of the internet, and with the technology ready, we can fix what we did wrong. After all, a closed metaverse controlled by Big Tech or the state will very likely result in a dystopian nightmare that we should avoid at all costs, as we will see.

We will also discuss what can go wrong in the metaverse. Not to scare you from entering the metaverse, but just as cybercriminals are active on the current internet, hackers and scammers will also constantly patrol the metaverse, on the prowl for their next victim. The metaverse will be hacked, and everyone must be aware of how the metaverse can damage society, organizations, and individuals. With more and more devices connected to the internet—it is expected that by 2030 there will be 125 billion devices connected to the internet, with 7.5 billion internet users—there will be ample opportunities for cybercriminals to hack you, your business, and the metaverse, inflicting damages totaling $10 trillion, already in 2025.[11] As described in the fictional story, it will be relatively easy for cybercriminals to pretend to be someone else in the metaverse; if someone looks like your sister and sounds like your sister, we are quickly to believe that she is your sister. But even this problem is relatively small compared to a metaverse flooded by harassment and toxic recommendation engines that create immersive filter bubbles, further dividing and polarizing society and harming individuals.

The first chapter will dive into what the metaverse is and could become because a shared understanding of this new concept is important if we all want to benefit from it. What are the characteristics of the metaverse, and how do these impact our experience? We will begin our journey at the start of the dotcom bubble when the internet arrived for the first time. Web 1.0 allowed personal computers to connect, and the internet arrived in our living room, but only sometimes would you go on

---

*In this book, the term *Big Tech* refers to Facebook (Meta), Amazon, Apple, Microsoft, and Alphabet, as well as the Chinese counterparts Alibaba, Baidu, and Tencent.

the internet. Web 2.0 arrived with the smartphone, although there is no set date when exactly the mobile internet started. It brought the internet closer to us, allowing us to be always online, but we still have to make an effort to "go on the internet," as in getting your phone or opening your laptop. The next iteration of the internet will be an internet that is always there. It is always on, and you are always connected to it, potentially even when asleep, e.g., your Apple Watch tracking your sleep. It will be ready to interact with whenever you want or need to.[12]

This immersive internet requires new hardware solutions, as without augmented reality (AR) and virtual reality (VR), we will remain observers instead of active participants of this virtual world. We will discuss what AR and VR are, where we are now, and where we need to go before it becomes mainstream and the physical and digital worlds truly converge. We will also dive into the key characteristics of the open metaverse and how we can create a metaverse that delivers the most value to society.

Then, in Chapter 2, we will explore how we can achieve an open metaverse that empowers its users instead of enslaving them and what the benefits of such a metaverse will be to society.

In Chapter 3, we will explore the rise of avatars and digital humans —2D or 3D representations of our identity in the digital world—and how these digital identities will redefine what it is to be human. We will investigate how avatars will change our identity and why reputation will become even more important in the virtual world. Of course, avatars cannot walk around the metaverse naked, so digital fashion and digital products will explode in the coming years, offering brands a new approach to connecting with their customers in ways that are sustainable and environmentally friendly.

Once we understand who we can be in the metaverse, we will discover what we can do in the metaverse in Chapter 4. Humans have always tried to escape reality, be it using story telling around a fire to reading a book, but now for the first time, we can create our own space and invite anyone from around the world to join and have a social experience away from daily life. Of course, users who prefer a solitary immersive experience can also find that in the metaverse. There will be millions of metaverse spaces similar to the current internet, and knowing your way around the metaverse will improve your experience. Therefore, we will dive into how to traverse the metaverse and have an immersive experience while listening to music, gaming, playing sports, shopping, and learning.

Of course, the metaverse will not only be for fun. For organizations, it will mean serious business. Increasing brand loyalty, developing digital twins, collaborating in virtual reality—the future of work will revolve around the metaverse. Chapter 5 will discuss how brands can step into the metaverse, including numerous examples of brands who have already ventured into it, and what brands can do to become successful in the metaverse. Chapter 6 will explore how location data and the Internet of Things (IoT) will be the driving force to propel homes, offices, factories, supply chains, and entire cities into the metaverse. Although many enterprise metaverse environments will be closed walled gardens to provide privacy and security, the consumer version of the metaverse will work only if the metaverse is an open and inclusive space controlled by users instead of Big Tech. Zuckerberg might have claimed the metaverse with his rebranding to meta, but he should never own and control it.

In Chapter 7, we will cover the economics of the metaverse, including nonfungible tokens. Already in 2021, there were multiple million-dollar digital real estate deals and exchange of digital assets, and that is just the beginning. With an infinite supply of digital land across various metaverse spaces, you would expect low prices, but that is not what is happening. Prices are at an all-time high, and the more the metaverse is in the news, the more this will probably continue. However, there is a caveat: this early gold rush will most likely, and should not, continue if we want to ensure the metaverse is inclusive and reduces inequality instead of enlarging it. How does digital real estate work, how does it impact the metaverse economy, and is it a good thing? What other aspects of the metaverse define how the economy will work? To understand how the economy of the metaverse will work, we will take a deep dive into NFTs: what they are, how they work, why they are so important, what the challenges are of NFTs, and why the current hype of selling JPEGs for millions of dollars is important, though not where NFTs' true value lies.

Finally, before finishing the book with a look into the future of the metaverse in Chapter 9, we will explore the dark side of the metaverse.

Similar that the existing Web has a Dark Web, the metaverse will inherently come with negative aspects that harm citizens, organizations, and societies. What are these problems, and more importantly, how can we prevent them from happening? We will discuss the dangers and ethical challenges of the metaverse, the most likely (mental) health impact on its users and the numerous privacy and security dangers. The metaverse will be fun and useful, but only if we build it right. Chapter 8 will discuss how to go about this and how we can fight back to keep the metaverse a pleasant environment that does not further destabilize society but drives humanity forward.

Our society and what it means to be human will change drastically in the coming years. We are at the cusp of building an alternate reality that is not bound by the laws of physics and where anything is possible. In this world, magic will become a reality. I hope that this book will give you a complete understanding of what the metaverse can become, how you as a consumer can enjoy it, and how organizations can benefit from it, without harassing and following those same consumers as organizations do on the Web today. If we get it wrong and don't learn from our mistakes, the dystopian metaverse portrayed by Neal Stephenson in his novel *Snow Crash* will become a reality. However, if we build it right, a world of abundance is upon us. Let the journey and magic begin; let's step into the metaverse.

Chapter 1
The Future Is Immersive

From Web 1.0 to Web 3.0

To understand how the metaverse will change us, we need to know where we are coming from and know what will drive the immersive internet. This requires us to go back in time, to the 1950s, when the second generation of transistor-based computers arrived on the market.[13] These big, mainframe computers replaced the vacuum-tube machines and started the development of the Information Age as we know it today. These machines were possible because a few years earlier, three scientists at Bell Labs—William Bradford Shockley, John Bardeen, and Walter Houser Brattain—had invented the transistor, for which they received the Nobel Prize in 1956.

Within a few years, the various components required to develop the personal computer, such as the computer chip and microprocessors, were small enough to catapult us into a new age. Over the years, developments in the hardware have continued to deliver ever-smaller solutions to such an extent that we now have machines that can create transistors of 1 nanometer in length.[14] One nanometer is one-billionth of a meter, or 40 percent the width of a strand of human DNA.[15] In other words, it's very, very small. These developments in hardware are required if we want to be able to access the metaverse using small, comfortable, and cheap devices such as virtual reality (VR) headsets, augmented reality (AR) glasses, or even smart contact lenses in the far future, which means that the mainstream adoption of VR and AR will still take a few years. In addition, the development of sophisticated hardware is only one of the prerequisites of the immersive internet.

The other component is, of course, software, and for the first algorithm, we need to go back to the 19th century. In the 1840s, Ada Lovelace created the first algorithm. She was an analyst and mathematician, and she is considered the first computer programmer. In her 1843 article, Lovelace correctly predicted that future machines might be able "to compose elaborate and scientific pieces of music of any degree of complexity or extent."[16] Of course, it took more than 175 years before computer programs could actually do so, but her foresight is remarkable and for that she is recognized as the mother of modern computing.[17]

One hundred and twenty years later, we moved from actually programming the ones and zeros to the era of programming languages. In 1964 researchers at Dartmouth College in Hanover, New Hampshire, released BASIC, an acronym for Beginner's All-purpose Symbolic Instruction Code: a family of high-level programming languages emphasizing ease of use and the programming language used in many of the first video games. A few years later, Hewlett-Packard released multiple computers that ran BASIC programs, and in the 1970s, Microsoft created a dialect of the programming language called Microsoft BASIC. This was the starting point of one of the most valuable companies in the world, and since then, Microsoft has come a long way. In 2021, Microsoft announced its entry into the enterprise metaverse and solidified this direction with the announcement of the purchase of the gaming company Activision Blizzard for almost $70 billion in 2022.

With hardware and software in place, the Defense Advanced Research Projects Agency (DARPA) was able to develop the first computer network, called ARPANET. In the 1970s, the ARPANET was extended with a host-to-host protocol and network software, resulting in the first applications for the network, including electronic mail. The original researchers were smart enough to develop an easy coordination mechanism enabling email messages to be sent to different computers regardless of the application used to send or receive the email. This interoperability enabled email to quickly become one of the main applications of the internet.[18]

ARPANET would eventually evolve into the public Web when it was split into military and civilian sections. A few years later, Sir Tim Berners-Lee proposed the concept of the World Wide Web while working at CERN in Switzerland. Berners-Lee wrote the three leading technologies that we currently use on the Web: HyperText Markup Language (HTML), Uniform Resource Identifier (URI, also known as URL), and Hypertext Transfer Protocol (HTTP). At the end of 1990, the first web page was put online, and in 1991, Web 1.0 opened up to the public. The rest is history, with millions of websites and billions of web pages nowadays. These standards have proven fundamental for the Web to evolve into what it is today. Similar standards will also be required for the metaverse if we want to create a metaverse that is interoperable and rewards content creation and ownership.

The fact that both ARPANET and the World Wide Web grew out of a closed *research* environment is important to understand why the internet works as it currently does. Over the years, those involved in developing the internet and the Web created many *open* standards, including TCP/IP, DNS, HTTP, etc. This creates a permissionless network, where anyone can easily connect to the network and share and receive information. Unfortunately, these standards and protocols have not propagated to all sections of the Web. As a result, the successor of electronic mail, mobile messaging, does not come with interoperability. While this results in strong network effects for Big Tech, it has also created the walled gardens we are now so familiar with for our mobile messaging. Up until 2021, it has not been possible to send a message from WhatsApp and receive it on Signal or vice versa. This lack of interoperability should be avoided at all costs in the metaverse. Fortunately, the European Union is proposing interoperable mobile messaging as part of the Digital Markets Act. In the metaverse, you want to be able to directly send your friend a text message from Fortnite that can be received on Roblox, or you want to be able to continue talking with your friends when switching from one world to another. Of course, platforms such as Discord can help here, but in the end, Discord is also a walled garden.* Nevertheless, those organizations

---

*Discord is a free voice, video, and text chat app with more than 250 million users that was originally predominantly used by gamers. In recent years, it has become the go-to platform for NFTs and the metaverse communities. Discord allows anyone to spin up a server and start public or private communities.

involved in creating the Web and the internet worked with the best intentions and envisioned an open, decentralized Web accessible to all.

Unfortunately, there was another design flaw of the Web. Over the years, those involved in the process forgot to create an identity protocol to use your offline identity online and a reputation protocol to be reputable and accountable online, even when you are anonymous.* They forgot this for a simple reason, but with grave consequences. Early on, when the Web was being designed, only trusted actors had access to the network, and there was no need for an identity or reputation protocol. As a result of this flaw, on the internet, "nobody knows you are a dog."[19] You can be anyone, while online actions do not have consequences. Moreover, data and identity are not owned and controlled by the person creating it. Consequently, it is currently impossible for users to transfer their data (identity and reputation) and digital assets from one platform to another, further fortifying the walled gardens that resulted in the monopolies of Big Tech.

When we move from the social, or mobile, internet (also referred to as Web 2.0) to the immersive internet, this quest for data will become only more important. It is data that will drive the immersive internet. The more we do online, the more we integrate the internet into our physical lives, and the further we merge the digital and the physical, the more important data will become. Already, data is the most valuable resource in the world, far more valuable than oil. Simply look at the type of companies that make up the top 50 most valuable companies in 2021; 18 are related to data or (digital) tech, and only three are related to oil and gas.[20]

Of course, this centralization of data and power is a problem for society. Big Tech owns and controls our data, and with that, they own and control us, as the controversy around Cambridge Analytica has clearly shown. They have long recognized the enormous power and money data brings. We have all fallen into their trap of free services and got addicted to it. As a result, Big Tech has become so powerful that governments are failing to break the power of those companies that deliberately and

---

*The level of anonymity as defined and required by the various privacy legislations around the world, such as the GDPR in Europe, may never be achieved. It is almost always possible to re-identify someone, even with just a few data points, as long as you have sufficient resources.

consistently breach consumers' trust, privacy, and freedom. With the advent of the metaverse, data will only increase in importance. Already in 2018, researchers found that a 20-minute VR game collects 2 million data points, including body movements.[21] It can, therefore, be expected that Meta also collects vast amounts of data when you use their VR headset. This data most likely includes where you look and how long, what emotions are evoked by what you are watching, and also what your hands look like, your room, the products in your room, and the people in your room. Although Zuckerberg said that privacy and security are important in his announcement on October 28, 2021, Facebook will likely continue to harvest human behavior data and put their predictive algorithms to work to sell ever-more personalized advertising and further disrupt our society with their toxic recommendation algorithms.[22] This was only confirmed when in February 2022, Meta threatened to shut down Facebook and Instagram in Europe if Europe would prevent the processing of Europeans' data in the United States.[23]

Meta is not the only company abusing our data. A famous saying is that if you are not paying for the product, you are the product. As a result, Web 2.0 resulted in an internet composed of walled gardens where it is impossible to move your own content and data from one platform to another simply because the data is too valuable. Nowadays, users are the data, and platforms are closed, preventing the interoperability of assets that are crucial if we want to deliver upon the promises of the metaverse. Even more, time and again, Big Tech has proven that it is difficult to trust them. In 2021, just after Zuckerberg revealed Meta, an Australian artist by the name Thea-Mai Baumann saw her entire identity on Instagram deleted because her Instagram handle is @metaverse. A decade of hard work suddenly vanished, and she had no way to get it back. Initially, Meta claimed that her account was blocked because she pretended to be someone else, and while Thea-Mai tried to reach out to Instagram to get her account verified, she received no response. Only when she involved the *New York Times* did Meta respond and restore her profile, claiming that the account had been "incorrectly removed for impersonation."[24] This is exactly why we need a decentralized, open metaverse to prevent companies like Meta from simply deleting someone's entire identity.

Fortunately, there is a light at the end of the tunnel. We have started decentralizing the Web, slowly taking back the power from Big Tech to the community. Obviously, this process is fiercely resisted by the incumbents, whether it is China banning all crypto trading or Big Tech eating up all the promising startups to avoid any competition. However, as we will see in the coming decade and throughout this book, the power of decentralization cannot be stopped. Just as hackers have not yet been able to hack the Bitcoin blockchain because it runs on millions of computers, Big Tech and authoritarian governments will not be able to resist the decentralization of the Web.

As we have progressed from Web 1.0 (read-only) to Web 2.0 (read and write but don't own), we are now seeing the first contours of Web 3.0 (read, write, and own). When building Web 1.0, the tools were more primitive and the level of knowledge required to publish a website was higher, but at least websites were published on owned servers instead of the cloud aggregators of AWS, Google, or Microsoft. With Web 3.0 we can revert many of the centralized tendencies of Web 2.0 and bring back power, identity, and control to the user, similar to how it used to be in Web 1.0. If we want to create a metaverse that is beneficial to society, and not just to Big Tech and a tiny elite, we need to embrace the decentralized Web 3.0 and limit the control and influence of Big Tech and prevent the likes of Meta from creating a metaverse just for them to harvest and abuse our data. At the heart of Web 3.0 lies the blockchain.

The distributed ledger technology was first mentioned in 2008 by Satoshi Nakamoto in the Bitcoin whitepaper.[25] Since then, the decentralized ecosystem has been developing rapidly. Blockchain is a fundamental technology that has the opportunity to completely change how we run our society.* In its simplest definition, a blockchain is a database, but contrary to a traditional database, which is *read*, *write*, and *edit*, a blockchain is only *read* and *write*. The fact that it cannot be edited results in a single source of the truth, and anyone with access to the blockchain can be certain that the data has not been tampered with.

---

*I have written about blockchain before in my 2018 book *Blockchain: Transforming Your Business and Our World*, which I co-authored with Dr. Philippa Ryan, Routledge, London.

The third evolution of the Web has the opportunity to enable an internet that will be a community-controlled, permissionless, persistent, and programmable, where you (the individual) own your data, credentials, identity, and content. It will be built upon decentralized data storage and computing power, which anyone can contribute to and earn tokens while doing. This ensures fault tolerance; reduces the impact of hacks, attacks, and data breaches; and ensures censorship resistance. Thanks to blockchain, data will be immutable, verifiable, and traceable resulting in radical transparency while protecting your privacy. Thanks to smart contracts, intermediaries in any industry will likely become less relevant. With that, fees charged by these intermediaries will disappear, and the peer-to-peer economy that will replace it will be governed by cryptography instead of humans. It is an exciting time but still a long way away, as it requires a plethora of standards and hard work, energy, dedication, and money to crack some of the most complex challenges of going from a centralized web to a decentralized one.

Web 3.0 will enable a new social contract around data and identity. As we will uncover, Web 3.0 is a prerequisite for an open metaverse, but not necessarily a necessity for *the* metaverse. Building the metaverse on top of the Web 3.0 infrastructure will enable us to move away from state and corporate surveillance and move toward empowered citizens who have complete control over their own data and identity, with lower risks of the data falling into the wrong hands. Blockchain can truly change how we deal with data and will therefore be a prerequisite for the open metaverse, especially because the amount of data we are creating is about to explode exponentially from zettabytes of data (10^{21}) to yottabytes (10^{24}) and eventually brontobytes of data (10^{27}, or one quadrillion terabytes) due to the Internet of Things,[*] 5G communications and beyond, and, most importantly, virtual reality and augmented reality.[26]

---

[*]The *Internet of Things* refers to a network of products, devices, or machines that are embedded with sensors and connected with the internet to share data for insights. Yuval Noah Harari refers to the Internet of All Things, indicating that it's no longer about your printer and weather station being connected, but you, the physical you with your wearables and trackers, smart rings, etc - Harari, Y. N. (2016). *Homo Deus: A brief history of tomorrow*. Random House.

From AR to VR to XR

It was the year 1955 when the American philosopher, inventor, film director, and cinematographer Morton Heilig released a paper entitled "The Cinema of the Future."[27] In the paper, he described an immersive multisensory machine, or *Experience Theatre* as he dubbed it, that included a stereoscopic collar display, a story-sound system, fans, odor emitters, and a motional chair. The *Sensorama* as it was called, and for which he received a patent, was a 5D personalized movie theatre avant la lettre.[28] Spectators were treated to an imaginary motorcycle ride through New York City. They would experience the city as it was in real life, with simulated noises and smells of people, cars and pizza, and fan-generated wind. Unfortunately, the invention was far too early for society, and Heilig failed to achieve financial backing for his invention, so the *Sensorama* never made it to the masses. Due to his work, Morton Heilig is considered the father of virtual reality.

Since then, virtual reality has been promised a breakthrough technology many times but never really managed to achieve what was promised. For a long time, the devices were too bulky and uncomfortable; the graphics were mediocre, to say the least; the experience made people nauseous; and the hardware was too expensive. It was far from a seamless experience that is required for a technology to go mainstream.

Everything changed when in 2010 Palmer Luckey, an 18-year-old entrepreneur, created a prototype for what later would become the Oculus Rift headset, the first VR headset with a 90-degree field of view (FOV). FOV is a crucial aspect of VR as it determines how much of an observable virtual world can be seen at any given moment. The wider the FOV, the more immersive the experience. The 2012 Kickstarter campaign for the headset was a major success, and Palmer raised $2.4 million to create the Oculus Rift. Only two years later, after seeing the enormous potential of the created VR headset and having received a demo of virtual reality by Jeremey Bailenson, founding director of Stanford University's Virtual Human Interaction Lab,[29] Zuckerberg bought Oculus for $2 billion. Since then, virtual reality has woken up from the VR winter and has rapidly gained momentum, leading to the metaverse announcement of Facebook on October 28, 2021, which brought worldwide attention to the metaverse movement.

Over the past years, we have seen a wide range of new VR headsets enter the market, targeting both the lower-end consumer market as well as the high-end enterprise market. Users can interact with 3D environments, which can be computer-generated using tools such as Unity or Unreal Engine,* or 360-degree recordings of real-world events. The objective of virtual reality is to provide the user with an immersive experience that can be explored freely, regardless of the laws of physics. VR is about endless possibilities where we are limited only by our own imagination. It is about how we interact with each other and the virtual world, which can be both for fun, such as games or social activities, or for work, such as virtual 3D meetings, remote guidance, collaboration or maintenance, or immersive trainings.

While virtual reality offers an immersive experience, it is certainly not the only technology that will enable the metaverse. The other is, of course, augmented reality, which saw its mainstream adoption in 2016 with Niantic's Pokémon Go's *Gotta Catch 'Em All!*

Where VR provides the user with a fully immersive environment, with an extended field of view, AR offers the user an additional digital layer on top of reality, often with a much smaller FOV. This digital layer offers endless possibilities because it can be used anywhere at any moment and deliver a unique experience depending on your location and where you are looking. From heads-up displays in the car (called that because they literally enable you to keep your head up while driving) to Google Glasses (infamous for its breach of privacy as it was unclear whether it was recording you), and from AR glasses MagicLeap or HoloLens to futuristic contact lenses projecting information directly onto your retina, augmented reality will radically change our lives. In fact, long-time industry expert Ming-Chi Kuo predicted in 2021 that by 2032, Apple will replace the iPhone with an AR device.[30]

While augmented reality is likely to have a bigger impact on our lives than virtual reality, it is also a lot harder to achieve, as you are dealing with the chaotic and ever-changing real world that you cannot control, and where it is necessary to sometimes hide digital objects behind real things for a realistic experience. This concept, which is called *occlusion*,

---

*Unity and Unreal Engine are game engines that enable developers to create 3D virtual worlds.

is an especially hard problem to solve.[31] In addition, where with virtual reality it is fine to wear a large and clunky device on your head, this is not ideal with augmented reality if you are walking on the street. It won't be very comfortable, let alone safe. We would need smart glasses that are easy to wear and preferably fashionable and provide you with a field of view that matches humans' field of view, which is almost 180 degrees forward-facing. While this has proven to be highly challenging to develop, the technology develops rapidly. In 2021 Snaps Spectacles AR were the most advanced AR glasses with a FOV of just 26.3 degrees and a 30-minute battery life (and at the time of writing, available only to select developers),[32] but at CES 2022, Kura announced their Kura Gallium AR Glasses with a FOV of 150 degrees, 95 percent transparent glasses, a weight of only 80 grams, and a resolution of 8K per eye.[33] So although the technology is improving, the high costs of AR glasses (the HoloLens and Magic Leap both cost a few thousand USD and also the Kura Gallium will cost around $1,200) and the challenge of occlusion will prevent mass adoption in the short term. Once the hardware does catch up (the launch of Apple Glass or whatever it will be called, will likely be a pivoting moment), augmented reality will have a far bigger impact on our society than virtual reality, and it will become the main entry point into the metaverse. Nevertheless, in the coming years, VR and AR devices will become as normal as carrying a smartphone with you.

These challenges, of course, do not mean that we cannot use AR today. Apple's ARKit enables a wide variety of AR applications simply with your iPhone, and the same applies to Google ARCore for Android phones. Already, there are countless apps available to experience augmented reality with your phone or tablet, such as obtaining information on landmarks while traveling or obtaining a very realistic, 3D digital replica of a real product created by simply scanning it with your phone. One interesting example is Mexico's new bills released in 2022, which now trigger augmented animations related to the country's history and culture when you scan them with your smartphone. This is a great way to offer a unique experience, provide an educational aspect, and improve the security to prevent counterfeits.[34] For now, though, augmented reality using your smartphone will be by no means as seamless and easy to experience as when we will have glasses, or eventually, smart contact lenses.

Without becoming too futuristic here, it is likely that five or ten years from now, if you are walking down the street and not carrying an augmented reality device, you will likely miss out on a lot of the action happening on the street, ranging from innovative street art on the walls to fantasy creatures flying through the air and immersive, personalized advertising (which you can subsequently block with AR ad blockers). Altogether, we can expect that five or ten years from now, augmented reality will become part of reality. If you don't have the wearable to participate, you will be left out of the physical world. AR will be the new reality. Lines will start to blur, and soon VR and AR will merge into extended reality (XR), and you no longer have to change devices if you want to switch between virtual or augmented reality.

Once we have reached that stage, probably the early 2030s, the metaverse will have arrived. Smartphones and laptops will likely become unnecessary as will separate VR and AR devices because for our entertainment, socializing, or work, we simply put on our sleek XR glasses.

VR and AR will help us bridge the gap between the digital and physical worlds we currently live in. Both are immersive technologies that allow users to experience digitally rendered content in both physical and virtual environments, and both will change how we socialize, play, work, and collaborate.[35] While virtual and augmented reality are important for the metaverse, they are not the only access points to the metaverse. Especially today, many of the metaverse experiences available offer a virtual experience but certainly not an immersive, 3D experience. The most well-known examples are in the field of gaming, where popular games such as Fortnite, Minecraft, Roblox, Decentraland, or Axie Infinity have attracted millions of users and raised billions of US dollars in funding by offering players a virtual, 2D social experience, which for some has become an important part of their lives. None of these platforms allow users to play the game in virtual reality or using augmented reality, but that has not stopped them from becoming the platforms that are currently driving the metaverse. It is, however, a matter of time before these metaverse spaces will also enable a 3D virtual environment. Platforms such as Somnium Space and Solice are already accessible using web browsers and virtual reality, and it is likely that in the future, we will see many more of such hybrid environments, catering toward the early adopters of VR and mainstream adoption using a web or mobile browser experience, bringing the metaverse ever closer.

What Can the Metaverse Become?

In 1973, legend Arthur C. Clarke coined his third law, stating that "any sufficiently advanced technology is indistinguishable from magic."[35a] Now that we experience the dawn of the metaverse, this will become truer than ever before. Although the metaverse is currently still in its infancy, in the coming years, thanks to the convergence of technologies, the metaverse will arrive at an exponential speed. Before the end of this decade, we will have converted the mobile or social internet to an immersive, omnipresent, persistent internet, where magic seems to happen constantly. The metaverse will usher in a new age, the Imagination Age.

Designer and writer Charlie Magee first coined the Imagination Age in 1993. It is a theoretical period after the Information Age when creativity and imagination become the primary drivers of economic value.[36] Especially because many of the jobs currently existing will be automated using artificial intelligence and robotics. The metaverse will unleash the Imagination Age in all its force, getting it out of the realm of theory and into the real world. The metaverse will reward creativity like never before, thanks to the transformative power of nonfungible tokens (NFTs). It will empower content creators to earn a living, and creativity will be rewarded based on how the community perceives it. In the metaverse, anyone can be an artist and share their creations with the world. But how can we define the metaverse?

Let's first get one misconception out of the way; there is only one metaverse. Similar to that there is only one internet. Of course, there can and will be infinite spaces, worlds, environments, or experiences within this metaverse where people can relax, be entertained, socialize, work, or collaborate. Some of these worlds will be walled gardens such as Meta's Horizon Worlds or Epic Games' Fortnite. At the same time, the majority of the metaverse, if we build it correctly, can be open, decentralized, community-driven, and user-controlled. Of course, not everything can be open and community-driven. Some environments will be secure virtual spaces accessible only if you have the right digital key, similar to how most offices are accessible only with the right physical key. In Chapter 2, I will go deeper into the debate of an open versus closed metaverse and the consequences of either direction.

Although the metaverse seems far away, nothing could be further from the truth. The metaverse has been years in the making, and many of the components and platforms that will be part of the metaverse have been around for years. This has become clear in the past two years. If there is one silver lining of the pandemic, it is that covid-19 catapulted us into the digital era. For years, organizations postponed their digital transformation programs for various reasons, but when the pandemic hit, organizations from around the world had to switch to remote work practically overnight, and many did so without any major issues because of the available technology. Every year, I write an annual technology trend prediction for the next year, and if I had predicted at the end of 2019 that three months later, most organizations would work from home, people would have called me crazy. However, that is what happened. Fortunately, the technology was ready for it, and many employees replaced their morning commutes for sleep-ins and breakfast, their 1:1s in the office for walking phone calls, and their meeting room huddles for home-office Zoom, Teams, or Google Hangouts. Of course, there were the various hiccups, such as a Texas lawyer appearing in front of a judge as a cat in an online court meeting. There were also the more serious data security issues, which fortunately were fixed relatively quickly. All in all, we did remarkably well. This shift to remote work, including online social gatherings, online pub quizzes, and even a complete virtual Burning Man festival, would not have been possible if the technology wasn't ready. Had the pandemic happened five or ten years ago, we would not have been able to make the switch so easily.

Since the start of the internet at the end of the 1990s, we have slowly transitioned from an analog species to a digital species: *Homo Digitalis*. Nowadays, for the majority of humanity, the internet has become the norm, and we spend many hours per day on the internet. For a large group of people, myself included, we spend most of our day online. However, we should not forget that even in 2022, there are almost 2.9

billion people who have never been "on" the internet.[37] Thanks to initiatives such as Elon Musk's Starlink, we will most likely give the remaining three billion people access to the internet, and the upcoming metaverse, in the coming decade. Once all humans have access to the internet, we can truly speak of a digital species.

We will experience the biggest change in our digital journey in the coming years—a true paradigm shift as we enter the metaverse. We will transition from being separated from the internet and required to make a conscious action to go on the internet to be fully connected with and immersed in the internet. The internet will become as pervasive as the air we breathe or the energy we use to power our devices. There will no longer be a need to "go on the internet." Instead, in the metaverse, the internet will just be there, waiting for you to interact with at any given moment, ranging from your smart glasses projecting your office while sipping your latte in your favorite cafe, your self-driving car informing your house when you are driving home, and your sleep tracker monitoring your every move while asleep and providing you with a detailed analysis of how you slept and automatically adjusting your virtual meditation session when you wake up. The metaverse is a complete convergence of the physical and the digital world, or as Satya Nadella, CEO of Microsoft, put it, we will "embed computing in the real world and embed the real world into computing,"[38] creating an additional layer in both worlds that we can interact with using any connected device imaginable, be it a smartphone, computer, AR/VR headset, IoT device, or whatever future devices we will invent.

The metaverse can be seen as the next iteration of the internet: a version of the internet that supports immersive, interactive, and persistent online digital experiences such as Decentraland, Microsoft Mesh, Pokémon Go, or Fortnite and anything that will be invented in the years to come. The metaverse is not a single place, let alone one specific virtual world as portrayed by *Ready Player One*. The metaverse will be the convergence of the physical and the digital world where all of our data— such as identity, personality, reputation, and assets, and also the entire history, feeling, and/or emotion of any (virtual or physical) place, organization or thing—can be interacted with, controlled, and experienced in completely novel ways so that people, and things, can create new, magical, experiences, interactions, and environments. The convergence of the digital and the physical worlds will enable yet to be developed applications similar to how the internet created completely new applications we could impossibly foresee in the mid-1990s. As Bayan Towfiq, CEO of Subspace, described it, the metaverse is "much more akin to [a gaming] console than it is to Mario the game that runs on top of it."[39] It will enable all kinds of new experiences to be created in the future. However, any company describing that they are building *a metaverse* would be the same as a company stating that they are building *an internet*.

In the metaverse, 2D and 3D content, spatially organized information and experiences, and real-time synchronous communication between humans and machines will seamlessly interact. Brands are already exploring such novel "phygital" experiences. For example, in early 2022, Nike and EA Sports created an experience that would offer players unique rewards in the Madden NFL game if they would run five miles in the real world, tracked with Nike's NRC app.[40] We can expect a lot more of such entirely novel experiences. As part of the metaverse, users, organizations, and things will be able to organize and interact with data that goes beyond the traditional senses of vision and hearing. For example, instead of reading or hearing about earthquakes happening around the world on the news, we might be able to feel them in real time using in-body sensors connected wirelessly to the world's seismographs. Does this seem farfetched? It shouldn't because that is exactly what Spanish artist Moon Ribas did already back in 2012 when she had sensors implanted in her body that allowed her to feel all of the earth's seismic activities. For seven years, she would feel the earth's vibrations in her body.[41] Such new experiences are also part of the metaverse and could become commonplace in the future.

By utilizing a variety of technologies, ranging from artificial intelligence, machine learning, the Internet of Things, 5G (and soon 6G), to of course VR and AR, the metaverse will enable us to create any kind of immersive experiences that transcend the real and the virtual world, and we will be limited only by our own imagination. Although the physical and the digital world are already converging daily—think of virtual backgrounds on Zoom or buying physical products with crypto—the metaverse will have truly arrived when we begin to stop distinguishing between the virtual and physical worlds and we see them as one.

The metaverse will see a huge variety of virtual or augmented worlds, experiences, or environments. Like the internet, the metaverse will be community-driven and the content creator-focused, with the difference that we have a second chance to create a more equal society by sharing the benefits of the metaverse with the community and content creators. For the metaverse to deliver the most benefits to society, it will need to be open, and data and identity will need to be **personal** (it is about you and it is yours), **portable** (as in interoperable, which means you can take your identity, reputation, assets, and data from one platform to another), **private** (you control your identity, assets, and data), **persistent** (data, identity, or created experiences do not change without your consent, and you can jump into an experience at any time, which can have evolved over time but not disappeared unless the creator decides so), and **protected** (your data and identity cannot be stolen).[42] In the next section, I will describe these characteristics in more detail. Although walled gardens such as Meta and Fortnite will exist for some time, I believe that in the long run, we should strive for an open metaverse that will benefit society as a whole and that will enable users to take their hard work and earnings from one environment to another. Of course, that does not mean that closed platforms will not exist in the metaverse, but as we will see in Chapter 7, the economic benefits for both shareholders and society are too big to ignore, and any walled garden would benefit significantly if they would open up and embrace interoperability, data privacy, and self-sovereign identities (for both individuals, organizations, and things).* If for some reason, as humanity, we are unable to create such an open metaverse, we might have amazing immersive experiences, but we will remain stuck in the Web 2.0 paradigm where Big Tech controls our data and identity, and most of the trillion-dollar value that the metaverse can unlock will remain accessible only to a small group of people and companies instead of the wider society. Instead of trying to fight for a bigger piece of the pie, even Big Tech would stand to benefit if we would just create a massively bigger pie by opening up. It is just common business sense.

An open metaverse will be a continuously evolving, decentralized, and creator-driven ecosystem, without physical and space-time

---

*In March 2022, Bored Ape Yacht Club creator Yuga Labs raised $450 million, despite only being one year old. Their $4 billion valuation can be contributed to the fact that anyone who owns a Bored Ape also owns all the copyrights and IP of that Bored Ape, allowing owners to create significant value from their investment.

limitations, where humanity and technology coexist in a balanced mutualistic relationship (i.e., where there is a win-win situation and there are no zero-sum games), enabling humanity to experience the real and the digital in ways we could never imagine.

Six Characteristics of the Metaverse

In the metaverse, we are bound only by our own creativity and the resources at our disposal. Because it is digital, anything can be created as long as we set our minds to it. After all, in the digital world, the laws of physics do not apply, even if we interact with the physical world. This change in perspective is crucial to have an open mind when constructing the virtual worlds and experiences in the metaverse. When developing a metaverse experience, be it a brand to engage with their customers, game developers who want to develop a social immersive game, or industrial companies planning to incorporate digital twins in their supply chains, you are no longer bound by real-world scarcity or limitations.

Consequently, mimicking the real world in the virtual world does not make sense at all. In the metaverse, there is infinite space. Users can easily teleport from one experience to another, so creating, for example, artificially scarce digital real estate, although beneficial to a small group of insiders and as a new way to raise funds for a startup (similar to the initial coin offering [ICO] hype in 2017), does not make sense at all if you take on this different perspective. In the metaverse, you can create what you want, where you want, for whom you want, how you want. This complete freedom for creators will undoubtedly lead to some fascinating experiences, but for the open metaverse to work, there are six characteristics that creators (individuals, startups, brands, enterprises, and even governments) should take into account when building for the metaverse, while, ideally, adhering to the five principles of data discussed just before:

- Interoperability
- Decentralization
- Persistency
- Spatiality
- Community-driven
- Self-sovereignty

Let's discuss them one by one to get a complete picture of how we can create an open metaverse offering unique experiences.

Interoperability

If we want to create a bigger pie, instead of obtaining a bigger slice of the same pie, interoperability will be key. It can make the network bigger and increase the external vale of a network to consumers. Lack of interoperability keeps users inside a platform once they are in, which is predominantly beneficial to the network owner. A great example is WhatsApp. Over the years, WhatsApp has achieved very strong network effects because the more of your friends with a WhatsApp account, the easier it would be to connect with your friends.

Lack of interoperability also comes with very high switching costs for the end user, which was most likely one of the reasons why Facebook paid $19 billion for WhatsApp in 2014. When in 2021 Facebook announced it would start sharing WhatsApp data with Facebook for more targeted advertising, something Zuckerberg promised in 2014 he would not do, there were a lot of users who had enough of the social messaging platform and decided to move to Telegram or Signal. While these platforms saw an increase in their user base, it did not have any big impact on WhatsApp simply because of these high switching costs. Because of the lack of interoperability among messaging platforms, moving to another social messaging platform is useful only if all of your friends also move over, and achieving that is nearly impossible. If we want to unlock trillions of dollars in value for society as a whole, we should avoid similar silos in the metaverse.

Interoperability is all about to what extent users can take out the value they created inside one platform and bring it to another platform and vice versa without any barriers. Interoperability would enable users to win, buy, or earn a digital asset in one environment and use it in another environment, whether physical or digital. Interoperability provides users with the means to transfer their data and assets from one platform to another and sell it to other users at the market value determined by the open market. The more seamless the experience is, the more overall value the metaverse will create for society.

Interoperability can be achieved by creating standards, protocols, and development frameworks that everyone agrees to use, similar to the standards and protocols that enable email or the application programming interfaces (APIs) that make it easy to connect disparate platforms. However, there are also challenges when it comes to ensuring interoperability for the metaverse and it will require more than just global standards, protocols, or frameworks. We also need to agree upon functionality and rules to enable interoperable assets that can be used in multiple virtual worlds.[43] Obviously, we want to prevent that you can use your rocket launcher from Grand Theft Auto during the meeting with your colleagues if you think that the meeting takes too long or your colleague is annoying you again. In addition, different worlds follow different designs, and taking an asset from a low-poly world (such as Minecraft) to a high-poly world (such as Fortnite), or vice versa, might break the user experience or the entire environment.*

From that perspective, a standard really is just an interoperability protocol that everyone decides to implement. It is an agreement for two things to work together, and as humanity, we have proven to be quite good at creating those. Think of the money standard that allows you to buy whatever product with US dollars or Euros, or the USB standard that allows you to easily plug one piece of hardware (for example, your phone) into another piece of hardware (for example, your laptop). Standards can mean anything, but in the case of the metaverse, a large part of the interoperability will be digital asset formats. The type of format and the information included in those asset formats have to be in agreed interoperability standards. This would enable you to take any asset across the metaverse, and any of the millions of upcoming metaverse spaces, worlds, or experiences would understand how to unpack, process, and use the digital asset. This immediately shows the enormous challenge ahead of us, and as Neil Trevett, elected president of The Khronos Group, said, "We need a constellation of standards."[44] Standard organizations such as the International Standards Organization (ISO) and The Khronos Group are working hard

---

*Low or high poly refers to the number of polygons in a model or world, which determines the level of detail and realism within an environment. A polygon is a two-dimensional shape with straight lines that enables developers to create any kind of digital model by combining polygons. The more polygons, the more realistic, and the more computing power required to render the avatar or digital asset.

on achieving the required interoperability standards. Still, despite all the hard work, in the end, it will be up to the market whether an open or closed metaverse will prevail. If Big Tech decides to push their own specifications and the market accepts those, we will end up with walled gardens that would limit the value the creator or end user could potentially achieve in the metaverse. Fortunately, we already see a move from company-owned standards to open standards, such as the shift from the .fbx standard to .glTF standard when uploading avatar files.*

An important aspect of interoperability is also the proof of ownership and trading of any digital asset. Fortunately, this challenge has largely been solved with nonfungible tokens, fungible tokens (cryptocurrencies), and (decentralized) marketplaces. I will cover these in-depth in Chapter 7 when discussing what NFTs are and how to achieve a vibrant and rich metaverse economy. For now, it is sufficient to know that the beauty of NFTs does not so much lie in the fact that you can purchase a JPEG for millions of dollars and show it off to your friends, but that it will enable us to undoubtedly verify and prove ownership of any digital asset as well as track the provenance of those assets across the metaverse. After all, if you possess the private key to your crypto wallet storing the NFT, it means you own that wallet and thus the NFT. This can best be compared to a postbox at the post office. Everyone can put something inside the postbox; you could even look into the postbox to see what's in it, but only the person who holds the physical key can open it and take out what's in it. If we can overcome the interoperability challenge, NFTs can become the fuel of the metaverse economy.

Decentralization

While interoperability enables the exchange of assets across virtual worlds or experiences, decentralization is all about who controls those virtual worlds, assets, and experiences and who reaps the benefits if it

---

*.glTF stands for *Graphics Language Transmission Format* and is a standard file format for 3D assets, similar to .fbx, which stands for *Filmbox*. While the .fbx format is a proprietary file format developed in 2006 and owned by Autodesk, the .glTF format is an open standard created by The Khronos Group and will soon be an ISO standard. Most companies are switching to .glTF as their important format, including Meta, Microsoft, and Ready Player Me.

becomes a success. The vision for the Web has always been one of full decentralization, where the power lies with the individuals and not with Big Tech or governments that can use centralized platforms to control, exploit, and manipulate individuals. Digital ownership and control of data are key here, and it will be vital that we fix the flaws of Web 2.0 and create a metaverse controlled by no one and owned by everyone.

This is where blockchain comes into play and the various blockchain technologies that have been developed in the past decade. The metaverse should rely on a decentralized single source of the truth when exchanging value among stakeholders, whether they are consumers playing various games or enterprises as part of a supply chain. In a decentralized metaverse, thanks to cryptography, data becomes immutable, verifiable, and traceable, foregoing the need for a trusted intermediary managing the source of truth of the information at hand. This means that the provenance of either data and (digital) products will ensure efficient value exchange and full transparency. Thanks to blockchain, settlement of transactions can take seconds.* With every digital asset, smart contracts enable us to embed rules and governance into the code, which are then enforced automatically. Smart contracts are scripts for processing transactions and/or decisions. They can be seen as *If This Then That* statements compiled into bit code (although a lot more complicated). Smart contracts are small software programs that will execute automatically once the preconditions, which were agreed upon by two or more actors, are met.[45,46] Smart contracts have three distinctive characteristics: they are autonomous, decentralized, and self-sufficient (they can accumulate and spend value over time).[47] Once a smart contract is on a blockchain, it is final and cannot be changed (i.e., they become immutable, verifiable, and traceable, although if the code allows it certain parameters can still be changed).[48] This will make governance automatic. The ledger can act as legal evidence for data and increase the importance of data ownership, data transparency, asset provenance, and auditability across the metaverse.

---

*This very much depends on which blockchain you use. Some blockchains offer indeed near instant settlement of transactions, but the most well-known blockchains—the bitcoin blockchain and Ethereum—are significantly slower, with the bitcoin blockchain processing around 4.6 transactions per second in 2022 (compared to Visa, which processes on average around 1700 transactions per second, or Alibaba, which can process more than 500,000 transactions per second on Singles' Day).

Smart contracts will increasingly remove the need for human judgment and minimize the need for trust. When multiple smart contracts are combined with artificial intelligence and analytics, it becomes possible to automate decision-making capabilities altogether. This will result in a completely new paradigm of organizing activity and building communities governed by code, so-called decentralized autonomous organizations (DAOs). DAOs will be an important part of the metaverse, and they could revolutionize how democratic processes work and how communities are formed.

Smart contracts are a critical aspect of an NFT as it embeds the rules that are linked to it. As a creator of the NFT, you can decide what rules you attach to an NFT, for example, how people can use the NFT online and what rights (if any) are attached to it, etc. Chapter 7 will discuss NFTs in depth and how users can monetize the digital assets they own.

Decentralizing the metaverse will be crucial for its success, especially if we require interoperable digital assets. Decentralization in the context of the metaverse is all about proving ownership of (digital) assets and having full control over your identity, reputation, and data (self-sovereignty). However, decentralization is not about using blockchain technology to decentralize computing power, bandwidth, or data storage, yet. While these solutions are already available, it will be a long time before we can use blockchain as a digital infrastructure to power the metaverse because interactive, real-time immersive experiences will require (ultra) high-definition, low latency, and extreme bandwidth, which cannot yet be delivered by blockchain technology.

Nevertheless, decentralization is crucial for the open metaverse as it would empower the end user, let creators connect directly with fans at scale, limit censorship, and ensure cryptographic trust in a trustless (as in no intermediaries) environment.[49]

Persistency

The metaverse will be an always-on, persistent internet where experiences, whether virtual or augmented, remain available and online for anyone to experience who has access to it and for as long as the creator decides. This persistency applies to augmented reality experiences and to virtual worlds, which would enable virtual experiences that could evolve over time and are always there for users to explore. Like the real world, a persistent metaverse should stick around, even if you leave. For example, if you have augmented reality experiences pinned at a certain location in the real world, they are always there unless the creator decides to remove them. So, a flying dragon above Times Square can be seen by anyone looking up with AR glasses or their phone or tablet and the right app on their phone or glasses. Depending on their physical position on Times Square, they will see a different perspective of the same dragon. If we take this a step further and you visit Times Square in virtual reality, you would also see the same dragon flying above the world-famous square. In a truly persistent metaverse, which is probably at least a decade away, those in virtual reality can see the avatars of the people watching the dragon in Times Square, and the avatars of those viewing the dragon in virtual reality would become visible for those looking through AR glasses in the real world. It would be a truly persistent XR experience, co-present in the real and virtual worlds.

The key to a persistent metaverse is that content can be deleted only by the creator, similar to how in the real world buildings are persistent and can be removed only with permission from the owner. This could also pose a risk as this technology could also be used by criminals or terrorists, who could potentially publish defamatory, offensive, or illegal content, e.g., a terrorist recruitment poster, which then also becomes persistent and impossible to remove. Therefore, platforms that allow users to drop augmented experiences in the real world should have certain rules that prevent users from just dropping any content, but that is similar to your local government that does not allow the development of just any building.

A persistent metaverse would create infinite (monetization) opportunities for artists and content creators to enrich the digital and virtual worlds, as their efforts can be rewarded, and revenues can be received instantly without the need for banks. For example, Banksy could drop a virtual painting on a high-traffic location in London, and you would only be able to view it if you are at that specific location and would pay a small amount of money in crypto.* Since the virtual painting would be persistent, it would remain there indefinitely unless Banksy deleted it.

From a technical perspective, the metaverse also requires persistent real-time connections with a high degree of accuracy. Whether you are viewing the dragon above (virtual) Times Square with 10 or 1,000 people simultaneously, each viewing it from their own perspective should not matter, which is a difficult technical challenge to solve as it would require many-to-many connections to ensure high levels of concurrency.[50]

Spatiality

A metaverse that is not spatial is a metaverse with limited opportunities. Any virtual world, space, or experience should incorporate spatial anchors to make objects inside those virtual or augmented experiences persistent so people can find them and provide an experience that is more akin to the real world, which can be further reinforced using spatial audio. Spatial data will enable users to interact with digital items, whether placed in the virtual or real world, in the most natural way using our five senses (or even future senses, as mentioned earlier). Spatial computing would translate physical actions (movements, speech, gestures) into digital interactions in the virtual or augmented experience. The keyword here is *location*, which determines where users (avatars) or digital assets and spaces are to be placed or moved in the physical and/or virtual world.

Each thing, user, or space should obtain a unique identifier, governance and interaction rules (ideally embedded in the code using smart contracts recorded on the blockchain), and verifiable provenance for stakeholders to interact with and have a perfect copy in either the physical or digital world. To get back to the example of the dragon above Times Square, spatial data would make the dragon persistent, enable users to experience it from different perspectives, and even hear audio based on their location relative to the dragon in the air. Spatial data would also

---

*Of course, payment in fiat would also be possible, but since we are likely dealing with micro transactions, the costs of fiat money transactions would be too high and the process too slow. A central digital currency such as a digital dollar or digital Euro could overcome this, but that would then enable governments to monitor each and every transaction of its citizens.

open up new monetization opportunities by having, for example, different price strategies based on the distance to the virtual object.

Spatial data is not only about adding anchors to digital items but also about the physical to become more digital by adding sensors and having the physical item appear as an exact replica, or digital twin, in the virtual world for users to interact with. We will cover this in more detail in Chapter 6, where I'll discuss the enterprise metaverse, which is all about incorporating digital twins in business processes.

Spatial data will make both our physical and virtual worlds smarter by adding context and intelligence to any object, space, or user. It will enable real-time interaction and collaboration and provide an intuitive experience for both humans and machines.[51] It will also enable finding our way in the metaverse. Remember, in the metaverse, there is no Google, yet. Obviously, this will change in the coming years when either Google or a future startup will step into this void and enable users to find whatever they need across millions of experiences and digital objects. Without these spatial anchors, the metaverse would be a floating, non-persistent, and chaotic world, and it would be impossible to find anything.

Community-Driven

Humans are social creatures by nature, so it comes as no surprise that the metaverse will primarily be a social experience, not counting exceptions. Even those VR experiences that can be experienced only alone often add a social component such as a leader board or other gamification techniques. For any metaverse experience, the community will be crucial, whether an experience is designed around a community or created by the members of that community. To that end, the metaverse is not any different from the real world where people come together and form a community around whatever topic, as belonging to a group has always been crucial for individual survival.

This can be a niche community such as a metaverse space for wine lovers or a very broad community focused on massively multiplayer online role-playing games (MMORPGs). The metaverse can bring communities to another level, where community members can have real-time, shared, immersive, and even owned experiences. A core trait of successful games, such as Fortnite, Axie Infinity, or Minecraft, is enabling social experiences,[52] and the same will be true for the metaverse.

Brands that want to step into the metaverse must acknowledge the existing community and not pretend to know better than the community. Respect for, learning from, and interacting with the community are crucial to success in the metaverse. Today, brands and organizations find their community on social media platforms, and websites are, most often, merely a showroom of what the brand has to offer. Almost all brands interact with their community on those social media platforms where their users are, instead of bringing the community to the company's website. The same will apply to the metaverse, and brands should go there where their community is. In addition, the metaverse offers an opportunity to create unique, immersive brand experiences that are created *with* the community and potentially even controlled and owned by the community. We will dive deeper into how brands can become part of the metaverse in Chapter 5.

Self-Sovereignty

The final main characteristic of an open metaverse is self-sovereignty, which means that the individual remains in control over their online identity and data, instead of the platform or website. A self-sovereign identity and/or reputation has long been the objective of Web 3.0, and it is one of the most important characteristics that we have to get right if we want to create an open metaverse. In the past decades, self-sovereignty has not been on the agenda as we too much enjoyed the free services provided by Big Tech. As a result, we have ended up in a situation where users have digital identities that are not self-sovereign but controlled by companies who can delete your (online) identity with a click of the button, as we have seen with the Australian artist Thea-Mai Baumann who saw her entire Instagram deleted by Meta. The lack of self-sovereignty leads to privacy violations, data breaches and manipulations, and more serious problems such as identity theft or identity impersonations. Self-sovereignty is crucial if we want to achieve an open, decentralized, and interoperable metaverse.

Identity consists of many different attributes, constantly changing and evolving in terms of priority and durability. Some attributes such as birth dates, place of birth, biological parents, and Social Security numbers will stay with a person for their entire life. Others, such as an employee number, student number, address, or telephone number, could change periodically. Other attributes could be very short-lived, such as a username on a forum or website. Each of these attributes has different, uniquely identifiable characteristics, and the combination of them constitutes a person's identity (although the person might perceive that differently).[53] Identity is a complicated concept, and within the metaverse, identity will become far more complicated as identity can take all forms or shapes thanks to avatars. Users will most likely have multiple avatars for various metaverse experiences; one could show up as a hyper-realistic dinosaur in one space, a digital human for work meetings, or a pixelated low-polygon avatar in a Minecraft or Sandbox-like environment. All constitute the same person but in different environments. This is nothing new as in the physical world we do exactly the same (albeit we might not dress up as a dinosaur if we visit a friend).

If identity consists of ever-changing attributes, a self-sovereign identity restores the control over who has access to those attributes to the consumer or device, which owns that identity. So instead of social media companies or governments owning a person's identity attributes, the consumer is in full control and determines, for each interaction, who gets access to which attributes or data points.[54] Self-sovereignty is the idea that individuals, but also things in the near future, should have control over their own data, identity, reputation, and information on the internet without having to rely on any one company or government entity for protection or any intermediary controlling their data or identity. People can regain sovereignty over their identity and data using blockchain technologies, including zero-knowledge proofs.[55]

For example, when entering a metaverse community that requires a minimum age, we could use a self-sovereign identity to prove that we are of a particular age without revealing our age. Instead, we would share a zero-knowledge proof, a cryptographically verified statement of *yes* or *no*, that we are older than the required minimum age, without sharing any additional information. Compare that to today's world, where you are required to provide your identity document or driver's license to prove your age, which includes a variety of very personal details such as your date of birth, address, name, or license number, none of which are necessary for the space to determine whether you meet the age requirement for the community. The entire process can be automated using smart contracts to create a seamless experience while protecting your identity. As a result of self-sovereign identities, consumers will become black boxes* for organizations, and only the user will determine what data will be shared with what metaverse space.

Within the metaverse, proving your identity, or proving that you are who you say you are, will become more important than ever before because, with avatars, it will be relatively easy to impersonate someone by creating a digital copy of the avatar they normally use. With advancements such as Reallusion Character Creator 4 or the Unreal Engine's MetaHuman Creator, it has become easier than ever before to create an exact copy of a celebrity, politician, or entrepreneur and using deepfake audio have him, or her, do and say whatever you want in any digital environment. Unless the celebrity, politician, or entrepreneur can cryptographically prove that they are the one who *owns* and *controls* the avatar or digital human, we will open a Pandora's box of disasters. In Chapter 8, I will dive deeper into the dangers of the metaverse that could ruin people's lives and bring significant damages to society.

Related to the impersonation of avatars are trust and reputation. How do you know that the person you are interacting with is who they say they are? How can we trust the avatar we are dealing with? That's where self-sovereign reputation comes into play. Many people discuss the concept of self-sovereign identity, but few discuss the concept of a self-sovereign reputation, which is as important because we want to ensure that we are trustworthy even if we are anonymous and change our identity, as in our avatar, on a regular basis.

---

*A black box refers to algorithms, which are generally black boxes; whatever happens inside an algorithm is known only to the organization that created it, and quite often not even. As a result, it is often unknown how an algorithm arrived at a certain decision, which is problematic as algorithms will make more and more (important) decisions in society. If consumers would become a black box, it means that only the consumer would have access to their data and organizations would need to ask for permission to obtain access to the data.

The answer lies in ensuring *anonymous accountability* in the metaverse, which is possible only if we have a self-sovereign, verified identity. This would enable users to remain completely anonymous to the outside world while building up a reputation across platforms. It would work that a user could obtain a unique code from, let's say, a bank, who has verified that person as part of their *know your customer* (KYC) process. This unique code can include a variety of data points, such as when it was provided and by which bank (to ensure only trustworthy banks can provide these codes). The information is stored on a blockchain and connected to a user's metaverse identity, which is linked to their crypto wallet. If a user switches avatar, the same verified connection will remain, and based on their actions, the user builds up a reputation that is portable from one platform to another as it is connected with the user's identity, even if that user interacts anonymously. When combining anonymous accountability with self-sovereignty, users can be held accountable, even if they interact anonymously. This would increase trust in the metaverse and place the power to reveal one's identity with the user instead of an organization. Of course, this sovereignty should focus not only on identity or reputation, but users should also be sovereign over their data, digital assets, and creations, ensuring that ownership of these lies with the user instead of organizations or governments. Therefore, digital wallets will play a key role in ensuring self-sovereignty within the metaverse.

If we can make self-sovereignty a cornerstone of the metaverse, it will bring us a step closer to a truly open and decentralized metaverse, owned and controlled by the community instead of corporations. It would enable us to move from programmatic information exchange as part of Web 1.0 and Web 2.0 to programmatic value exchange as an intricate part of Web 3.0, whereby users can build code components on top of their sovereign assets that do interesting things with those assets to increase value for the overall system, without being dependent on intermediaries that could cut them off from the ecosystem. In other words, self-sovereignty is a paradigm shift from today's identity and data system, empowering users and creators to take their lives into their own hands.

An Open Metaverse Means Freedom

An open metaverse is all about value exchange and human beings being able to interact with one another and have complete control over how they organize their lives in the metaverse. Any platform building something for the metaverse should incorporate these characteristics in some form or shape if they want to contribute to the open metaverse and be there for the long run. To understand how this would work in practice, let's have a look at a fictional example.

The Freedom Platform is a new digital world that enables users to socialize, relax, work, and collaborate in an immersive, spatial environment. Users can register with the platform using their digital wallet to create an account. Once registered, they can select one of the available avatars, create their own avatar using the on-board creator tool, or add their own creation by simply uploading it. Their avatar is minted as an NFT and stored inside the user's wallet. Users who want to be verified can use the decentralized application (dApp) to connect with their local bank to become fully verified. Users can then decide to interact anonymously on the platform or share their identity.

Within The Freedom Platform, users can build worlds, buildings, and experiences similar to existing virtual worlds such as Decentraland, The Sandbox, or Wilder World. The user can either interact with the platform using a 2D immersive experience on their desktop or tablet or go truly immersive and explore the world in virtual reality. Some experiences can also be dropped into the real world, and using spatial anchors connect the real and the virtual world. For example, artists can create a unique sculpture inside the platform and drop the same sculpture on Trafalgar Square in London. The sculpture is connected to an NFT that the artist holds, and users can pay to view the sculpture in both the virtual and the augmented worlds using the platform's native crypto token FRDM, which the artist instantly receives.

Multiple companies also have set up shop inside The Freedom Platform, which allows them to have immersive meetings with their staff located around the world. Employees can join a meeting remotely using their desktop and webcam or using a VR headset, while those employees inside the office can use their AR glasses to instantly project their colleagues' avatars that have joined remotely. Spatial audio will create a more immersive experience for all participants, ensuring a productive meeting.

Both a company's virtual headquarter and an artist's sculpture are persistent and remain available for anyone to view or join if they hold the right keys, preventing unwanted guests from joining the company's meeting. Since the platform is decentralized, nobody can delete the content created by others, though there are, of course, rules in place that prevent certain behavior. Artificial intelligence and smart contracts govern these rules, and a user's reputation can be affected in case rules are persistently breached.

Within The Freedom Platform, anyone can come together, create a community, and set up a decentralized autonomous organization to build an experience together. The experience is owned and controlled by the community, and any revenue generated from the experience is shared instantly among the community based on their input.

Over the years, the platform evolves into an ever-growing virtual and augmented experience. Thanks to the interoperability standards, users can easily export their avatar and assets to explore other worlds, obtain assets in those worlds and expose them as virtual trophies within their The Freedom Platform home or as augmented digital trophies in their real-world, physical home.

Of course, this is only a fictional example. Still, it shows how future platforms could incorporate the six characteristics of the metaverse to build a platform that offers true benefits for society. Those who created the platform also benefit due to the increased price of the FRDM cryptocurrency, thereby rewarding them for taking the risk to create such a unique world.

An Endless Blue Ocean

The future is guaranteed to be virtual and augmented. It already is. We no longer need to memorize all kinds of facts because we have Google. We do not have to prepare our road trip anymore because we simply tell our car where we want to go, and in the not-too-distant future, learning a new language will also become obsolete as instant translations will become the norm. Because of the convergence of emerging technologies such as blockchain, artificial intelligence (AI), the Internet of Things, and AR/VR, we have an opportunity to rebuild our society and fix some of the flaws of Web 2.0. AI will be the glue that makes everything stick together and allows it to function according to its design, while blockchain is a necessity if we want to ensure interoperability and true ownership of digital assets. The Internet of Things is required to connect the physical world with the virtual world using digital twins, be it machines, factories, or even humans, and AR and VR will deliver new channels to explore all this digital content.

The metaverse will enable the Imagination Age, where content creators will be able to monetize their work and contribute to a rich, vibrant, and magical immersive internet. Humans are sensory beings, so the shift to the metaverse is a natural iteration for humanity. In the years ahead, computing devices, whatever they are, will become world aware and communicate with each other. Thanks to spatial and contextual computing, any device connected to the metaverse will understand its (virtual) environment and be able to interact with it.

As a result, the metaverse will be an infinite blue ocean of opportunity similar to the original internet. We will have millions of virtual spaces and augmented experiences across the metaverse and our physical world. All niches and groups that exist in the real world and on Web 2.0 will likely find their way to the metaverse and create their own niche immersive communities. We are currently at the very start of the metaverse, and platforms such as the fictional The Freedom Platform are at least still five years away because of the infrastructure required to deliver such a world. You could even argue that in 2022 we are where the internet was at the end of the 1990s, way before Facebook or Amazon, although it won't take as long to achieve the full potential of the metaverse due to the convergence of the various technologies. In the coming years, it will become easier to build immersive and augmented experiences, especially if we manage to create the "constellation of standards" required to run the metaverse smoothly.

If we do, the metaverse could add trillions of dollars to the global society. The estimates vary, but PWC released a report in 2019 estimating that VR and AR have the potential to boost GDP globally by up to $1.5 trillion in 2030, up from a projected $476.4 billion in 2025.[56] I believe this is grossly underestimated, as, by 2030, virtual reality will have become hyper-realistic, and augmented reality will become the standard way to interact with the metaverse.* Every citizen, every organization, and most governments will live, work, and interact in the metaverse. Digital fashion will become the norm, and content creators will be able to monetize their work in ways we cannot yet imagine. Direct-to-avatar will have surpassed business-to-commerce (B2C) business models, and immersive commerce (iCommerce) will be significantly bigger, even surpassing eCommerce.

Digital twins are beginning to already create new ways for enterprises to optimize their operations and supply chains, driving up the value the metaverse will deliver to the global GDP. Some studies forecast 50 percent of the children alive today will have jobs that do not yet exist or are just appearing in the market, ranging from virtual metaverse tour guides to digital stylists welcoming you in virtual stores and helping you select the best fashion item for your avatar.[57] The metaverse will have its own global economy, bringing globalization to another level as artificial borders will likely play less of a role in the metaverse. How we organize this economy will directly impact the value that it can deliver for our society, but concepts like decentralized finance will be an important part of it, thereby empowering content creators to put their assets to work and generate more value.

The metaverse will likely disrupt all industries and create revenue opportunities in iCommerce, events, advertising, hardware/software, fashion, and many more, creating new companies along the way and delivering tremendous value similar to the ~$15 trillion market cap of Web 2.0 companies.[58] The metaverse will have as big an impact on society as the internet had, if not bigger. It will completely change how we

---

*While this book does not cover much of the Chinese metaverse, which will be significantly different due to its regulation and censorship, Morgan Stanley estimates that it could be an $8 trillion market in the future - Arjun Kharpal, "China's tech giants push toward an $8 trillion metaverse opportunity — one that will be highly regulated," CNBC, February 13, 2022, visited February 14, 2022, www.cnbc.com/amp/2022/02/14/china-metaverse-tech-giants-latest-moves-regulatory-action.html.

work, live, and socialize. Those organizations that are too late to adapt will likely cease to exist in the years ahead. The metaverse is a paradigm change, and in the coming chapters, I will discuss what that will mean for being human and how it will impact organizations and our society. However, let's first discuss how we can create an open metaverse.

Chapter 2
Creating an Open Metaverse

Open vs. Closed

As discussed in Chapter 1, interoperability is the key enabler to significant value for society as a whole, enabling users to seamlessly move assets (including your identity) from one platform to another. But what does this really mean? What is the difference between a metaverse constructed of open platforms versus a metaverse that consists only of closed walled gardens, and what lies in between? Is some hybrid metaverse possible, with both open and closed digital experiences? As it appears, the spectrum of open versus closed is not exact, but there are multiple layers and aspects that determine how open or how closed a certain platform or experience is. One thing is clear, though: an open metaverse will deliver significantly more value than a metaverse consisting of closed platforms, let alone a metaverse consisting of a single, closed platform such as The Oasis as portrayed in *Ready Player One*. In fact, The Oasis was created, owned, and controlled by one person, which would mean the equivalent of one company owning the entire internet. Although some companies do their best to be portrayed as being the metaverse, it is not very realistic and, ideally, will never happen.

The less extreme variant is a metaverse that exists only of closed walled gardens, which is basically what we have today. The vast majority of organizations on the Web are centralized companies running platforms or websites, some of which have grown so big due to network effects that they are considered Big Tech. Despite the vision of the early internet, it is currently not possible to take your data or digital assets from one website to another. You cannot download your entire TikTok history, including all your comments and friends, and upload it onto another platform and continue your digital influencer activities. TikTok owns your data, and they make it very hard for you to leave because your data is worth way too much to them. Big Tech has done very well in making a seamless user experience, including federated authentication to log in with Google or Facebook on third-party websites, thereby gobbling up even more data. Users trade their privacy for convenience, and, naturally, Big Tech will do whatever it can to prevent this model from changing.

A metaverse consisting of closed walled gardens would basically be a more extreme version of the current Web. Since the immersive internet will result in more than 100x data collection compared to today, Big Tech will become more powerful and have more control over our lives than ever before. It will be social media and toxic recommendation engines to drive shareholder value on steroids. If you think social media radicalized people and polarized societies in 2D, imagine what could happen in 3D. Virtual echo chambers and alternate virtual realities could fracture society with everyone living in their own (virtual) world, reinforced by a toxic vicious circle of advertising and recommendations.[59] Using augmented reality, we could automatically overlay avatars to people on the street based on their race to create our own reality, further dividing society. If we want to keep our society pleasant and livable, this is the part we need to change and prevent from happening. We should move away from a shareholder model that drives toxic recommendation engines focused on keeping people engaged as long as possible to a stakeholder model that rewards all parties and considers the wider impact on society. We should potentially prevent some applications from being launched, and we should enable a seamless experience for users to move from one platform to the other, taking hard-earned digital assets, data, and identity with them, rewarding all those who create the value instead of just the platform owners.

Of course, this does not mean you will be able to import those assets, data, and your avatar into anywhere. When it comes to virtual worlds, augmented experiences, or even digital twins, these will be either private or public and can be either permissioned or permissionless. There are three options.

- *Permissionless and public:* Anyone can join at any moment. You might need an account to join, but you do not have to obtain permission to join a virtual world or see an AR experience.
- *Permissioned and public:* You need some approval to join a public experience or network. This approval can be given after payment or using a special invitation.
- *Private spaces:* By definition these are permissioned and secure, similar to the intranets of organizations and to how some of the largest organizations create private 5G networks.

Each digital space has its own rules, created, monitored, and enforced by its founders, owners, the community, or the wider organization. Similar to the real world, there will be a large variety of completely open, permissionless platforms, but also plenty of permissioned, closed private spaces, your virtual office, for example, and anything in between. The extent to which you can import and export your avatar and identity, your digital assets, and your data depends on the rules and governance in place. A decentralized social media platform will have different levels of openness and permissions than a digital platform to track your health, your home, your local airport, or a government building, for that matter. Unfortunately, you won't be able to teleport into the virtual world of the Pentagon.

The platforms that embrace the Web 3.0 paradigm will use distributed ledger technologies, such as blockchains and NFTs, to give the user complete control over their data and identity. In contrast, closed platforms might focus on other benefits and prevent users from owning the value they have created. However, we cannot force people to move to closed or open platforms. It is more a Darwinian approach where those platforms that offer the most benefits to the end user will win—both closed and open platforms in a healthy Darwinian competition with each other.

I do hope, though, that open platforms will become the norm instead of the exception, simply because of the value and benefits they bring to users and society. Wealth and influence will become trapped if a walled garden is truly closed. If the digital value you have created is nontransferable, it does not have any value for the wider economic system.

As Jamie Burke, founder and CEO of Outlier Ventures, explained, a good way to picture this would be through a Fortnite gamer walking into a bank to obtain a short-term loan or a mortgage.[60] The Fortnite gamer could have invested years and hundreds of dollars, thus amassing a huge chunk of wealth through avatars, skins, assets, and prize winnings. However, to a bank, much of this wealth is a sunk cost that cannot be considered as a form of collateral when obtaining a loan or mortgage. This is the same predicament facing a majority of those involved in the digital economy, such as social media influencers. Despite having property rights to digital assets, they are trapped by design, with much of the digital value and assets owned not being recognized by today's financial system. This constitutes a form of financial exclusion, even when the gaming and digital ecosystem around it is in the sums of billions and billions of dollars. If users cannot take their assets from one platform to another, whether in the real world or the digital realm, it will just remain disconnected stuff that does not add any value to society. The user is financially excluded from the economic system, although potentially the user could have contributed a lot of value. As long as that value is not recognized, creating a truly inclusive economic system will become very difficult.

That is where economic interoperability comes into play. You have to be able to transfer assets out of a platform and freely transfer them at market value in an open market, if for no other reason that it creates tremendous value for the economic system. For example, research by Outlier Ventures showed that people spent 10 times more on a blockchain-based game that allows users to transfer their assets out of that platform than they do on a non-blockchain-based game.[61] Take the *Play to Earn* game Axie Infinity as an example. Despite having a player base of around 3 million, the game generated more revenue than any game on the planet, making almost $760 million in revenue in the 3rd quarter in 2021 alone.[62] It was launched in 2018, and within a few years, it exploded to 1 million

daily users, grew to $364 million in revenue per month,[63] was valued at
$3 billion in October 2021[64] (in addition to a highly fluctuating billion dol-
lar market cap of Axie Infinity's ASX token, changing from $9.77 billion
in November 2021 to $3.89 billion in mid-February 2022.[65]), and enabled
a large group of people in the Philippines to give up their jobs and move
to Axie Infinity full-time. Initially, they were able to make more money
with the game than with a job, but due to the market demands and crypto
volatility, earnings for most players dropped below the minimum wage.[66]
Despite these challenges, the overall economic and societal impact of
Axie Infinity is bigger than Fortnite, which made $5.1 billion in revenue
in 2020 with 80 million monthly users[67] and where the profits ended up
with only a small group of companies and individuals. According to Jamie
Burke, people will place a premium on transferable digital assets versus
nontransferable assets, so it is just good business and societal practice to
embrace interoperability. Yes, maybe it will result in the elite of Big Tech
earning hundreds of millions of dollars instead of billions of dollars, but
I'd say that should be a sacrifice they should make to improve society and
advance humanity.

While the transferability of NFTs contributes value to the economic
system, there are use cases when you would want to prevent or limit this
transferability.[68] One use case where nontransferability would be required
is when NFTs are used for the issuance of government documents (e.g.,
driver's licenses) or university degrees. If you would be able to transfer
the NFT proving you completed a degree to someone else, the system
would lose its value quickly. Another use case would be the *Proof of
Attendance (PoA)* NFT, which proves that a person has personally participated in a particular event. Say you have attended a massive interactive
live event and the sponsor of the event provides everyone with a PoA that
offers a discount when you go to the physical store of the sponsor and
show it. Taking this a step further, the *Proof of Attendance* can actually be
a digital fashion item, says Lindsey McInerney, former Global Head of
Technology & Innovation at Anheuser-Busch InBev, such as a digital
T-shirt that your avatar can wear similar to festival T-shirts in the physical
world, but which updates automatically if you attend more events.[69] Users
could display these NFTs, not so much to show off their wealth but that
they attended some event personally. Especially if the NFT comes with

some kind of utility, such as the discount at a store, it could be wise to limit the transferability. The platform POAP offers event organizers to easily create *Proof of Attendance* tokens and hand them out to their visitors. Completely preventing the transfer of NFTs is also not desirable as users should still be able to transfer NFTs from one wallet to another wallet, e.g., for security purposes. That is why POAP recommends developers and organizations implement their own checks, such as checking on-chain whether the current owner is the same as the original recipient.

Of course, an open economy driving more value than a closed economy is nothing new as the same applies to real-world economies. In the past 500 years, we went from relatively closed economies to a global, interconnected and open economy where standards, protocols, and trade agreements have resulted in economic growth for those countries open to it. One only has to look at the closed economy of North Korea to confirm that closed economies perform far worse than open economies. From that perspective, the metaverse is just history repeating itself.

In recent years, more and more platforms have been developed that aim to build an open equivalent of the current Web's most prominent platforms, though most of these platforms have yet to become mass adopted. For example, Steem.it tried to replace Medium, and Status.im aims to replace WhatsApp, but due to the strong network effects of these walled gardens, the switching costs are high for users. In addition, another reason for the low adoption rate is that decentralization requires hard work for the user, and most people prefer convenience. Many people will find it too much trouble, too complicated, or too much of a responsibility to deal with a fully decentralized wallet, where the user is responsible for their private keys and where mistakes can be very costly.

The user experience (UX) of Web 3.0 has been challenging and requires a high degree of technical literacy.[70] As the UX gets better over time and decentralized wallets become accepted and trusted by the masses, open platforms will become a better alternative to the current centralized, closed, but very convenient, platforms owned by Big Tech.

Wallets can, of course, be completely decentralized, where you alone are responsible for keeping your private keys secure, or it can be a managed wallet, the equivalent of the bank keeping your wallet secure, which is a bit of an oxymoron: a centralized entity securing a decentralized asset. People lose their passports, phones, and physical keys all the time, so keeping your private key—a long string of letters and digits that is impossible to remember—secure will seem very challenging for many people. Of course, there will be a hardcore group of people only using truly decentralized wallets, but the majority will certainly not do so. We have to acknowledge this and develop the platforms, and regulations, to protect those people who will opt for managed decentralized wallets because losing your entire digital identity is a much bigger problem than losing your passport.

Once the decentralized Web offers as much convenience and as seamless an experience as Web 2.0, we might also be able to convert the hardcore "lazy" users who prefer convenience above anything else. Ideally, the better the UX of decentralized tech becomes, the less relevant closed walled gardens that continue to block interoperability become. After all, what is the value of something that you invested all your time, money, and energy in if you cannot take it out and monetize it?

As more closed platforms either open up or close down, interoperability becomes the key feature of the metaverse. Of course, that does not mean that all platforms will enable the transfer of all assets, as even within interoperability, there are multiple layers. For example, hyper-realistic platforms will not allow low-polygon avatars, and vice versa, as it will break the experience, and you can be sure that any virtual world owned by Walt Disney will not allow any avatars dressed as Nazis to enter their experience.

The Hybrid Web

The vision of Web 3.0 is one of a decentralized internet, owned, run, and controlled by the community. The idea of Web 3.0 is to democratize data and move away from a centralized server model to a decentralized, peer-to-peer, and large network of nodes seamlessly operating and running the Web's applications. Although we should strive for such a model, I do not believe that this completely decentralized metaverse in all its facets is attainable in the next decade or two for multiple reasons.

First, the metaverse must be backward compatible. Existing and future platforms will need to be able to connect with the legacy of Web 2.0, which means there will always remain a centralized component to the metaverse. We cannot simply hit the delete button on everything that has been built before the arrival of the metaverse or migrate everything from AWS or Microsoft Azure to decentralized storage platforms, such as the InterPlanetary File System (IPFS), Storj, or FileCoin, that reward users for sharing any excess storage and as such create a storage system that is not owned by one company but by thousands of users.

Second, for the foreseeable future, distributed ledger technologies will not be advanced enough to handle metaverse platforms. Delivering hyper-realistic, live-streamed, volumetric video data is very hard, let alone having hundreds of thousands of users inside that same immersive experience, all interacting with each other. Imagine having 100,000 avatars all present at one event. It means 100,00000 movements, all influencing each other from 100,000 locations around the world, shown from an almost infinite number of perspectives. We are talking bandwidth, latency, computing power, and architecture at unprecedented levels, which even today's centralized system cannot handle. That is why, today, in most of the virtual worlds, you are present only with a few dozen other users at max. As soon as the space becomes multidimensional, the technical challenges become exponentially more complex. How do you serve the data? How do you make it social and appropriate and accessible and not hackable? It becomes even more complicated if you want to have a truly real-time experience. Let's say you have a shared object, a soccer ball in a game, and two people are trying to kick it at exactly the same time. If there are even a few milliseconds of delay, the trajectory of that ball can change, thereby directly impacting the outcome. For the foreseeable future, handling such activities will be impossible for distributed ledger technologies.

Next, the internet started as, and still is, an open protocol, but consolidation happened within less than a decade, resulting in an oligopoly that runs the world. This happened because creating digital platforms and websites was really hard at the start of the internet. Hence, it made sense to group together, create economies of scale, and raise tons of capital to build the tools to build the internet. Those platforms, the AWS, Google,

Facebook, or WordPress of this world, became the Big Tech of today. The same will likely happen with the metaverse. Building today's decentralized virtual worlds and augmented experiences is really hard. Creating decentralized and immersive platforms such as Decentraland or Somnium Space is significantly harder than spinning up a website with WordPress. So, I would not be surprised if the same thing would happen with Web 3.0, and we will have a small group of platforms that will make it very simple to create virtual or augmented experiences. Of course, these platforms should be open; they might even be owned, partially, by the community, but it is more likely that they are controlled and owned centrally by the investors of this world who funded the platforms to begin with.

Finally, even if the technical challenges are overcome, decentralized autonomous organizations (DAOs) start centralized. Nothing can be decentralized from the first moment as someone needs to develop a certain idea and create the foundation centrally. Of course, to grow, it can be funded using the community who consequently own and control the DAO, but unless there are programmatic restrictions in place to limit the level of ownership an individual user can have, it is possible that even a DAO can eventually become controlled by a select group of people. It is part of the human instinct to try to grow influence within a particular community. If there are no checks and balances that prevent that, even systems that start decentralized can quickly become centralized. The same is also happening in the crypto world. While its objective is to create a decentralized ecosystem, the reality is that economies of scale and inequality quickly result in some form of centralization. For example, 50–60 percent of Bitcoin's mining power (the hash rate) is controlled by five to six mining pools (a group of miners sharing their computing power),[71] while the top 10,000 wallets control more than 4 million bitcoins or 21 percent of the circulating supply.[72] The same happens in the NFT space, where a small group of whitelisted buyers (buyers who are notified before anyone else when a new NFT drop becomes available) makes the most profit; 78 percent of sales by whitelisted buyers result in a profit, while 78 percent of the sales by un-whitelisted buyers result in a loss.[73]

As a result, I believe that the metaverse will be built on top of a hybrid Web. The next iteration of the Web will probably never be fully decentralized. Instead, the best we can hope for is a hybrid Web with the best of both worlds seamlessly connected. The centralized network's speed, bandwidth, and computing power enable real-time, hyper-realistic visualizations, advanced AI capabilities, and in-network applications enabling fast-paced innovation combined with a self-sovereign identity and true ownership of digital assets, your data and how you want to monetize those using blockchain technologies.

According to Ryan Gill, founder of the Open Metaverse Association, "the internet has been built by web developers, the open metaverse is being built by game developers."[74] While platforms such as Unity, Unreal Engine 5, or Blender have made it easier to create immersive platforms, these experiences still require the best, game-like infrastructure ranging from fast fiber-optic internet connections to the best gaming consoles. Therefore, for the metaverse to become a success, the Web itself has to become intelligent and an active participant. There will be centralized platforms that will help you create your digital assets, be it augmented experiences, avatars, immersive virtual scenes or spaces, digital wearables, etc., and then allow you to export them as a decentralized, interoperable asset linked to an NFT controlled by the owner of it. Serving those digital assets will require (ultra) low-latency, stable network connections, extreme bandwidth, and low redundancy, which has to be done using the centralized server model we know today as it will be impossible to use your avatar in a decentralized way, for example, in an MMORPG.* To ensure self-sovereignty, this can be governed by smart contracts in such a way that the moment you stop playing or extract your NFTs, it automatically deletes the accompanying centralized copy of that asset, bringing together the best of both worlds of self-sovereignty and unique immersive experiences.

An Open Economic System

The best that can happen to the metaverse is a metaverse consisting of centralized platforms and decentralized communities where interoperability is possible everywhere. This does not mean there won't be any

---

*In case you forgot this acronym, MMORPG stands for massively multiplayer online role-playing games.

powerful, centralized Big Tech. It does mean it will lower the switching costs for consumers or make them negligible, which will benefit both the consumer and society as organizations have to work harder to keep users happy. This is the most beneficial to all parties and will bring the most value to society, though it is maybe less attractive to those billionaire founders who care only about their personal wealth. Some decentralized communities will be pure DAOs and be completely open. In contrast, others are centralized platforms with their own rules and regulations but where you can still import your assets that remain under your control, though not all.

Economic interoperability is the key to an inclusive metaverse that can bring value to all internet users. Although there will be different levels of economic interoperability, depending on the platform, its rules, and its governance mechanisms, freely transferring property rights (be it your identity, digital assets, content, data, etc.) is possible only with the right internet protocols and global standards as discussed in Chapter 1.

Protocols and standards can result in additional value across large ecosystems. For example, an energy company can build an AI model using data from its 100 wind turbines to predict when they require maintenance and how much energy they will deliver. However, if the industry as a whole could create an AI model of the data from all of the world's wind turbines (who fall in the same category), it would make a much better AI model, delivering more value to humanity as a whole. To enable this, organizations would need to collaborate and share their data in ways that protect proprietary insights. Independent protocols and standards that the industry has agreed upon would help avoid any mistrust between participating energy companies. The same applies to the metaverse. Protocols and standards can help ensure that users join any platform without fearing that their identity or digital assets will be stolen or hijacked. That is where standard organizations such as The Khronos Group or the International Standards Organization (ISO) come into play. They can collectively create open standards and protocols that are embraced by everyone and controlled by the community instead of Big Tech pushing their proprietary specifications.

Of course, when it comes to standards, "it is certainly easier and faster for one company to write a proprietary specification, get three people to sign off on it and to ship it out" than it is to "bring a whole industry along with you and get broad agreement from potentially hundreds of companies. But getting that agreement, it's not a bug. It's the feature," according to Neil Trevett, elected president of The Khronos Group.[75] Although standards take time, it is still the fastest route to ensure an open and inclusive metaverse that delivers the most value to all nearly 8 billion humans.

The metaverse offers us a unique opportunity to fix our past mistakes and re-create a better, more inclusive, and more equal future. We are at a point in history where we have a choice. We can create a metaverse where everyone can be part of unique, immersive experiences, have access to unique ways to earn a living, and have complete control over our identity, data, and digital assets, or we can stick to what we have, including all problems that come with it.

An interoperable metaverse will enable users to monetize those assets, to sell them, borrow against them, use them as collateral, create derivatives, or rent them out. The opportunities are ample, and it will create an entirely new 24/7 economy as we will see in the following chapters. However, it also brings a responsibility to us as it requires us to stand up against closed platforms that limit an open economic system and interoperability and be willing to potentially pay for services instead of sticking to free services where we pay with our data. We should vote with our data and wallet, a decentralized wallet preferably.

Chapter 3
Be Who You Want to Be

The Rise of the Avatars

The ARPANET was not only crucial for creating the internet, but it was also used to play a first-person shooter maze game between multiple universities that included the world's first avatar. In the early 1970s, three NASA employees—Steve Colley, Howard Palmer, and Greg Thompson—created the multiplayer game MazeWar, where a graphical eyeball moved around the maze, pointing its cyclops gaze at wherever it was going.[76] It was the first visual representation of a digital character. Since then, avatars have evolved significantly to represent real and nonexisting users in a virtual world. In the not-too-distant future, avatars will also enter the physical world using augmented reality or holographic projections.

An avatar can be anything from a 2D pixelated image such as CryptoPunks or a character of the Bored Ape Yacht Club to a character in games like Fortnite or Minecraft to hyper-realistic 3D digital representations of humans, called *digital humans*. Above anything else, an avatar is a visual representation of an identity. This identity can be of a real person who needs a representation in a virtual world, or it can be a representation of a nonexisting digital user, a digital agent, also known as *nonplayer characters* (NPCs), which a computer instead of a person controls. Avatars are crucial to the metaverse as they enable us to bring our identity to the virtual world, interact with others, and take our virtual identity into the real world.

Users will have different identities in the metaverse depending on the (virtual) setting, similar to the physical world. In real life, with your friends, you behave and dress differently than in a business setting. The same applies to the virtual world. Depending on the community you want to go to or join, you would dress your avatar differently or select a completely different avatar. The exciting aspect of using an avatar to portray your identity is that you are no longer bound to your physical identity, which opens a world of new opportunities to express yourself.

We have already broadened our perspective of what identity means in the past years. What started as man versus woman, there are now a wide variety of gender identities, including nonbinary, transgender, or gender-fluid. In fact, there are many gender identities.[77] However, not all identities are accepted everywhere, sometimes even with grave consequences. In the metaverse, this will be different. In the virtual world, if you can come up with it and create it, you can be whoever you want to be, whenever you want. This will likely result in an identity explosion, as in the metaverse, people have the complete freedom to decide whatever type of avatar they want to use and how they want to dress their avatar.

In the metaverse, you can be who you want to be. You can show up as yourself, or you can show up as anything that you can imagine, from a cute fluffy rabbit to an enormous robot or a purple flying centaur. Anything goes, as long as you are happy with it. The fact that an avatar might not look like a human should not make a difference. In fact, it can help people to better portray their identity and better show how they feel at any given moment, changing your avatar depending on your mood. An avatar can also be a showcase of belonging to a certain community. Many people are currently using their NFT as an avatar, be it a CryptoPunk, Bored Ape, or whatever, on social media as their profile picture, thereby showing (off) that they are part of a certain niche community, which is why in early 2022, Twitter enabled users to verify their NFTs by connecting their crypto wallet to Twitter.[78]

This will only be amplified in the metaverse as 3D avatars will become the norm. 3D avatars offer a wide variety of new ways to show who you are and to which community you belong. This can be in the form or type of your avatar, but it can also be by how your avatar dresses or what kind of digital wearables the avatar will possess. This will create an entirely new economy, as we will see in a bit.

We can expect a wide variety of avatars within the metaverse, and which type of avatar is available in what environment is often a design choice that has significant implications from a technical perspective. Platforms can use a ready-to-go platform such as Ready Player Me, which allows developers to easily integrate an avatar platform in their experience or develop their own avatar system as done by the likes of Roblox, Meta, or Microsoft. These platforms each take a different approach, where Roblox and The Sandbox have chosen for a more Lego-like appearance of their avatars, and Meta and Microsoft opted for avatars without legs. Both platforms use low-polygon avatars to reduce the required computing power and enable most consumers to play their game or use their environment on pretty much any smartphone, tablet, or computer. Simpler avatars have a lot of advantages and will make a game or environment easier to play. As Timmu Tõke, CEO and cofounder of Wolf3D, the company building Ready Player Me, said, the "closer you go to realism, the easier it is to mess it up."[79]

The number of polygons determines how realistic an avatar, or any digital asset for that matter, is. An avatar in VRChat on Quest cannot exceed 10,000 polygons[80]; otherwise, it will not be displayed, while the hyper-realistic assets in the video game The Matrix Awakens (which is not only a game but also a demo showcasing the possibilities of Unreal Engine 5 and promoting the movie) have millions of polygons each, which explains why only users with an Xbox Series X or PS5 can play this game.[81] It will be a while before such hyper-realistic experiences become available in virtual reality. There are currently few platforms that enable hyper-realistic, high-polygon avatars such as digital humans, simply because the computing power required to handle such avatars is too much for the vast majority of consumers. They are primarily used in professional games, movies, or recordings. In addition, hyper-realistic avatars are very challenging to make. Although new solutions such as Unreal Engine's MetaHuman or Reallusion Character Creator 4 simplify this process, it is still a challenge, and expensive, to create one. It will be a few years before hyper-realistic digital humans such as the virtual

Keanu Reeves of The Matrix Awakens become commonplace and available to the masses.

Apart from the compute and bandwidth requirements of hyper-realistic avatars, there is another important aspect why currently most platforms opt for cartoonish avatars, and it has to do with a concept called the *uncanny valley of the mind*. Humans are very good at distinguishing social potential in items that imply humans to any extent. Give any object, for example, a fridge, two eyes, a nose, ears, and a mouth, and it signifies social potential to us. However, suppose that "social" object doesn't behave in a sufficiently human way. In that case, we are immediately disappointed, according to Rabindra Ratan, associate professor at Michigan State University, who has been researching avatars for years. That is why digital assistants such as Siri, Alexa, or Cortana do not have a body. We would get angry at them when they messed up if they did. Without this embodiment, we can forgive them easier if they make mistakes. The same applies to the currently available virtual worlds; (hyper) realistic avatars would be more prone to lag and clunky behavior due to the available bandwidth and computing power. (Hyper) realistic avatars that look mostly realistic but not quite enough fall in the *uncanny valley* and put people off. This sensation is basically a mismatch between how our brain expects a hyper-realistic avatar to look and behave and its actual behavior, and if this is not in sync, it will put us on edge and make us feel uncomfortable.[82] Of course, if people feel uncomfortable while playing a game, they won't be playing that game for very long. Hence, organizations will have to take this sensation serious if they want people to use their environment for an extended period of time, which is why we currently have cartoonish avatars, some even without legs, that behave realistically; it is simply the best approach given the current hardware constraints. With our devices getting better and our internet connections getting faster, hyper-realistic avatars will become more commonplace in the future.

The type of avatars and their impact on development and computing power can easily be portrayed in a simple matrix, as shown in Figure 3.1, where we have two axes: the x-axis shows a scale from a low number of polygons to a high number of polygons, and the y-axis depicts a scale from cartoony avatars to hyper-realistic avatars. Based on the design choice made, the exponential graph shows the most likely required computing power and the time it takes to design the avatar.

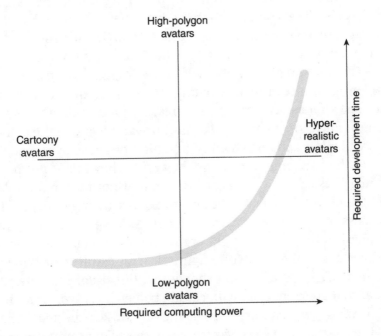

Figure 3.1 Type of avatars

Another design decision is whether, as a metaverse developer, you want to focus your time on building a unique avatar system or you want to implement a plug-and-play solution such as Ready Player Me. This startup aims to develop the default avatar system for the metaverse,[83] and with this tool, users can easily create avatars by uploading a photo, or users can design their avatar themselves from a myriad of options. At the end of 2021, they connected their platform to more than 1,000 apps and games, enabling users to create their avatar once and take it to a wide variety of experiences, exactly the interoperability required for the metaverse. After all, users might have multiple avatars for different environments, so it won't be a user-friendly approach if you have to create a new avatar every time you enter a new experience or platform. That would be the equivalent of opening a new email account every time you want to register for a new website.

The avatar is a crucial aspect of the metaverse as it is your identity in the digital world. It should travel with you from one platform to another. This visual identity will determine who you are in the metaverse, but most likely also how you feel and how you behave. Identity is a fascinating concept and one that many people have thought long and hard about, including me. What does identity mean? What does it mean to be you? How do you want to portray yourself in this (digital) world?

If identity is already a fascinating sociological and anthropological area for researchers, expect identity to take on a completely new meaning as more and more people will create an avatar to use in the metaverse. Avatars will allow people to hide behind their physical layers and experiment with their identity in the digital world. They might not be happy with their physical appearance, or they might not be comfortable with their sexuality yet. People will be able to explore their identity a lot more than is possible in the physical world. For example, if you are a woman in the physical world, you might opt for a male avatar, or if you are an introvert in the real world, you might select an extravert-looking avatar for the metaverse. Research has shown that the visual characteristics of an avatar that are associated with certain behavior will result in the individual behind that character engaging in those expected behaviors, which is called the *Proteus effect*. As such, the avatar's appearance (skin color, height, body, digital clothes, etc.) can directly result in changes in the behavior of the person behind the avatar.[84] According to a 2007 study by researchers Nick Yee and Jeremey Bailenson, participants who were assigned taller avatars exhibited greater confidence in a virtual environment. Interestingly, the changed behavior continued in subsequent physical interactions.[85] Consequently, the metaverse will enable people to explore their identity like never before. Simply selecting an avatar that showcases the character traits an individual would like to possess can result in a change in behavior in both the virtual and real world. It will give people the freedom to explore their identity in a relatively safe environment, especially if this can be done anonymously. Most likely, in the beginning, people will switch between different avatars often, trying to figure out which avatar best fits their identity and personality before settling on a selection of avatars that they will use across a variety of platforms.

The rise of the avatars is unstoppable, and the more people who step into the metaverse, the bigger the explosion of creativity when it comes to identity. Literally anything goes, and users are bound only by their own creativity when displaying who they are in the digital world. Of course, this would work only if you, and only you, are in complete control over it. Self-sovereignty is crucial if we want to fully exploit the potential that a digital identity has to offer us. As discussed in Chapter 1, this means that the user has full ownership and control over their identity, data, and digital assets. This is where blockchain and NFTs come into play. Although Ready Player Me is a great platform for bringing interoperable avatars, they are still owned and controlled centrally. If Ready Player Me gets hacked or goes bankrupt for whatever reason, users will lose their avatar and, with that, their identity. Timmu Tõke from Ready Player Me indicated that the funds of their series A round of $13 million at the end of 2021 would be used toward NFT wearables and virtual fashion for the avatars.[86] While that is a great start, I believe that the platform will become truly valuable if users can own not only their avatar customization assets but also the avatar they created, which should then, of course, also be stored decentralized and linked to an NFT.

While we move from 2D avatars in a 2D internet controlled by Big Tech to 3D avatars in an immersive internet controlled by individuals, we will enter a world of unlimited creativity. You can be who you want to be, but of course, you want to make sure that you are unique and that you do not come across a stranger who uses the same avatar as you. Naturally, this does not apply to using default avatars if you are exploring a new environment and cannot be bothered to spend more than 30 seconds on selecting your avatar, but if you have settled on a small range of avatars that you use in various settings, you want to make sure that your avatar is truly you, and therefore truly unique. Obtaining these unique avatars will likely happen in multiple ways in the coming years. Of course, you can meticulously personalize your avatar using systems like Ready Player Me, but I believe we will see vibrant avatar markets popping up in the coming years. Within these marketplaces, you will be able to purchase off-the-shelf standard avatars that you can then personalize; purchase truly one-of-a-kind, ready-made avatars with an edition of one; or have an artist develop an avatar for you upon assignment. There will also be a vibrant secondary market because we will probably shed our digital skins and digital fashion items as fast as we change our physical clothes. Of course, this raises other interesting questions; how does it feel when you sell your avatar that you have used for years? Will it feel like a new start, or will you enter an identity crisis? These are fascinating topics to explore for researchers in the coming years.

Regardless, for an avatar to be truly unique, we need to be sure that others cannot steal or impersonate our avatars, which criminals will undoubtedly attempt, especially if you are a well-known person. That is where NFTs, and potentially biometrics, come into play. One of the main characteristics of interoperable avatars linked to NFTs is that we can verify that a particular avatar is indeed linked to and controlled by its official owner, who controls the private key to that wallet and had its identity verified. Otherwise, it would be too easy for criminals to disguise as a celebrity and scam people, similar to how criminals currently use fake social media profiles of celebrities to scam people. After all, if I can create a digital copy of myself, anyone can, and using deepfake audio, criminals can impersonate anyone in the digital world. Without some form of verification, it will become challenging to distinguish fake from real, a topic we will discuss in depth in Chapter 8. NFTs will enable platforms and other players/users to verify if an avatar is who they say they are and if the avatar is linked to a self-sovereign identity and whether the avatar is actually controlled by its owner. Biometrics can be used as an additional security layer to verify that the person controlling has not stolen the private key but really is the person who they claim to be. It would basically work like a more advanced *Verified* blue tick from Twitter, but then not available to some but to all who want to be verified.

An avatar is a digital representation of an entity that facilitates interaction with other people, assets, or environments. For an avatar to be a digital representation of you, not only should it be unique, interoperable, and verifiable, but it should also be controlled by you, ideally in a universal way across the entire metaverse. After all, there is no point in relearning how to control your avatar if you move from one platform to another. There are a variety of ways to move your avatar. The most commonly used is using your keyboard, either using your arrow keys or using the keys *a*, *w*, *s*, and *d*, potentially in collaboration with your mouse.

In the (near) future, we will switch to more advanced ways of controlling our avatar, using motion capture (*mocap*). Mocap is the process of using sensors and/or cameras to record the movement of people or objects and translate these movements to the digital world. There are a wide variety of motion capture systems available on the market.

- Simple, free, facial tracking systems using your webcam such as Animaze
- Multi-thousand-dollar advanced optics systems that can measure every move in precise detail
- VR treadmills to mimic walking or running in VR such as used in *Ready Player One*
- Full-body haptic feedback and motion capture tracking suits such as the TeslaSuit

In the coming years, it will likely become possible to use mocap to control your avatar across the metaverse and uniquely identify your avatar using full-body behavioral biometrics or facial recognition, adding the required additional security layer to verify that an avatar is controlled by its rightful owner. In addition, once high-definition and real-time replication of facial expressions can be translated to avatars, it will become possible for users in virtual worlds to connect faster and more authentically with others.

An avatar that is a unique representation of you, of course, needs to be dressed. After all, just like humans, avatars are born naked. The digital fashion market will be a multibillion-dollar market that has only begun, and it might end up even bigger than the physical fashion market. Creating your avatar might require a bit of effort up front, but dressing your avatar will be a lot easier. Using (unique) digital fashion and wearables, you will be able to create a truly unique digital representation of yourself, and the digital fashion industry is about to explode.

Digital Fashion

On September 13, 2021, Kim Kardashian donned an all-black attire by Balenciaga at the Met Gala.[87] Her stark black Balenciaga haute couture gown with matching mask drew a lot of conversation online, even within the Fortnite community. Multiple Twitter users from within the Fortnite community saw a close comparison between her attire and locked characters within the popular video game. They wondered why she was dressed like a video game character you haven't unlocked yet.[88] The rumors came clear when, a few days later, Balenciaga announced a collaboration with Epic Games, the developer of Fortnite, to bring the fashion house's signature clothing and apparel into the game.

Balenciaga's iconic collections inspired the clothing: the new Balenciaga Fit Set of outfits for players introduced fresh looks for four of Fortnite's fan-favorite characters—Doggo, Ramirez, Knight, and Banshee. The new outfits were completed with exclusive Balenciaga backpack back blings, pickaxes, and more, for players to express themselves in completely unique ways.[89] The clothes and wearables were available for purchase in Fortnite's usual game store as well as Balenciaga-themed Strange Times Featured hub. To accompany the digital apparel set launch, the two companies also debuted a community-driven living lookbook campaign via the same Strange Times Featured Hub inside Fortnite.[90] At the center of the campaign sat the digital Balenciaga retail stores appearing in Fortnite showcasing the virtual community's fashion on billboards, mashing up the player's self-expression with unexpected elements.

Both brands also debuted a limited-run collaboration of physical apparel exclusively available in select Balenciaga stores and Balenciaga .com. The new line featured hats, tees, hoodies, and more inspired by the community-favorite point of interest (POI) Retail Row and was on sale globally from September 20, 2021. Adam Sussman, president at Epic Games, expressed confidence in the collaboration by stating, "Self-expression is one of the things that makes Fortnite so unique, and there couldn't be a better first fashion partner than Balenciaga to bring their authentic designs and trendsetting culture to millions of players around the world."[91] It worked, as kids around the world started asking surprised parents for money to buy Balenciaga clothing.

Haute couture and the fashion industry have entered the gaming industry, and we have only just gotten started. The possibilities for digital fashion are as limitless as the potential for the metaverse, and it will be one of the biggest industries of the immersive internet in the coming decade. Even if your avatar is a dog man called Doggo in Fortnite or, especially, if you have to go into your virtual office for a meeting with your manager, your digital representation can't walk around the metaverse naked, although I am sure there will be niche communities where that is preferred or even required. After all, as with any new technology, we can expect the porn industry to embrace the metaverse just like they embraced the VHS, DVD, or the internet.

Another luxury fashion brand that embraced the metaverse is Gucci. Also, in 2021, Gucci collaborated with Roblox by selling several rare Gucci items on the Roblox platform. The fashion house created a unique virtual garden exhibit for two weeks, accessible exclusively on Roblox. The virtual exhibition was part of Gucci's Archetypes, a two-week immersive multimedia experience in Florence, Italy, that explored and celebrated the brand's 100th birthday. The physical exhibition dove into the world of Gucci's advertising campaigns and was largely comprised of inspirations such as music, art, travel, and pop culture. Each venue was divided into exhibition rooms by theme, which reproduced the diverse and fascinating world of Gucci's advertising campaigns. With cutting-edge technology, handicrafts by artisans with the utmost precision, and innovative interior designs, the exhibition presented the diverse and immersive space. It made visitors feel as if they were in the advertising campaigns of Gucci.

At the same time, Roblox's virtual Gucci Garden space was available to everyone on the world's favorite platform for pre-teens. Those who attended were able to view and experience the vision, aesthetics, and inclusive philosophy of the brand's creative director Alessandro Michele through the same 15 past advertising campaigns by Gucci. During the event, the fashion house dropped limited edition items such as virtual bags on the Roblox platform.[92] The Roblox experience mimicked the physical experience, enabling Roblox users to purchase digital clothing available for a limited period of time, creating a feeling of scarcity and increasing the prices. Some of these items were re-sold for ridiculous prices, with one Gucci Dionysus Bag With Bee eventually re-selling for 350,000 Robux, the platform's in-game currency, or $4,115, which is more than a physical bag's $3,400 retail value.[93] All the buyer got was a set of exclusive pixels to be used solely inside the Roblox platform, not the kind of interoperability one would expect from a $4,115 bag.

Balenciaga and Gucci are far from the only brands that have created digital fashion items for the metaverse. By the time you read this book, there will have been many new examples of fashion brands experimenting with digital fashion, and fashion houses will have experienced the benefits digital fashion brings to fashion houses, users, and even the environment.

Digital fashion is more sustainable as its pollution footprint is smaller since it only requires servers and computers, which can be powered by renewable energy, in comparison to its current fossil fuel–driven logistics and use of chemically treated fabrics by children creating the clothes in sweatshops. It is very scalable and offers limitless possibilities to experiment with new fashion styles. The opportunities are endless, which is why digital fashion could soon become the new fashion. If anything, fashion is about identity, and as a result, identity will go through a renaissance in the coming years. After all, in the physical world, we express ourselves with how we dress and what we wear, and the same will apply in the virtual world, but then with infinite possibilities.

In the physical world, fashion designers are limited by the available fabrics and the laws of physics when they design their clothes. These barriers do not apply in the metaverse. Digital fashion designers can come up with any type of garment or fabric to create exclusive and exotic designs never seen before. One such example is the virtual Glass Suit designed by Domenico Dolce and Stefano Gabbana in 2021. The digital fashion item was part of Dolce & Gabbana's Collezione Genesi NFT—a nine-piece NFT collection. It sold for almost $1.2 million to the digital-to-physical eCommerce platform Boson Protocol. For that money, the company received the original digital file of the suit and a physical version of it. The actual suit contains 100 percent silk and is woven with 72 embroidered glass workpieces, consisting of both Swarovski crystal and Murano glass. Apart from the Glass Suit, during the auction, the fashion brand also sold a digital gold dress for more than $750,000 and a digital silver dress for more than $600,000.[94] These designs from Dolce & Gabbana are great, but they do not yet embrace the full potential of digital fashion items.

If you would take digital fashion to its natural next level, it becomes possible to create fashion items from garments only available in the digital world and to add utility to the fashion items. One company exclusively focused on designing digital fashion is the company The Fabricant. The Dutch fashion house is a digital-only fashion brand and designs clothes only for the metaverse. It uses the latest advancements in artificial intelligence to create naturally looking and behaving digital fashion items, sometimes from novel garments such as liquid metal. According to Michaela Larosse, head of content and strategy at The Fabricant, digital fashion items are an emotional experience similar to physical clothes.[95] Whatever items you decide to wear in the metaverse, they allow you to explore different identities. You might be someone wearing very practical shoes in real life but trying a pair of 10-inch digital stilettos in the metaverse to see how that feels. In February 2022, The Fabricant also released a new platform called The Fabricant Studio, enabling everyone to create their own fashion NFTs. The Fabricant Studio is a blockchain-based platform that enables anyone to create, trade, monetize, and sport their own fashion designs while accruing $FBRC, the platform's token that allows users to influence future decision-making in the Studio. The Studio creates a decentralized fashion chain in which everyone can participate and profit from their art: AI weavers, cyber material designers, digital fashion creators, meta tailors, stylists, professional buyers, multilabel retailers, or simply fashion fans will all co-exist in the virtual world. Everyone will have the ability to define their role, expand their business, and benefit from the platform's growth in a decentralized manner.[96]

Both influencers and fashion brands can create garments and fabrics, and users can combine these to create new unique digital fashion items and sell them as NFTs. The Fabricant's objective is to democratize fashion creation and enable anyone to become a digital fashion designer as long as you have an internet connection. It is not unlikely that in the years to come, the next fashion powerhouses are metaverse-native digital-only brands, potentially created by a 14-year-old kid who designs their own fashion items that go viral. Of course, the platform will also enable traditional fashion houses to drop their fabrics onto the platform, co-create next year's style and clothes with the community, and bring them to market both digitally and physically—a true convergence of the physical and the digital into a *phygital* experience.

As more creators join the metaverse, we will see an explosion of creativity. Add in artificial intelligence, and we will get unique digital fashion items that can change based on your mood, the weather, or your physical state. There are literally limitless possibilities when we start to combine digital art and fashion with data from the physical world.

In the beginning, the digital fashion items will likely much resemble the physical fashion items, but in the years to come, we will see an explosion of creativity because a traditional suit might not look very nice on your 3D Bored Ape. New, not human-like, avatars will require different garments, fabrics, and styles. In addition, we might want to integrate new ideas into our digital fashion, for example, creating a digital jacket that is connected to your local weather and with fabric that changes color depending on whether it rains or the sun shines. Digital fashion that conveys a message and emotions simply by changing the fabric. Anything is possible. After all, digital clothes are just data that can be manipulated in any way required by connecting it to sensors in the real or digital world.

Apart from giving you an identity, digital fashion items will also start to come with all kinds of utility. Brands could use this to reward buyers in novel ways, for example, by giving you additional powers depending on the platform; i.e., you could buy Adidas or Nike shoes that will enable you to run faster in a platform or buy a Red Bull jacket that allows you to fly in certain environments. Such additional in-game experiences will make the items more valuable. Utility can also include a discount on the physical equivalent of the digital item, incorporating a social responsibility or sustainability benefit for the user, VIP access to unique brand experiences, (digital) community events, or anything else, as long as it offers engagement and a unique experience for the users.[97] The more utility added to the digital product, the more valuable it will become. The possibilities to add utility to digital fashion items and wearables are endless, and it will be interesting to see how this space will evolve in the years to come.

Of course, not all fashion items have to be unique items. That would simply be not affordable to the masses. Therefore, we can expect digital haute couture to become cheaper than physical haute couture, excluding exceptions as we have already seen, which is most likely because of the current gold rush, if anything. Large fashion brands such as Nike, Adidas, H&M, or Zara will likely sell their physical products also as digital products to generate additional revenue and ensure visibility in the metaverse.

Your Nike shoes (designed by RTFKT, the digital sports shoes designer brand purchased by Nike at the end of 2021) or your Zara dress might have unique features, but they are mass-produced digitally, minted as NFTs, and sold in the metaverse for you to wear at a reasonable price. You would probably be able to re-sell your digital fashion items on a secondary market for those people who do not want to pay the full price, together with digital scratch marks from using them across various platforms. Potentially even with the provenance attached to the NFT that could give them additional value if they have been used in a certain challenge or were worn to a unique experience that provided it with additional utility.

Creating digital fashion items using tools such as developed by The Fabricant is the first phase of digital fashion. As we discussed, digital fashion items and digital wearables should be interoperable, so you can take your $1.2 million Glass Suit or your $5 Zara dress from Fortnite to Microsoft Mesh to The Sandbox, which gives it additional utility and makes it useful instead of it just remaining a JPEG or a GIF file. After all, it is highly unlikely that you would purchase a physical fashion item or wearable that you can wear in only one location and nowhere else, so we should not accept the same in the metaverse. However, creating fashion items that you can wear in different environments is a lot more complex than doing so in the physical world. It will be complex to achieve interoperability because the Glass Suit or the Zara dress will look different in each environment and will have to comply with each platform's technical and design requirements but should still resemble the original so people can recognize it across platforms. With so many different virtual worlds and a lack of standards, the best solution would be a tool that allows users to create an asset once and automatically adopt it for the various available platforms. For example, you create a digital wearable or fashion item once, and it is automatically converted to work seamlessly in a variety of worlds; i.e., you turn a hyper-realistic dress into a low-polygon Roblox dress with a click of a button and drop the NFT in different platforms. Once we are able to crack this challenge and take our digital garments and wearables from one platform to another, the items automatically adjusting to the required technical and design constraints, it would significantly increase the value of those digital items and wearables and grow the metaverse economy.

iCommerce

The sale of all these digital (fashion) items has ushered in new business models. Instead of direct-to-consumer, we have now entered the realm of direct-to-avatar (D2A). D2A means that these digital products will never leave the virtual world. Digital fashion brands that sell NFTs with utility in specific metaverse environments are just the start. In the coming years, we will see the convergence of physical and digital shopping creating an entirely new form of commerce: immersive commerce or iCommerce.

iCommerce includes the direct-to-avatar business model and the digital-to-physical (D2P) and physical-to-digital (P2D) business models. D2P will enable users to experience a product virtually before the physical version is delivered to your door, while P2D means that when you buy physical sneakers, you will also receive a digital version for your avatar. However, iCommerce is not just about duplicating the physical products that you sell into the digital world or the other way around. Brands that will follow that path will most likely not succeed. The metaverse is not an additional marketing opportunity but a completely new distribution channel with its own rules and requirements. Generation Z is digitally savvy, but Generation Alpha will be metaverse-savvy. They know how to navigate the immersive internet and appreciate its ease of use. They have grown up playing Roblox or Minecraft, and they want brands to be there where they are, offering native immersive experiences. That will not be on YouTube, Twitter, or Facebook. Brands must take a different approach if they want to succeed. iCommerce provides endless opportunities to engage with customers, but brands have to really think out of the box about how they want to be perceived in the metaverse and what their brands stand for if they want to be successful with iCommerce. It is a different ball game altogether, and we will cover this in-depth in Chapter 5.

One of the key characteristics of iCommerce is that it will deliver new opportunities for consumers to explore or experience a product, whether digital or physical, before purchasing it. For example, in the coming years, we will be able to watch an immersive volumetric movie (a movie captured three-dimensionally so you can watch it using VR goggles or 3D displays) or sitcom or play a metaverse game and, with a click of the button, select a product that is part of the show or game and have it either drop-shipped to our physical address or added to our NFT wallet to use in other games. As Lindsey McInerney, explained, we will be able to attend a massive interactive live event together with our friends and all receive a personalized digital T-shirt for our avatar and have the physical version shipped to our homes.[98] If we take this a step further, iCommerce is also about a shared experience; my friend and I can both attend a virtual event and decide to order a beer at the virtual bar, which is then delivered physically to our homes using Deliveroo or Uber Eats within 15 minutes so we can have a shared experience while being geographically apart.

iCommerce has the opportunity to revolutionize buying clothes online and, most importantly, drastically reduce the large number of returns. A well-known and expensive problem for the fashion industry that is environmentally unsustainable is the high number of returns by customers who decide to order a large number of clothes to try at home. These online and offline returns cost retailers almost $400 billion per year, and less than 50 percent can be re-sold at full price,[99] and many of these brand new returned clothes end up in a landfill.[100] Digital fashion can contribute to reducing returns, thereby positively influencing the fashion's impact on the earth's climate. In the metaverse, we will be able to try new clothes in a virtual store and have our avatar try the clothes we are interested in to know if the clothes will suit us. Using a virtual mirror, we can see ourselves in the new clothes and even take pictures or videos and share them with our friends to hear their opinions before buying the items. In the more distant future, our hyper-realistic avatars may come with specific physical data about our bodies to ensure that all physical clothes we order will be tailor-made and always fit perfectly, further reducing the required returns.

When you enter the virtual store, you will be assisted by virtual agents. In the high-end virtual stores, these agents will be controlled by real people working from home, advising you on what to wear and helping you find the right clothes, while in the cheaper stores the virtual shopping agents will be controlled by AI. You can then either order these for your avatar only or have the physical items shipped to your physical address. Since you have already tried them on virtually, you know what it will look like (at least if your avatar is an exact digital copy of you), and you are less likely to return most of the clothes than in today's world because you already know whether it suits you.

iCommerce is not only about these purely virtual experiences. It is also about bringing the digital into the physical world. An example is using magical mirrors as is happening already on a large scale in China. These intelligent dressing mirrors can show you wearing different outfits suggested by the mirror, which you can then purchase by scanning a QR code. In addition, when taking clothes into the fitting room, the mirror can suggest additional matching items for you.[101] The next step would be that your avatar would receive the digital version as well, potentially with additional benefits, as mentioned before.

iCommerce has more advantages for organizations. Not only can retailers experiment and co-create their products digitally with customers to create better products, but it also means purely digital brands can go physical, drastically lowering the entry barriers to start a fashion brand. For example, the metaverse-native digital fashion brands we discussed can become so popular in the virtual world that people are requesting digital items to be created as physical items. The moment the first metaverse-native brand develops physical fashion items will be a wake-up call for the fashion industry, and it won't be too long for it to happen.

Digital products will usher in a new era of limitless opportunities for retailers and customers. It will make the retail industry richer, literally because (fashion) brands will be able to make a lot of money and figuratively because it will enable consumers to explore new identities using digital clothes and wearables and have a richer (brand) experience. Already in 2017, way before the crypto boom or the NFT boom, trading virtual (fashion) items in video games was a $50 billion industry,[102] and this will grow exponentially in the coming years, especially if those virtual items become interoperable, have utility, and can incorporate their provenance to encourage re-selling on secondary markets.

A Cambrian Explosion of Identity

The metaverse will enable you to be who you want, regardless of physical restraints or considerations. It will enable individuals to explore their identity in ways never possible before. The more we step into the metaverse and the more the physical and the digital worlds converge, driven by continuous advancements in (digital) technologies, the more fun the world will become. It will result in unique niche communities that come together either virtually or phygitally (with some joining in person and others joining digitally).

Already, there are fascinating examples of niche communities that indicate what we can expect. As Konrad Gill from NeosVR explained to me, there are furry communities on the NeosVR platform that organize hugging parties, and they like to hug each other in virtual reality.[103] Or there is a Japanese group that organizes virtual sleep-over parties. They have created a digital house, a cute place, and they organize pajama parties where they sleep in the virtual world together to beat the loneliness of the lockdown during the pandemic. Nothing stops people from coming together if they have a shared interest in the virtual world.

Of course, there will be various groups and organizations that will oppose this identity exploration, and there will be digital communities that will restrict exotic identities from participating. Each virtual world or augmented experience will come with its own rules as we will discover in the next chapter. Some communities might allow you to enter only if you have a Bored Ape as an avatar, while going to work and meeting your boss as a Bored Ape might be less of a good idea. In the end, it will all depend on the rules set by the communities you interact with. Some companies won't care how you show up virtually for work, and it could potentially help during brainstorm sessions if everyone shows up as an animal. In contrast, others would require a more realistic digital replica for professional meetings. Then again, there will be metaverse spaces that only allow low-polygon human-like avatars such as The Sandbox or Roblox, while others will opt for more alien-like avatars or animal avatars.

Personally, I am looking forward to this Cambrian explosion* of identity and creativity in the upcoming Imagination Age. It will be a colorful world of unique and creative communities, each with its own requirements and characteristics. Within the metaverse, you can be who you are and be where you want to be. It will make both the virtual and physical worlds more fun. Imagine if you would meet up with your friend in the physical world while being geographically apart, and she would show up as her digital twin with a unique virtual dress made from liquid metal, projected as a hologram in your living room using your augmented reality glasses. I am sure it would result in a lively and fun discussion that would make both happy.

---

*A Cambrian Explosion refers to the era of time ~541 million years ago when suddenly many new complex animals appeared. Within a timeframe of 20 million years, a blink of an eye on evolutionary time scales, there was a burst of new life, inconsistent with the time before.

Chapter 4
Be Where You Want to Be

Virtual Worlds

In 1970, at the University of Essex, Roy Trubshaw and Richard Bartle (professor, author, and game researcher) created the world's first multi-user dungeon (MUD). A MUD is a multiplayer, real-time virtual world, but instead of being graphics-based, it is text-based. Players read the descriptions of the virtual rooms, characters, or objects and perform actions by typing commands in a natural language.[104] In 1980, the game became the internet's first multiplayer online role-playing game, when the University of Essex connected to the ARPANET.[105] MUD was created, of course, for fun and relaxation, but there was more to it, according to its co-creator Richard Bartle. They attempted "to bring fairness to a virtual world that [they] perceived wasn't there in the real world,"[106] and they created MUD as a political statement to offer people a virtual world "where people could go and shed what was holding them back"; or in other words, they created MUD because "the real world sucked."[107] Of course, this is a familiar theme in most science-fiction books and movies. For example, the virtual world The Oasis in *Ready Player One* was also an escape for people because the real world ended up becoming a dystopian place. Virtual worlds do indeed offer people an opportunity to get away from reality for a moment. Depending on how we shape the real world, the future iterations of these virtual worlds can become a full-time escape from the real world or a place to enter just for socializing, entertainment, or work but not to escape the physical reality, explained Benjamin Bertram Goldman, an executive producer and thought leader in the metaverse.[108] We should try to avoid a dystopian future at all costs, or, as Raph Koster, an American video game designer and entrepreneur, said during his keynote at the 2017 Game Developers Conference, *Snow Crash* is unrealistic but "what's coming is far weirder and in most ways, less cool. It's also dangerous and challenging in a way that *Snow Crash* never touched."[109]

Since the creation of the first MUD, virtual worlds have changed significantly. Although MUDs still exist, there are numerous games out there with 100 + players online most of the time,[110] today's virtual worlds are anything but text-based. Over the years, they have improved significantly, and with technologies such as Epic's Unreal Engine 5 becoming available, we can expect ever-more realistic virtual worlds.

One of the first globally known virtual worlds is probably Second Life. Created by Linden Lab in 2003, at its peak, it reached approximately one million regular users and close to $1 billion in annual virtual goods transaction volume.[111] It even created the world's first real-world millionaire from selling virtual real estate as its virtual currency, the Linden Dollar, can be exchanged for real-world currency.[112] The player Ashe Chung (real name Ailin Graef) achieved millionaire status already in 2006,[113] many years before virtual real estate was popularized again in 2021. Today, Second Life still exists, and in 2020, the CEO of Linden Lab, Ebbe Altberg, shared that Second Life still had 900.000 active users, driven primarily by the pandemic.[114]

Imaginary worlds are a great way for people to briefly escape reality, which humans have done since the beginning of our existence. Whether we use stories that we pass on from parents to children around a fire or books to drift away in a different reality for a few hours, escaping reality appeals to us. With today's technologies, these virtual worlds have become more realistic and offer opportunities that we have never had before. It has become possible to create immersive and persistent experiences that you can tap into at any moment and have a great experience, together with your friends. Although virtual reality is, by definition, a solitary activity, it is by no means a solitary experience.

One such virtual experience was the digital edition of Burning Man in 2020 and 2021. Burning Man is a global community that comes together once a year in Nevada's Black Rock Desert for a week to build "a temporary metropolis dedicated to community, art, self-expression, and self-reliance."[115] Like any other event in 2020, Burning Man was canceled due to the pandemic when Doug Jacobson and Athena Demos decided to create a virtual edition. The virtual edition took place in AltspaceVR, a social VR platform founded in 2013 and acquired by Microsoft in 2017. AltspaceVR is a digital events platform available in virtual reality or on your computer for those without a VR headset. It enables artists, creators, and brands to come together and create any virtual experience, and that's what Athena, Doug, and the rest of the team involved exactly did. They re-created the famous Playa, including its well-known layout, caravans, tents, bars, etc. They invited so-called *Burners*—those participating in Burning Man—to create digital art and experiences that people could visit from within AltspaceVR. They received hundreds of digital experiences that users could explore. User-generated content has always been important for Burning Man, and with the digital version, participants did not disappoint either. Using portals, people could easily move between the various digital installations and have a good time together from the comfort and safety of their homes. What started as a way to replace the physical experience of Burning Man during covid-19 now turns out to become an annual additional digital Burning Man event. Although it was a great experience, according to Doug, it also showed that the metaverse is not here yet. The graphics were moderate, the loading times of the different digital experiences were long depending on your internet connection, and the onboarding process was challenging. They spent a lot of time educating *Burners* to become familiar with the platform and help them create their avatars, understand how to move around, and have a good time together. In the end, it worked out well, and with technologies improving, the digital version of Burning Man will become closer and closer to the real deal.

One of the key characteristics of the digital Burning Man event, and for any virtual or augmented experience for that matter, is that the virtual world is synchronous, is persistent, and allows people to interact with each other as avatars.[116] As discussed, ideally, these virtual worlds are interoperable and decentralized, though that is currently more the exception than the rule. Today, there are thousands of virtual worlds already, ranging from closed walled gardens such as Meta's Horizon Worlds, Microsoft's Minecraft or AltspaceVR, Fortnite, or Roblox to decentralized and open virtual worlds such as Decentraland, The Sandbox, CryptoVoxels, or upcoming worlds such as Somnium Space, Solice, or Dreem. For an overview of available virtual and augmented worlds, see xrshowcase.xyz or ExtendedCollection.com.

Building a virtual world, whether an immersive digital environment or an augmented experience, is akin to building a new society. What rules you implement, what governance structure you embed, and how you set up the virtual economy will determine the virtual world's success and the impact it will have on the real world. As we have seen from thousands of years of trying to build real-world societies around the world, this is highly challenging, and there are many directions a virtual world can take. Regardless of what virtual experience is built, there are real-world consequences that we need to take into consideration, according to Benjamin Bertram Goldman, an executive producer and thought leader in the metaverse.[117] From the first virtual, text-based worlds to today's immersive digital experiences, players perceive virtual worlds as real worlds, and users treat those virtual worlds as if they are real.[118] The more time we spend in these virtual worlds, the bigger the consequences, for example, on our mental health, as we will cover in Chapter 8. More importantly, virtual worlds mimic how real human societies work (after all, both are built and used by humans), and unless you have thought hard and long about the code of conduct, the governance structure, and the economics of the virtual world, you should not open a virtual world.[119] Especially because increasingly, virtual worlds interact with real-world economies and societies, and we should be aware of the unintended consequences of those interactions.

Niantic's Pokémon Go provides an excellent example of such consequences. When the game was launched in 2016, the success affected peoples' lives in unexpected ways.

- The proximity to Pokéstops increased the value of physical real estate.[120]
- Relationships were broken up as some users were caught red-handed cheating because they caught Pokémon while visiting their ex.

- There was an increase in robberies as criminals discovered the game as well and were awaiting Pokémon players at popular Pokéstops.[121]

Unfortunately, there was limited to no possibilities for people to report bad behavior or bad locations to the game developers, further driving these unintended consequences.[122] More recently, games like the Play-to-Earn game Axie Infinity, where players can earn yield in the form of tokens when playing the game, resulted in large groups of Filipinos giving up their jobs because they can earn more money playing the game than doing a "real" job. These are just a few of the consequences game developers likely did not foresee when building their virtual worlds, and it is likely that similar unintended consequences will appear in the virtual worlds of tomorrow.

Virtual worlds can be a lot of fun, and the metaverse will most likely have positive effects on society, including fostering social contacts, offering new forms of entertainment, and enabling more efficient digital collaboration for organizations. However, virtual worlds can also be damaging. As in any society, virtual or real, some people refuse to abide by the rules and display bad and damaging behavior. This is nothing new. Only a few years after the launch of Second Life, there were reports of virtual pedophilia in the digital world, when users dressed up as children avatars offered virtual prostitution in an area that mimicked a children's playground.[123] There have also been plenty of reports of virtual harassment, ranging from Second Life's first millionaire Ailin Graef being attacked by a swarm of pink flying penises back in 2006[124] to the virtual groping of a woman while shooting zombies in the VR game QuiVr in 2016[125] to a female beta tester of Meta's VR platform Horizon Worlds reporting sexual harassment in 2021, which, to make matters worse, was supported by other people on the platform, according to the victim.[126] Although the harassment occurred in virtual reality, it felt real and was a horrible experience, according to the women. Unfortunately, such acts of online harassment, including stalking, physical threats, and sexual harassment, are on the rise,[127] and most platforms place the responsibility to avoid such acts on the user instead of preventing it from happening altogether. QuiVr came up with a forcefield, a Personal Bubble, that a harassed player can activate to instantly dissolve and mute a nearby player.[128] While Meta initially stated that it was basically the user's fault for not utilizing the safety features built into Horizon Worlds,[129] in February 2022 Meta brought social distancing to the metaverse and announced a mandatory distance between virtual reality avatars as a default setting.[130] Both approaches are shortcomings of the virtual worlds because it can easily be baked into the code to prevent groping from happening at all. After all, it is a virtual world, and implementing such measures is as simple as writing a few additional lines of code. Even more, users who do display such behavior should be penalized automatically by instantly banning them from the platform for a period of time. This could start with a warning and a ban of one to two minutes, but the time banned could increase if the user continues to display bad behavior, resulting in a permanent ban for those users who continue to go against the code of conduct of the virtual world. Perhaps we should open source an antiharassment standard that virtual world developers can easily implement, because as Jordan Belamire, the woman sexually harassed in the game QuiVr, described, she "lasted three minutes in multiplayer without getting virtually groped," while her brother-in-law "played multiplayer mode a hundred times without incident, but [her] female voice elicited lewd behavior within minutes,"[131] and we should avoid such bad behavior from becoming commonplace in the metaverse at all times.

Of course, the same problems will also exist in other virtual worlds. As we have seen with Web 2.0, whenever users can generate content on a platform or interact with each other, problems of bad behavior appear. User-generated content (UGC) is what powers the Web and what makes the Web beautiful, but it is also what damages society, harms people, and polarizes democracies. A persistent and interoperable self-sovereign identity and reputation, as described in Chapter 1, would certainly help alleviate these problems because when virtual actions have real-world consequences, without giving too much power to Big Tech, people might be less inclined to showcase bad behavior. Of course, this would still leave the question of content moderation to prevent harmful content, which has not been solved in centralized platforms and will likely continue to be a problem in the metaverse, as we will discuss in Chapter 8.

If a code of conduct, self-sovereignty, automatic enforcement of rules, and an open source antiharassment standard could keep virtual and augmented experiences safe, a seamless user experience, interoperability, scalability, and authenticity could keep a virtual world fun and engaging. For the metaverse to achieve mass adoption, a seamless user experience that enables users to simply put on a headset or glasses and start interacting with it is key, which is why game designers and UI/UX designers will play an important role in developing the immersive digital experiences of tomorrow. Regardless of what one thinks of a walled garden such as Meta's Horizon Worlds, they have done well in the user experience. This virtual world, together with the seamless integration of their hardware (Meta Quest), is an added benefit to the Meta platform. While at launch, Meta, and other platforms, limited the number of people who could join a single virtual environment simultaneously, as the hardware and software become more advanced, this limit will eventually increase and enable a more social and immersive experience with hundreds or thousands of people at the same time.

In the end, virtual and augmented experiences should become as easy to play and interact with as apps on our smartphones if we want to achieve mass adoption. This means a lot of work needs to be done to ensure a seamless and affordable experience. Mass adoption will require affordable devices and a user experience that everyone can understand and interact with. As the technologies will improve and economies of scale kick in, the metaverse will become more accessible. Moreover, creating 3D immersive experiences and assets is currently available to only a small group of designers who master the complex tools available on the market. While tools such as Reallusion, Blender, Unity, and Unreal Engine 5 have made it already significantly easier compared to a few years ago, we are far away from reaching an ease of use similar to publishing a website using WordPress or creating and sharing a video clip using TikTok.

When it comes to the metaverse, we are truly at the start of the internet, when creating a website was hard, and the experience of building a website or buying something online was available only to a small group of innovators and early adopters. Nevertheless, we can already see the impact the metaverse has and will have on activities such as gaming, sports, entertainment, education, and work, so let's dive into these topics to see how the immersive internet will change how we play, entertain ourselves, and learn.

Gaming in the Metaverse

According to 2021 research by Accenture, the global gaming industry is valued at $300 billion, consisting of $200 billion in direct spend and $100 billion in indirect revenue.[132] Although maybe not widely known, this is 20 percent more than the global film and video market, which includes global box office and streaming video from Netflix, Disney, or Amazon.[133] The gaming industry is huge and is about to get a lot bigger. Around half of the total value of the gaming industry in 2021, ~$155 billion, can be attributed to software, meaning actual games, including in-game revenue. Gaming is a large global business, and with already 2.7 billion gamers in 2020,[134] or 35 percent of the global population, the gaming industry is likely to grow in the coming years, among others due to the metaverse. It is important to note that while gaming might be big business, gaming is not the metaverse. As Matthew Ball, managing partner of Epyllion Industries, described in one of his metaverse articles: "while the metaverse may have some game-like goals, include games, and involve gamification, it is not itself a game, nor is it oriented around specific objectives."[135]

Nevertheless, games are an important aspect of the metaverse and can even be considered a starting point of the metaverse. All the components that enable high-quality games, such as 3D computer graphics, graphics processing units (GPUs), gaming consoles, the cloud, etc., can now be applied to enable the metaverse. Games like Fortnite, Minecraft, or Roblox have been around for 5 to 15 years, way before the metaverse became the talk of the town. In these past years, these games have amassed large numbers of players, driven not only by all the lockdowns during the pandemic but also by the stickiness of gaming. For example, already in 2020, Fortnite, which launched in 2017, had more than 80 million monthly active players[136] and 350 million registered accounts,[137] while in 2021 Minecraft, released in 2009, had around 141 million monthly active users.[138] Roblox, launched in 2006, had a staggering 202 million monthly active users,[139] of which the vast majority are Generation Alpha (over half of all US kids under 16 play Roblox[140]). For many, especially before Facebook's Meta announcement in October 2021, these large numbers are or were a surprise, but for others, playing these games is a daily practice.

There are plenty of examples of children throwing their birthday parties on Roblox and asking for digital gifts because the pandemic prevented physical birthday parties. Fortunately, the massive attention to the metaverse since the autumn of 2021 has put this into the limelight, and now many are trying to understand how the metaverse works and what role games will play.

Although neither Fortnite, Roblox, nor Minecraft are the metaverse—as there is only one metaverse as we discussed—they do share some elements of a metaverse space. Within these platforms, there is a consistent identity spanning the various closed sections of the platforms (although interoperability across these games does not yet exist); it offers a unique experience, some of which are for social purposes only; and there is a strong creator-focused economy that rewards content creators, although in most platforms, assets and earnings cannot be taken outside the respective platforms.[141] Despite not open and decentralized, Roblox comes closest to a functioning metaverse environment. Technically it is not even a game but a social platform that provides the tools for anyone to create a game and socialize, create, play, and interact with others for free. Millions of games have been created, some of which have reached billions of visits[142] and brought in millions of dollars of revenue for its creators.[143] We have gone from physically buying a game to playing games using your console to games streamed from the cloud and paid for using a subscription to actually building your own game and earning money with it.

The success of these games has resulted in new gaming platforms appearing, some of which do take an open and decentralized approach, where digital assets are recorded on-chain to ensure true ownership of them, including platforms such as Decentraland, Upland, Utopia, or The Sandbox. These blockchain games* introduce true digital ownership using NFTs to offer a different experience while at the same time creating new business models and monetization opportunities using crypto for its players. Interoperability between these blockchain games is likely

---

*Blockchain games are video games that incorporate blockchain technologies to record certain elements of the game on a blockchain and that use crypto to drive the in-game ecosystems. Transactions are made using the game's native cryptocurrency, and users receive NFTs of their digital assets that players can both trade or transfer outside the game.

still a few years away. Still, the opportunity for users to truly own their digital assets, and for the community, eventually, to control the environment, is a great step in the right direction away from Big Tech and centralized control. Of course, not everyone will be drawn to these new approaches as it does require more work from the user (for example setting up your crypto wallet) versus a seamless experience on the centralized platforms. Though I do hope that over time more people will see the benefits of having full control over their data and identity, which requires a bit more work versus a seamless experience owned and controlled by Big Tech.

There are different types of blockchain games, including the following[144]:

- Pet games, which include the famous CryptoKitties launched in 2017 and more recently the Play-to-Earn game Axie Infinity
- Fan Economy games, such as NBA Top Shot, which focuses on buying, selling, and collecting NBA official authorized collectibles
- Sandbox games, including Decentraland, The Sandbox, or CryptoVoxels, where anyone can create any digital experience, but all are focused on the possession of virtual land

All of these games bring a fundamental shift in the business models of games, moving away from value extraction in closed environments such as Fortnite or Minecraft to value capture in open ecosystems.[145] As a result, blockchain games allow for layer 2 applications built on top of the original game that benefit from the public transaction details available on the blockchain. For example, suppose you are interested in recent digital real estate sales across all blockchain games or the availability of NFT art. In that case, you could simply query the blockchains and display the data visually on your website for anyone to see and interact with. This would simply be impossible using traditional games as this data would likely be deemed proprietary. Of course, the added benefit of truly owning your digital, gaming, assets, made possible by NFTs, is that you can monetize them, which we will cover in-depth in Chapter 7 when discussing the economics of the metaverse. What is certain is that gaming, and the economics of gaming, will be transformed in ways we cannot yet imagine in the years to come.

Most of the games discussed so far are currently available as virtual 2D worlds accessible only on your desktop, tablet, or smartphone. While there are, of course, plenty of virtual reality games available, there are only a limited number of blockchain games that are also accessible using virtual reality. Some of these games, such as Somnium Space or Solice, have only recently launched, but likely more will follow in the coming years. The same applies to augmented reality blockchain games, such as AR crypto treasure hunts (think Pokémon Go but then decentralized), which offer tremendous opportunities for game developers, brands, and players. Whether these blockchain games are available in 2D, 3D, or augmented reality, these experiences should eventually embrace interoperability to create a metaverse that brings value capture to another level and is accessible to all.

Sports in the Metaverse

While gaming is a market that creates a lot of value globally, the sports industry is another form of entertainment that is well-known for creating value. Already a $620 billion global market, watching or participating in sports (events) could take on a whole new meaning when the sports industry steps into the metaverse. The sports industry is no stranger to augmented reality, as sporting events on TV have had digitally added and targeted advertising on the field sidelines for years. Now that there is a convergence of technologies such as data analytics, the Internet of Things, AI, and VR or AR, it could completely transform sports.

Imagine your favorite sports club, be it, for example, in football, baseball, basketball, or soccer, and you would love to attend a live match. In the metaverse, you can do so from the comfort of your home without missing any of the experience you would have when attending in person. While, of course, nothing beats a live experience, a metaverse experience would provide unique benefits that you would not be able to get when watching the match inside the stadium. For example, apart from most likely paying a much lower fee, you can watch the match in VR, and in the long run, potentially also in AR as a holographic projection, from any viewpoint—be it alongside the pitch or hovering above the players—while receiving additional live insights about what is happening. You could literally be standing next to your favorite player while they score a goal.

Early 2021, Nickelodeon tried a different, but very much fun, approach. They partnered up with the Dutch sports data visualization company Beyond Sports to turn a live NFL playoff match into cartoony-style block form based on *SpongeBob SquarePants*.[146] The entire environment, including stadium, players, pitch, etc., were turned into block form, and using real-time data the players in the block world moved exactly as the players in the real world, but with all kinds of fun elements added to it, including slime canons. It was an absurd way of game reporting that was vibrant, fun, completely unique, and a mix of video game simulation and an actual NFL game.[147] It was an indication of what is to come and where users can experience sports in whatever way they want.[148]

Reporting sport matches in block form might not be for everyone, and hyper-realistic immersive sports might seem farfetched, but the metaverse will certainly revolutionize how we watch sports. With instant replay already available for years and new developments such as Intel True View technology, being in full control of how you want to watch a game is closer than ever before. Intel's system places dozens of small smart cameras around a venue, capturing the field and the game from every possible angle and generating massive amounts of volumetric data, including height, width, and depth information.[149] These terabytes of volumetric data are then converted into volumetric video that gives the editor full control of what to show from which viewpoint, at any depth or distance. The natural next step would be to give this control to the viewer, assisted by AI, who can decide how to watch his favorite team. Theoretically, Intel's system should be powerful enough to completely replace all traditional cameras while giving editors and viewers more control than ever before. Add in spatial audio, and all of a sudden, you can stand on the pitch, among the players, while watching the match like never before and hearing the players talk to each other from different angles. Of course, all this volumetric data can be analyzed by AI to give sports teams new insights and improve their play in ways that would give the Oakland Athletics baseball team and their general manager Billy Beane, portrayed in the movie *Moneyball*, a run for their money.

What would apply to physical sports would also apply to the eSports industry. eSports is a form of competition using video games, where individuals or teams participate in multiplayer video games with the objective to win or be the last person standing, depending on the video game genre. Most of these eSport championships revolve around first-person shooters, Battle Royale, or real-time strategy games such as *Dota2 Counterstrike* or *League of Legends*. It is a billion-dollar industry with world championships followed by millions of enthusiasts and million-dollar prizes. Although these games are just 2D games, the next iteration of eSports is already here.

The metaverse will unite eSports and physical sports into a larger omniverse, where they are currently sovereign ecosystems. Games such as *Echo Arena* merge physical activity with a virtual reality multiplayer game. Players need to duck, jump, dodge, throw with accuracy, and use quick reflexes in physical reality to win the game. It combines physical activity and technology in completely new ways, and it is increasing in popularity.[150] It could easily become as popular as traditional sports as the digital environments can be displayed on 2D devices or viewers could watch a game in virtual reality. Suddenly, participating in the real-world Olympics while playing Quidditch for your national team becomes a possibility!

Of course, the sports industry is also looking at utilizing crypto and NFTs to increase fan engagement. During the 2022 Olympics, the International Olympics Committee jumped on the NFT bandwagon, creating a blockchain game called Olympic Games Jam: Beijing 2022, which allowed users to compete in different Olympic sports, wear custom avatar skins and earn rewards. Interestingly, the game was not available in China, due to its restrictions on crypto.[151]

The 2022 Australian Open tennis tournament also released NFTs including the AO Decades Collection—six NFT collections celebrating the history of the Australian Open.[152] While most of these NFTs were nothing more than images or short video clips, one NFT would give its owner an all-paid trip to the Australian Open in 2023. At the same time, the Australian Open also released NFT art linked to live match data. The 6,776 unique items of the AO Art Ball collection gave people a possibility to own a piece of the Australian Open. The organizers linked the

6,776 NFTs to a 19cm × 19cm plot of all tennis courts, and whenever the winning shot of any of the 400+ matches landed on one of those plots, a unique NFT would be minted in real time, including the metadata of the match. Contrary to the AO Decades Collection, these NFTs came with utility such as limited-edition wearables, merchandise, and other future benefits. The 6,776 tennis balls were created using artificial intelligence to ensure a unique combination of colors and textures. Finally, the Australian Open also opened a tennis experience in Decentraland, for fans to explore virtually from anywhere in the world and complete challenges and interact with players.[153] The Australian Open digital experience is a great example of how the metaverse can enrich the sports experience, and it won't be long before you could watch a live game inside one of the virtual worlds and experience matches in completely new ways similar to the Nickelodeon NFL game.

Media and Entertainment in the Metaverse

Of course, all the changes we can expect for the sports industry also apply to the media and entertainment industry. The entertainment industry was hit hard due to the pandemic, with concerts canceled worldwide. However, as we have seen from the introduction, massive interactive live events have now appeared, and in the coming years we can expect these events to become bigger, more interactive, and a massive money-maker for artists and virtual world owners while offering unique experiences to fans. Fans can see and hear their favorite artists in completely new ways, while NFTs and crypto will reduce the dependency on intermediaries, and artists can connect with and sell their music to fans direct. As such, they can retain a larger share of their revenues while at the same time reaching millions of fans at once with (live) virtual concerts. Of course, centralized platforms will also take a cut of artists' earnings, but that is similar to the physical world where the costs for a stadium or concert hall also need to be paid for.

Apart from the two virtual events discussed in the introduction, there have been a wide variety of virtual events already. The very first concert was on February 2, 2019, when Marshmello, an American electronic music producer and DJ, delivered the first virtual concert in Fortnite. 10 million fans played Fortnite and attended the Marshmello concert, with millions more joining the live stream on YouTube.[154] The next big concert on Fortnite was by hip-hop star Travis Scott in April 2020. His *Astronomical* tour of five 15-minutes concerts saw an eye-dropping 27.7 million concurrent players participate live, with a total of 45.8 million visits.[155] These five concerts reportedly earned him $20 million, not bad for a few hours of work,[156] especially if this is compared to his *Astroworld* tour in 2019, which grossed him $1.7 million.[157] These massive interactive live events are here to stay. At the same time, we have only just explored the possibilities of these concerts.

These initial concerts took place in a 2D virtual world that people could attend on their computers. In the coming years, we will also see live virtual reality concerts, which will bring the experience to another level—allowing fans to feel as if they are there and sharing the experience while attending the event remotely. If the graphics and spatial audio are good enough, it could almost look like the real deal, though the experience will probably be a lot more visual and out of this world. Especially because with such virtual events, whether 2D or 3D, it is possible to align the visuals with the rhythm of the music, creating an additional sensation. Of course, similar to physical events, merchandise in the form of skins, digital fashion, or wearables for your avatar can be sold as NFTs during the event, adding to the revenue-making opportunities for the artist and others involved.

A few years down the line, we will probably be able to have your favorite artist deliver a personalized concert right in your living room using a holographic projection thanks to your AR glasses. Combined with AI, your favorite artist can address you by your name, and you can even have a simple, conversation, further personalizing the experience. The possibilities are endless.

Of course, not only famous singers can benefit from the opportunities in the metaverse. Anyone can create a digital twin and deliver a unique performance in the metaverse, whether you are a stand-up comedian, a famous entrepreneur delivering a keynote, or a celebrity author doing a book launch. I can imagine that 5 to 10 years from now, we will go to the local theatre, and you will be handed AR glasses that will give a completely new meaning to theatre, merging the physical actors with magical digital creatures to deliver a unique experience. The metaverse will completely revolutionize media, culture, and entertainment and enable a wide variety of unbelievable experiences, unlike anything we have seen before. Magic will become real.

Apart from delivering virtual experiences that can generate a lot of money for (famous) artists and platform owners, NFTs will enable all artists to increase their revenue opportunities. Research by the Ivory Academy showed that 80 percent of the music creators earn less than $275 per year, while the top biggest record labels made $12 million, per day.[158] Thanks to NFTs, artists can now interact directly with their fans and increase their music revenue.

Naturally, the music industry jumped onto the NFT bandwagon in 2021, and many famous artists were the first to explore these options. Singers such as Grimes, Kings of Leon, and Eminem, to name a few, minted songs and album art as NFTs to raise money directly from fans. Eminem even made $1.7 million for his first NFT music collection, while Grimes sold a digital-art NFT.[159] Fortunately, NFTs are not only for famous singers. Also, up-and-coming artists can benefit from NFTs and crypto to raise funds for creating their albums and thereby growing their community. NFTs are a great new source of income to replace the minimal revenue most artists generate from streaming platforms.

The platform Royal.io, for example, enables musicians to sell fractionalized royalty ownership to their fans. When the artist earns, the fans earn too, a concept called *Listen to Earn*. With each NFT, apart from a small share in royalty, the singer can add special perks that further strengthen the bond with the fans. As an artist, with NFTs, you are in control, and you can create engaging experiences that further increase your fan base. An artist can use NFTs to sell an asset, or multiple, and sell them directly to their fans, creating a direct economic relationship with them instead of going through some intermediary. The artist can see who owns those NFTs and drop them another NFT or digital wearable or digital gift as a reward for their continuous support. It could be a limited edition of a T-shirt that the fan can wear within virtual worlds and gives access to a backstage meeting with the artist. NFTs empower content creators, help them depend less on intermediaries, and create a stronger connection with fans. Upcoming artists can use platforms such as Royal.io to share their royalty with their early fans and use those funds to further increase their presence.

The same would apply to movies, where you can create NFT movie tickets before a film has been made. This would help kickstart a movie and give the owner a stake in the movie's success. After all, if the movie becomes a success, the NFT movie tickets can become collector items similar to the real world.

The startups GrooveUp and Portal take it to another level and let artists even reward fans for streaming their music with tokens or NFTs, administered automatically using smart contracts. This *Stream-to-Earn* business model is another attempt to break the power of the large record labels.

With virtual concerts and the NFTs to directly engage with fans, the money-making opportunities will likely shift away from the record labels to the artists and virtual platforms. They will empower artist to be more in control *if* the artist wants to go the extra mile and connect directly with fans without the help of record labels. Whether the metaverse and NFTs can reverse the existing inequality remains to be seen, depending on the power of the record labels, but at least it gives (upcoming) artists a novel way to connect with their fans and reduce the dependency on record labels to become successful.

Of course, creating this direct relationship with fans applies to any brand, and companies that want to get involved in the metaverse should think about how they want to evolve the relationship with their customers. Brands should reward consumers for attending, buying, sharing, or displaying their product or service in the metaverse. It is early days and not yet battle-tested, but brands and startups should experiment to determine what works and what doesn't.

Education in the Metaverse

When I advise organizations or deliver my keynotes, I always tell people that we live in exponential times and that the world is changing faster than ever before. While I firmly believe this, it is not the case for the education industry. In the past 100 years, the world might have drastically changed, but the way we teach our children remains exactly the same as 100 years ago; a large group of kids in a classroom, sitting forward-facing, listening to a teacher who explains something, gives an assignment, or has a discussion with the students. To make matters worse, the pandemic forced children worldwide to learn from home, sitting hours in front of Zoom or Teams and being home-schooled by parents. Zoom fatigue is a real thing for professionals, so for children, with their limited attention spans, online learning during the pandemic was challenging for children, parents, and teachers.[160]

I would argue that teaching children is the most important task we have as society; after all, the children will be the innovators of tomorrow. The fact that we have not innovated our teaching methods in the past 100 years while having all these technologies available is remarkable to me. We stick to the old paradigm of teaching children traditional subjects in a traditional way, most of which will become useless in the next decade. Instead, we should teach our kids the research and analytical skills so they know how to form an opinion and self-educate, how to be adaptive and deal with rapid change, and how to use and apply technology (responsibly) by teaching them programming, robotics, and ethics. Above all, we should embrace the latest technology, from AI coaching to virtual and augmented experiences, to prepare our children for a world that will look fundamentally different by the time they finish school.

Moreover, research has shown that passive teaching methods are ineffective in transferring knowledge. The least effective method is a lecture. Long-term retention rates of the knowledge shared in a typical lecture where the teacher stands in front of a class and talks are around 5 percent, while reading about a topic only marginally improves the retention rates to 10 percent.[161] However, participatory teaching methods drastically improve the memory retention rates, with group discussions bringing it to 50 percent and learning by doing to 75 percent. Hearing and reading can be useful in some use cases, but the best would be to learn by doing, and that is where AR and VR come into play. After all, practice makes perfect.

Imagine a history teacher that offers VR classes combined with a discussion with the group after the class has experienced Ancient Rome using virtual reality. It would allow students to actually go into a virtual environment, interact with the teacher and fellow students, pause or play back a scene or session, and notice new things every time they visit or replay a scene. It would allow the children to experience a new environment in a safe and controlled environment and explore knowledge from a different perspective while being fully engaged. We could teach children the world of quantum mechanics by literally stepping into the microscopic world or showing the effects of climate change on any environment. The potential is endless, and it most probably would result in a fun learning environment and the best ratings ever for the teacher and school. Moreover, celebrity teachers will be able to teach millions of kids simultaneously in an immersive environment, as long as the required hardware becomes available to as many children as possible. Perhaps we should organize the equivalent of the One Laptop per Child project, which attempted to create a $100 laptop for children in developing countries, but then for a VR/AR headset offering children around the world an equal opportunity to learn in an immersive environment, which would of course also require us to solve the issue of internet connection in remote locations.

Using virtual reality, it will be a lot easier to keep children and students fully engaged and attentive without the fear of them wandering off compared to a Zoom, Teams, or in-person lecture. Of course, it would most likely not be healthy for kids to spend more than one to two hours per day in virtual reality, although more research would be required to understand how virtual reality impacts the brains of children. Metaverse-natives will be wired differently, literally, which is not necessarily a bad thing.

If virtual and augmented reality can significantly improve education for children, it also has the potential to revolutionize corporate training or skill-based learning (such as fixing your washing machine with augmented reality).[162] Digital twins or replicas of factories can be used to train (new) employees in a safe working environment until they master the skills to go out in the real world and work with the (advanced) tools.

Jeremy Bailenson, founding director of the Stanford Virtual Human Interaction Lab (VHIL) and founder of the VR training company Strivr, called education and training the "home run" use case. His company worked with Walmart to train employees using immersive experiences, resulting in a 30 percent increase in job satisfaction and a 15 percent increase in knowledge retention rates.[163]

The potential for workers around the world to learn new skills and learn how to operate complex machines without risking being harmed or damaging the physical machine are practically endless. From employee onboarding, to learning safety and security processes, to preparing for rare and unexpected, events to improving customer-client interactions, virtual reality will offer new ways to learn a new skill faster and more efficiently.[164]

In the coming years, ideally education around the world will be brought into the 21st century. Using novel concepts such as *Play-to-Learn* using immersive experiences or eSports to train skills such as team skills, collaborative working, hand-eye coordination, or strategy-making has the opportunity to revolutionize how our children, and employees, learn. Taking it one step further, we could disentangle curricula and allow students to create their own curriculum from various resources, as long as these verified courses are connected to NFTs. Collect sufficient NFTs, and you could receive your diploma, certified on the blockchain.

Schools and universities have to embrace the technologies described in this book to give children and students the education that prepares them for a radically different society in the years to come. Not doing so would be a missed opportunity for both children and society.

Power to the Creators

Regardless of what virtual world you will be in, user-generated content will play an increasingly important role in the metaverse. Whether this involves designing and creating games, immersive songs, volumetric media, educational environments, or the virtual worlds, art, and avatars that will liven up the next version of the internet, the metaverse will be a creator economy, and UGC will be everything. Thanks to technological advances in creating immersive and augmented experiences, the metaverse will catapult us into the Imagination Age, and NFTs and crypto will enable creators to earn a (substantial) living, as we will also see in Chapter 7.

Within the metaverse, user-generated content will most likely be visual and audible, and potentially even tactile at some point. People will craft narrative experiences, but what we can expect 5 to 10 years from now is impossible to say. At the start of the mobile Web, people also had no clue what the amazing potential was of an app economy. The first apps were, in retrospect, rather ridiculous and useless. But that is a normal process. It was just us trying to figure out what was possible and what that new ecosystem meant. The same will apply to the immersive internet. In the coming years, we will better understand what is possible with VR and AR, and content creators will be able to take full advantage of these new capabilities resulting in amazing experiences.

Of course, users will need to be able to find all this immersive and augmented content. After all, there is no Google yet in the metaverse to locate all the spatial experiences. Most likely, this will work with some kind of portal system, within one platform that can be solved easily. More challenging will be to connect millions of platforms to each other so users can teleport directly from The Sandbox to Fortnite to *NeosVR*, for example, ideally together with their friends. To achieve this, we will probably need some kind of hub model, which directs you from one platform to another. Naturally, this should be done in an open source, decentralized manner to avoid any centralized entity controlling who can traverse where from one place to another. If done well, it might be possible that from the user experience, it is a seamless experience, similar to how we go from one website to another.

The metaverse will open significant opportunities for artists and creators, but it will also be a place for brands to fully engage with their customers, fans, and future clients. However, we should of course avoid for the metaverse to become an advertisement dystopia, where similar to the current Web, ads follow you if you traverse from one virtual world to another (unless of course, you want them to and you have given your informed consent to allow this). How brands should step into the metaverse is the next chapter's topic.

Chapter 5
Unbounded Creativity for Brands

Beyond flash

"Technology is a glittering lure. But there's the rare occasion when the public can be engaged on a level beyond flash—if they have a sentimental bond with the product."

Don Draper, *Mad Men*

This quote by Don Draper is probably one of the most well-known quotes from the show, and it still holds true. In today's world, thanks to the tsunami of data, it has become easier than ever before to target exactly the people you want. Spend enough money on hyper-targeted and personalized ads, and you are guaranteed to get eyes on your ad. But those eyeballs don't necessarily mean success. On the internet, the attention timespan of people is only a few seconds, and the infinite scrolling trap ensures people will have forgotten the ad again the moment something new pops up on their screen. The quality of the majority of advertising online is (below) average, which means that the moment something comes by that creates an emotional bond with them, something with actual substance, it will stand out and have an impact.[165]

During *Mad Men*'s time, in the 1960s, the era of mass marketing had just begun. Thanks to radio and television, it had become possible to reach large groups of people with a single company's message. This also meant that the message better be good because it was not possible to adjust the message per target group. It had to be a concise and clear offer that resonated with the intended audience. Over the years, this mass marketing worked well for brands, which is why when the internet arrived, brands at first were reluctant to develop an online presence.

This seems unthinkable today, but during the internet's beginning, plenty of brands did not see the need for a website. Then when eCommerce became a thing, brands were reluctant to open an online store. Even at the start of the pandemic, there were plenty of brands that had not yet invested heavily in an online channel and ran into problems when the brick-and-mortar shops had to close due to the lockdowns around the world. Those companies that had not updated their supply chain to the digital era before the start of this pandemic faced a lot more difficulties in adjusting to the new normal than those companies with a digitally optimized supply chain and eCommerce channel.

The same applied at the start of the social media era and the mobile internet. Again, brands had to be convinced that it was a good idea to develop a mobile app, create a presence on social media, and build a community on Twitter, Facebook, YouTube, or, more recently, TikTok.

Time and again, brands have been reluctant to embrace new opportunities. At the same time, the few frontrunners and innovators who did embrace the new reality were successful in the long run, even though they made mistakes when exploring the new possibilities. In comparison, the graveyard lies full of companies that failed to innovate or embrace the new reality. Now that we have entered a new era of connecting with consumers, the metaverse, brands should avoid making the same mistakes again. The immersive internet offers an opportunity to engage with customers in authentic and unique ways, offering experiences to create new sentimental bonds with your products. One brand that seemed to have learned from its mistake is Warner Music Group. Early 2022, it announced a concert-focused theme park in the Sandbox, embracing this new paradigm early on, which is a considerably different approach than two decades ago, when Warner fought hard against the rise of file sharing and Napster.[166]

Another brand that seemed to have learned from previous mistakes is JPMorgan Chase. In 2017, JPMorgan's CEO Jamie Dimon called bitcoin a fraud,[167] and in 2022 they opened a lounge in Decentraland that includes a tiger wandering in the lobby in order to capitalize on what it says is a trillion-dollar opportunity.[168]

While it is very early days when it comes to the metaverse, those brands that decide to step into this immersive world today will be the frontrunners tomorrow. This new virtual and augmented world requires a different approach when connecting with (future) customers, so practice makes perfect. Those companies starting early will have a head start on the majority who will be late to the game. The rules of marketing are changing, and the era of unauthentic, pushy marketing and advertising is over. Especially Generation Z and Generation Alpha no longer accept ads that follow them around the Web, greenwashing to pretend you care about the environment, or hyper-targeted, intrusive ads that indicate that you know the customer better than they know themselves.

While we are about to leave that marketing era behind us, a door opens to a new form of marketing. Consumers are now getting accustomed to the reality of shopping and socializing digitally, through social media but also using AR filters, video games, or immersive, interactive, and real-time content. In this phygital world, consumers play online games together, wander around the virtual world to be with friends, attend digital events, visit new virtual locations, and interact with brands to buy (digital) goods and services. This new virtual and augmented world, together with the fact that the average human attention span is currently down to only 8 seconds,[169] requires brands to redefine how they interact with and sell their products to consumers. Organizations will have to redefine their marketing efforts and offer (future) customers a unique and authentic digital experience; where co-creation and even co-ownership become the norm and community-driven marketing is the key to success.

With the development of an immersive ecosystem, companies will have new ways to increase brand loyalty and engage with their (future) customers in unexpected, exciting, and fun ways. In the coming years, the metaverse will become a significant component of successful brand strategies, and those companies that refuse to jump on the metaverse bandwagon will lose out. Although the immersive internet can be perceived as another channel to connect with customers, business as usual is not the way to go.

The Power of an Immersive Community

In the metaverse, two things will separate the "cool" brands from the "uncool" brands: creativity and authenticity. This has always been the case, but it will become more important than ever as anything will be possible in the metaverse. While the first metaverse initiatives of brands included translating real-world products and experiences into the virtual world, mimicking the real world in the virtual world will be a mistake. In early 2022, Samsung launched the virtual brand store 837X in Decentraland, which pretty much was a digital copy of their physical 837 store in New York. Although the 837 flagship store in NY is an experience in itself, replicating it in the metaverse misses the opportunity to expand the customer experience via the immersive internet. Brands should focus on creating highly visual, experimental, and engaging experiences unlike we have ever seen in the real world to far exceed physical world marketing expectations and take advantage of the unbounded digital possibilities. Turn your business into an experience that connects with the emotions of your customers. This presents a fantastic opportunity for brands to reinvent themselves and come up with a new narrative, directly collaborating and interacting with customers instead of just selling to customers.[170] It would involve carefully creating and nurturing a community by offering personalized entertainment and value that stimulates digital self-expression by metaverse-natives and acknowledges the need for an authentic and unique connection.

The global beer brand Stella Artois did just that during the pandemic. When, just like all events, horse racing events such as the Kentucky Derby were cancelled, virtual horse racing gained global attention. Although virtual horse racing has been around for some time, the rise of NFTs enabled users to truly own and breed virtual horses and have them compete against each other in virtual races for real money. The platform

ZED RUN offers such races and saw a 1,000 percent growth since the start of the pandemic.[171] Similar to brands sponsoring physical races, Stella Artois decided to jump in and sponsor digital horse racing, as it was "a natural fit that mirrored Stella Artois' partnership with premium horse racing," explained Lindsey McInerney, who was responsible for the campaign when working at AB InBev.[172] They partnered with the platform, creating a unique set of digital horses, including themed skins, and a 3D racetrack, offering a unique experience for users and positioning the beer brand as innovative and a thought leader in this space.

The metaverse is an entire digital layer on top of our existing world. As such, it will be far more disruptive for brands than social media or the mobile internet ever was. These virtual or augmented layers offer brands countless opportunities to connect with consumers and deliver a unique experience that can build customer loyalty. While the earlier-discussed need for interoperability will further increase these opportunities, until we have achieved that crucial stepping-stone, the current virtual and augmented worlds already offer brands great ways to create meaningful, two-way interactions with (potential) customers. One of the most exciting brands to step into the metaverse is Walt Disney, and in December 2021, they filed a patent for a "virtual-world simulator" to bring their theme parks into the metaverse. According to the patent, users would be able to move in "highly immersive individualized 3D virtual experiences without requiring those users to wear an augmented reality viewing device."[173] Walt Disney has always been far head of the pack when it comes to digital transformation, starting with their MagicBand+ wrist device that they introduced already in 2013,[174] so we can expect digital magic from the Mickey Mouse brand.

Before brands go down this rabbit hole, it is important to have a very clear idea of what they want to *be* in the digital world. It requires a deep understanding of the company DNA, the target group, their expectations, and where (future) customers are hanging out in this virtual world as the metaverse is so much more than creating a (static) website, app, or interacting on social media. Done well, it will enable organizations to build deep and long-lasting loyalty that directly impacts and contributes positively to a brand's reputation and bottom line. Done wrong, it could significantly damage the brand.

In Chapter 3, I discussed the example of how Gucci created a unique, interactive experience on Roblox, resulting in digital luxury items eventually selling for more than their physical counterparts. While this was a great exploration by Gucci into the metaverse, it was not flawless as it did not incorporate the platform's core players: children and pre-teens. Fifty-four percent of Roblox users are younger than 12 years,[175] and while the kids playing Roblox would undoubtedly have loved to wear virtual Gucci, hundreds or even thousands of dollars for a digital item is, of course, out of reach for 99.99 percent of the kids active in the game, and most likely their parents as well. What made matters worse is that, in line with the concept of creating scarcity for luxury products, most of these exclusive items dropped by Gucci in the game were available for only a limited amount of time. They were dropped at times when the children playing Roblox, the primary target group, were in bed, missing out on a lot of the fun. So, while adults got super excited about digital products selling for thousands of dollars, the future customers of Gucci, the children actually playing the game, were frustrated and felt left out. Gucci's story was great PR but might not have resulted in a strong connection with future customers. Considering the actual players of a virtual world is crucial, especially if you want them to have a positive brand experience.

Mistakes aside, the benefits of the immersive internet for brands are numerous.

Endless New Touchpoints

Already, a wide variety of virtual and augmented worlds pop up across the metaverse. In the coming decade, this will likely explode as the technology to build such environments will become more accessible. Consequently, instead of just a few major platforms as Web 2.0 offers today, there will be a wide variety of large and small communities that can be targeted in unique ways. Each of these new touchpoints will offer unique brand engagement or product placement opportunities including dropping the latest car in a virtual world for users to test-drive, creating digital fashion as we have seen in Chapter 3, and delivering a fun way to bring forward one of your brand's unique selling points (USPs). While this offers a lot of opportunities for brands, it could also result in fragmentation, making it costly to reach customers.

Wendy's *Keeping Fortnite Fresh* brand activation in 2018 is a perfect example of the latter. In 2018, Fortnite introduced a new event called Food Fight, enabling players to represent their favorite digital restaurant. Teams of the digital restaurant Durr Burger (Team Burger) and Pizza Pit (Team Pizza) had to fight each other, with the last person standing being declared the winner. Wendy's decided to join the game to make its advertising the audience's entertainment.[176] They discovered that the burgers from Durr Burger were stored in the freezer, which is against Wendy's policy never to use frozen beef. Wendy's saw an opportunity to advertise its "fresh, never frozen beef."

The fast-food chain got on Twitch, created a character that resembled the brand's mascot, dropped it into Fortnite, and started destroying all the freezers in the game's Food Fight mode instead of killing other players. Wendy's live-streamed their quest on Twitch, inviting hundreds of thousands of players to watch and join them destroying freezers instead of killing other players. Over the course of nine hours of streaming, 1.5+ million minutes were watched on Twitch (the equivalent of nearly 3 years watching Twitch nonstop), and there was an increase of 119 percent of brand mentions across social media, with everyone learning about Wendy's USP. This unique freezer fight was a successful guerrilla marketing campaign by Wendy's, which even resulted in several awards, including eight Cannes Lions—the Oscars of the advertising world.[177]

Continuous and Real-Time Insights

The first metaverse marketing campaigns of several luxury brands, such as Gucci, Balenciaga, or Dolce & Gabbana, are great examples of increasing the brand experience. However, digital fashion can also be used to better understand what customers like or don't like before actually launching a new fashion line. By carefully analyzing which options and what combinations are selected by users playing games such as Fortnite or Roblox, fashion houses, both luxury brands and nonluxury brands, can quickly learn what resonates best with which group of customers (based on who is wearing what when dropping, free, digital items in a game) and adjust their physical offerings accordingly.

Moreover, immersive digital product demonstrations, or product customizations, where consumers can try out and create a product before actually buying it, can be a data goldmine for brands. Even if consumers decide not to buy the product, it will be a great opportunity to interact with (future) customers and learn valuable insights about what customers deem important. Of course, there is nothing new about online product demonstrations or product configurations; these have existed for years on the Web. However, an immersive, 3D version of it would significantly improve the brand experience and provide additional insights that go beyond what can be achieved with traditional surveys.

Already launched in 2017, IKEA's Place app is a leading example of using augmented reality to offer a unique experience for customers while, undoubtedly, generating a stream of additional user data for IKEA. It was one of the first examples of a mobile shopping app that took full advantage of ARKit, Apple's augmented reality framework, allowing users to try out furniture digitally to better understand how that new couch or table would look in their house. Linking such digital customer interactions directly to your organization's business intelligence would offer invaluable, real-time insights into who is interested in what, when, where, and why.

With the amount of data generated in the metaverse to be 10 to 100x compared to the current Web, not stepping into the metaverse as a brand would be akin to driving blindfolded.

Increased Sustainability

As discussed in Chapter 3, thanks to VR and AR, the decision-making process while shopping online can be made more fun, engaging, and eventually also more sustainable by reducing the number of returns and "try-before-you-buy" virtual experiences. At the end of 2021, the augmented reality company Snap worked with Tommy Jeans to create a virtual try-on for their clothes. Using Snap's AR glasses, customers were able to try the Tommy Jeans men or women puffer jacket and easily change the jacket's colors to see which style worked best for them.

Users could then instantly click through to the website to buy the product they had virtually tried at home.[178]

Of course, the metaverse offers more opportunities to reduce the CO_2 emissions of an organization, especially when it comes to travel or collaboration, but we will cover that in the next chapter.

Virtual World Considerations

Although virtual worlds offer countless possibilities to wow the customer, determining where to start is an important decision. The process to decide where to build your virtual or augmented brand experience is strikingly familiar to the process you would follow when opening a brand experience or store in the physical world.

Whenever an organization decides to open a new physical store, there are various important metrics to consider. These include the neighborhood's demographics, the foot traffic, how safe the neighborhood is, where your competitors are located, how accessible the area is, the cost of doing business, rules and restrictions, etc. To a certain degree, these are the same metrics you need to take into account when selecting the virtual world where you want to open up your virtual brand experience:

- How many people use the platform
- How popular is it
- How long people stay on the platform
- How often they come back
- What the demographics of the users are
- What activity is going on at the platform
- Whether there are any scams happening
- What the rules and restrictions of the platform are
- How expensive is it to set up your virtual shop

In this early stage of the metaverse, companies should try different platforms. Each platform operates differently, with different users, rules, and brand expectations. The more a brand explores these various digital worlds, the faster they will understand how the metaverse works for them and what digital experiences work best for (future) customers.

The Era of Experience Marketing

When organizations want to venture into the metaverse to connect with consumers, it is wise to involve the creators, the artists, and the influencers who already have an in-depth understanding of the various virtual or augmented reality applications. By involving the community as early as possible, brands can avoid (potentially costly) mistakes such as Gucci's. This also means that if you are new to the metaverse and want to enter a new community, be sure to be humble as a brand, even if you are a multinational organization. Brands have the tendency to enter a creative community and turn it into the Super Bowl, according to Justin Hochberg, founder of the Virtual Brand Group. Instead, brands can stand to benefit a lot more if they become part of the community and do not bombard the community with advertising messages. This applies especially to the metaverse.

Moreover, since the metaverse is still a work in progress, for at least the coming years, even if you join with the best intentions, there are risks involved. For example, when McDonald's created a set of 10 NFTs to celebrate their McRib at the end of 2021, they quickly found out that minting NFTs is something different than frying burgers. The McRib NFTs were described by McDonald's as "digital versions of the fan-favorite sandwich."[179] Unfortunately, sometime after the announcement, a racial slur was discovered in an early transaction linked to the Ethereum address associated with the official McRib NFT collection.[180] A racial slur linked to McDonald's is now on the blockchain indefinitely. The company stated that they had no idea how it happened, but a fun brand experience quickly turned sour. Regardless of whether it was an insider or someone completely unaffiliated with the brand, the metaverse is not without risks for brands. Having a good, shared understanding of what you are doing is thus important. Of course, in these early days, this means involving those who have been in this space for years, who understand the various continuously evolving environments, and who can guide the organization into this exciting new opportunity. It also means associating yourself with new and existing virtual worlds instead of creating your own ecosystem, at least for now.

Brands that do step into the metaverse have an opportunity to demonstrate leadership, associate themselves with innovation, and tap into new communities and channels, especially if they display authentic behavior and closely align their immersive experience with the community they intend to reach. Gen Z and Gen Alpha are the creator generations. They are ready to participate and generate content with you, so as a brand you should create such opportunities. One retailer that did so is the fashion brand Forever 21. The American fashion retailer developed a unique community-first brand experience for Roblox, launched at the end of 2021, which allowed Roblox users to operate their own Forever 21 store. By creating a unique brand experience and offering value to the Roblox community, the retailer attracted significant coverage in traditional media while truly merging the physical and digital space. According to Justin Hochberg, CEO of the Virtual Brand Group, who architected the metaverse strategy and experience for Forever 21 with their metaverse adventure, the brand actively worked with Roblox creators, designers, and influencers. It gave them a platform to showcase, and sell, their own designs. Within the Forever 21 brand store on Roblox, they created a section called Collab 21, where each month, Roblox users are allowed to showcase their own Forever 21 designs, which other Roblox users can then purchase. They also created a Tycoon-type game, enabling players to design and fully operate their own Forever 21 store. Unlike most brands currently exploring these virtual worlds, Forever 21 plans to stay in the game for the long term. To create a continuous interaction with the user base, the retailer announced *Forever 21 Day*, launching new brand experiences, such as a live event, limited NFT drop, or collaboration with a different brand or celebrity, on the 21st of each month. In addition, one of the main features of the campaign, which Justin calls the *Infinite Marketing Loop*, is that Forever 21 will release new collections simultaneously in the physical and digital world, enabling users to match what they wear in the real world with what their avatar wears, merging the physical and the digital brand and creating a continuous gamified experience that connects the physical and digital worlds. This continued collaboration with Roblox has paid off for the retailer, with a 92 percent positive sentiment, a 20x social amplification compared to other brands that launched around the same time, and 2.5x media exposure in 30 days than all other company-wide Forever 21 efforts over 90 days. In addition, the number-one Forever 21 item on

Roblox sold almost 1 million units, which was created by the community, and Forever 21 will produce this as a physical item at zero R&D costs.[181]

Forever 21's Roblox experience shows how marketing has changed at the dawn of the metaverse. The immersive internet requires a different perspective when reaching your target group. Brands would need to rethink how to create content, how people can interact with that content, and the capabilities and utility of that content. From promoting artistic creativity to community building, we can expect a broad range of marketing innovations in the coming decade as we move from social media marketing to metaverse marketing and brands learn new ways to engage and enlighten consumers. Ways that brands can do so already include organizing digital events, launching a series of NFTs, dropping digital products, creating a cross-platform brand experience, or a combination of the above.

When you want to start as a brand, starting with small experiments is recommended. For example, in 2021, Taco Bell, an American fast-food chain, made tens of thousands of dollars after releasing a series of NFTs.[182] While profits were modest for the well-established brand and the GIFs of a taco did not offer any utility, it shows that if a fast-food restaurant can sell NFTs of floating tacos and make money, then other companies can create unique NFT campaigns to offer a brand experience for users.

Coca-Cola went a step further. In July 2021, Coca-Cola launched an NFT collection that fetched $575,000 within 72 hours in an online auction. The company relied on the power of its brand and large global community of Coca-Cola enthusiasts to push forward its collection to raise money for charity. Coca-Cola auctioned four multisensory, friendship-inspired NFTs via the OpenSea marketplace on International Friendship Day. It was auctioned off as one loot box, a play on the popular video game feature involving sealed mystery boxes. Not only did the winner become the owner of these four NFTs, but the winner also received a real-world physical fridge stocked with Coca-Cola bottles and additional surprises—a great example of an NFT that is more than just a digital image and actually has some utility. The NFT auction resulted in a strong buzz in the crypto community and portrayed Coca-Cola as an innovative brand that knows very well where its customers are.[183]

The more an organization experiments with metaverse marketing, the better the brand will understand what works best for them and their community. What better way to experiment with metaverse marketing than during the metaverse fashion week? From March 23–27, 2022, the metaverse fashion week was held in Decentraland, bringing digital runway shows, shopping, after parties, and panel talks to the virtual world. Over four days, more than 50 luxury and digital brands stepped into the metaverse for a unique experience.

Selfridges, the UK retail chain of high-end department stores, displayed 12 unique NFT dresses by Paco Rabanne and was inspired by Op Art movement pioneer Victor Vasarely. The exhibition mimicked a physical exhibition happening around the same time in Selfridges in London. The luxury fashion house Dolce & Gabbana unveiled multiple outfits designed explicitly for the metaverse, presented using avatars looking like cats. Many brands also sold their (digital) fashion items to fashion week visitors. Brands such as Tommy Hilfiger and Hugo (the Gen Z brand by Hugo Boss) partnered with the Web 3.0 startup Boson Protocol to enable users to buy physical products as NFTs during the fashion week.[184] This allowed users to dress their avatar in Tommy Hilfiger or Hugo while also receiving the physical item at their home. This created a great combination of the physical and virtual converging into a phygital experience. Not only did fashion brands join, but also the beauty brand Estée Lauder participated, giving away 10.000 digital wearables as NFTs, which were based on its famous Night Repair Serum, giving avatars an aura of sparkles and gold glitters.[185]

As the event took place on Decentraland, the entire event was blockchain-based, ensuring the interoperability of the NFTs that users bought. However, reviews from attendees also indicated that the graphics were below-average, and there were plenty of glitches compared to other digital fashion shows, which is because Decentraland is blockchain-based and as such has restrictions on 3D design capabilities.[186] Despite these glitches, more than 100,000 unique attendees attended the digital fashion week, and they saw a large variety of brands experimenting with metaverse marketing and NFTs in unique ways. If done correctly, NFTs are a fantastic marketing tool, and the brands that joined the metaverse fashion week have learned valuable lessons on how to connect with Gen Z and Gen Alpha in the metaverse.

Metaverse marketing is all about offering an experience, which should revolve around storytelling. Storytelling has always been at the heart of a brand's journey and how they connect with consumers. In an immersive digital environment, the narrative around a digital asset is as important as the asset itself. Due to the near-infinite possibilities in the digital world, brands have an opportunity to generate unique and engaging content that brings happiness to people. To refer once more to Don Draper, "Advertising is based on one thing: happiness." It keeps people engaged and wanting to belong to a brand or community. It is about the ideas behind it that determine the success and impact on a brand's sreputation and bottom line.

Creativity, Community, and Co-Creation

Although the metaverse is an excellent channel to connect with and sell to customers, the metaverse should not end up as an advertising dystopia where brands are everywhere and everything is commoditized. Brands need to think hard about what to do and how to connect with customers and avoid being perceived as creepy. Of course, for large brands such as McDonald's, Nike, Gucci, or Coca-Cola, this is easier to achieve as they have already built a community. New and smaller brands should first focus on building and expanding a community before venturing into the metaverse (unless it is a metaverse-native brand, of course). Above all, brands should avoid advertising their way into the metaverse. After all, if we copy the advertising practices of Web 2.0 to the metaverse, the next iteration of the internet is guaranteed to become an advertising nightmare. The amount of available data will explode compared to today, enabling even more personalized and intrusive ads that follow you wherever you go, be it in virtual reality or using augmented reality when you are going shopping in the physical world, as described in the fictional story at the start. From billboards that blow up into your face if you are looking at it for more than two to three seconds, commercials that constantly interrupt the volumetric movie you are watching in VR, to persuasive immersive advertising where AI-human characters constantly approach you with a personalized ad while you are going about your own business,[187] a metaverse optimized for advertising is not something we should want or accept. Of course, advertising will exist in the metaverse, but it should be aligned with the experience. Interactive billboards while playing Fortnite or other games will distract from playing the game and most likely annoy players. In contrast, branded experiences or fun guerrilla marketing campaigns such as Wendy's Keeping Fortnite Fresh can be more successful. Similar to the existing Web, ad blockers will also exist in the metaverse, but they have to become a lot more advanced to block out all the sponsored messages. The best approach would be to reward users for their attention by offering a unique experience instead of pushing branded messages in our (virtual) faces.

An interesting use case of how brands can promote their message is the partnership between the Bored Ape Yacht Club (BAYC) and Adidas. The BAYC is a collection of 10.000 Bored Ape NFTs, and each Bored Ape doubles as the Yacht Club membership card that gives you access to members-only benefits. The BAYC has been very successful, with the most expensive Ape, Bored Ape #8817, selling for $3.4 million in October 2021.[188] One of the reasons why these JPEGs are so expensive is that they come with utility (other reasons being the novelty of NFTs, famous owners, etc.). More importantly, contrary to most NFTs, they provide the owner with the copyrights to monetize their Bored Ape. As we will see in Chapter 7, not many NFTs come with copyrights, and often owners buy nothing more than a token that directs to the location where the JPEG is stored. As a result, multiple Bored Ape owners have already started monetizing their Ape, including the Bored Ape Yacht Club band created by Celine Joshua and Jimmy McNeils in collaboration with Universal Music Group. The band, called KINGSHIP, consists of four Bored Apes, and they will be releasing new music, NFT fan memorabilia, community-based products, and other experiences to create artist-fan engagement.[189] Around the same time, Adidas also purchased a Bored Ape, kicking off a partnership with some of the most well-known personalities in the NFT world. Their Bored Ape was dressed in Adidas clothing to position the brand at the forefront of creativity.[190] Adidas made these digital clothes available as NFTs, offering owners the physical equivalent to match their digital items. Moreover, Adidas announced their digital headquarter in The Sandbox as well as a partnership with Coinbase, where they will likely also sell their digital sportswear as NFTs.[191] Their campaign is called *Into the Metaverse*, and by combining a variety of touchpoints, the brand has garnered a lot of media attention and positioned the brand as a thought leader and innovator.

Of course, Adidas is not the only major sports brand that entered the metaverse. Nike also embraced it thoroughly. The company started by creating a fully immersive digital experience that connected with their physical offering. From February 4 to 11, 2021, customers visiting Nike's House of Innovation in New York could explore a virtual creation of the Smith Rock State Park in Oregon. The experience was limited to within Nike's walls using geofencing but allowed visitors to have an augmented reality experience using their phones.[192] The activities within the location were made as interactive and fun as possible to intrigue customers and digitally tell and deliver a story by using AR and QR-code scanning. At the end of the same year, Nike brought this to another level when they opened their virtual headquarters on Roblox, called NIKELAND. The virtual experience enables Nike fans to connect, create, and share experiences and compete in the virtual world. Inspired by Nike's real-life headquarters and building on top of their earlier experience, Nike created a world that merges the physical and digital worlds. Users are encouraged to go run in the real world, and their physical activity is translated into unique movements in the Roblox game.[193] Of course, users can purchase digital Nike products for their Roblox avatar, especially after the company purchased virtual sneaker maker RTFKT at the end of 2021.

As the examples show in this chapter, embracing the metaverse early on and collaborating with the metaverse community has paid off for brands, at least when it comes to the media attention they have received. The future of marketing is creating a storyline that embraces the various communities and virtual worlds and merges them into a unique narrative. The metaverse is all about creativity, community, and co-creation. Co-creation can help brands foster stronger loyalty and engagement by involving customers in the product-creation process as done by Forever 21 and enabled by The Fabricant Studio, as discussed earlier. Gen Z and Gen Alpha expect brands to become part of their community without taking control of the community or flooding it with one-directional ads. It is a multilayered approach that requires organizations to think differently when reaching out to consumers.

In the metaverse, all brands should reconsider their marketing activities or risk going the way of the gramophone. They should take this opportunity to move away from paying money to display ads and instead invest their money into building a relationship with their community: to co-create, engage, and establish unique brand experiences that offer utility and extend the physical experience into the digital world and vice versa. It will be a collaborative effort between brands and customers, and those brands that include their customers in the creative process will win.[194]

Chapter 6
Exponential Enterprise Connectivity

A Changing World

While the pandemic brought fear, anger, despair, and grief to the world, it also drastically changed how we work. As soon as lockdowns happened worldwide, entire industries switched to remote collaboration practically overnight and, to the surprise of many, without too much trouble, keeping the global economy afloat after the initial shock was over.

For many, working from home became the new normal. Meetings and events moved from the physical world into the digital world. Suddenly, employees had to be onboarded via Zoom or Teams, investments had to be made without ever seeing founders in person, and annual general meetings had to be moved to the digital realm. While for many Millennials and Baby Boomers, this was a brand new experience, connecting virtually had been common practice for Gen Z and Gen Alpha. For years, these generations have grown up in the digital world; they have been socializing, interacting, trading, playing, partying, flirting, working, experimenting, presenting, and collaborating in closed virtual worlds such as Roblox, Minecraft, or Fortnite. In the coming years, these generations are hitting the workforce, especially Gen Z, and they are expecting a different way of working; they will not accept a 9 to 5 job in a cubicle.

In May 2021, amidst the pandemic, Anthony Klotz coined the term The Great Resignation.[195] Based on his research, the associate professor of Management at Texas A&M University noticed that the pandemic had caused people to reflect on their lives. More people started to value family time, having seen the benefits of remote work, reduced commuting time, and the ability to focus on passion projects. The Millennials joined Gen Z in their need for a digitally fueled work environment that empowers them to have complete control over how they organize their lives.

This awakening, combined with an ongoing pandemic, will result in more people deciding to follow their passions. People resigning from their current jobs and looking for a new job are no longer geographically bound to work where they live. This is good for employees, as suddenly, the world is their oyster. However, the same applies to those organizations fully embracing remote work. They, too, will be able to fish in a much bigger, global, talent pool. Employers have access to more employees from anywhere globally, and they can even opt for replacing those jobs with ever-improving AI or robotics, depending on the job to be done. Nevertheless, organizations that want to continue to attract talented individuals will require to change their culture and work practices.

With employees no longer restricted to what is available in their geographical neighborhood, they can become more selective and embrace the digital nomad lifestyle like never before. Especially as cryptocurrencies become the norm in the next decade, these digital nomads can get paid in crypto instantly, anywhere in the world. Interestingly, a digital nomad earning a salary from, let's say, the United States or the UK but living in a developing country is worth a lot more to that country than dozens of tourists who stay only for a few days, spend only a limited amount of money on their trip and go back home, while causing a lot of the troubles that tourists generally do. Remote work has a lot of benefits, but what's stopping a lot of people from opting for this lifestyle is often the fear of missing friends and families. That is about to change in the coming decade.

As the metaverse kicks into gear, remote working technologies will become more advanced and intuitive, making collaboration, and socializing with friends and family across the digital highway a lot more comfortable than using the current versions of Zoom or Teams. As the technologies improve, *work from anywhere* will replace (the hybrid model of partially) working from home, first for knowledge workers who have already become accustomed to this new paradigm but later also for operational staff as digital twins and virtual and augmented reality tools become advanced enough to seamlessly operate a hydrogen plant or even an entire factory from the comfort of a tropical island. Of course, before we can settle in on that comfy beach chair watching the sunset while working, organizations need to change their mindset and cultures and drop the *work from here* mode.

All organizations, even those who prefer to remain stuck in the old paradigm, will have no choice but to change if they want to remain relevant to the workforce of tomorrow. We are at the start of a seismic shift in global employment whereby The Great Resignation can become a catalyst to a world where people are more empowered, may decide to play to earn instead of work, and they can do so from anywhere, at any time they want. Pieter Levels, serial entrepreneur, and a well-known digital nomad, even predicts that by 2035 there will be one billion digital nomads, thanks to exponential improvements in technologies, including 6G and supersonic travel.[196] Although 1 billion digital nomads might be on the high end, we will certainly see an increase in the coming years.

As soon as we have left Covid behind us and travel becomes as seamless again as it used to be, *work from anywhere* will change how we travel, live, and work. Moreover, once the metaverse is operational, digital collaboration tools will make working remotely feel as seamless as working in the office. Advanced VR headsets and AR glasses will enable hybrid meetings whereby those colleagues dialing in using virtual reality will appear as holographic projections on the AR glasses of those meeting in person. At the same time, using a future version of Intel's True View technology, as described in Chapter 4, the colleagues meeting in person will be seamlessly copied to virtual reality as hyper-realistic avatars, including their movements and facial expressions, enabling hybrid collaboration that mimics the all-physical meetings of the past. Welcome to the enterprise metaverse and the future of work.

The Future of Immersive Work

Technically, the term *enterprise metaverse* is not the right term. After all, as we established in Chapter 1, there is only one metaverse. For lack of a better word, I opted to use this term to indicate the difference between the metaverse used by consumers for fun, play, shopping, and entertainment versus the metaverse used by organizations to enable work and collaboration across time and space.

While all the entertainment in the metaverse will fuel our endorphins and drive our dopamine through the roof even more than social media does, for better or worse, the enterprise version can actually make work more fun and especially more efficient. In fact, from an enterprise perspective, we are already living in version 0.1 of the metaverse, with Zooms and Teams sort of merging the physical and digital worlds and collaborative tools such as Slack or Miro enabling digital collaboration. Including new phenomena such as Zoom fatigue, which is a type of fatigue caused by increased eye contact with monitors, increased cognitive workload, restricted physical mobility, and self-evaluation when visualizing yourself constantly on a real-time camera feed.[197] However, these are mere windows into each other's reality and not a complete convergence of the physical and digital worlds. Neither do they provide an immersive experience, though, of course, both Zoom and Microsoft have announced immersive virtual experiences. When it comes to most of the available tools today, they are kind of flat, i.e., 2D, and not really immersive, i.e., 3D.

With organizations required to embrace the metaverse as it comes online, the augmented employee will become the norm. We have reached an inflection point, where the augmented employee becomes the norm and benefits from a wide variety of technologies, including, of course, immersive technologies such as VR or AR but, more importantly, also technologies such as artificial intelligence, robotics, or digital twins. An augmented workforce is a blend of human workers and technology seamlessly collaborating for a better outcome.[198] As a result, the future of work will be more effective and efficient, meaning fewer employees can do the same amount of work, which is being amplified by the pandemic. It is a narrative that happens after almost all crises. Once a crisis is over and business is back to normal, the economic production generally restores, but those people fired won't be hired again.[199] It means that companies find other ways to restore production and, increasingly, rely on technology instead of humans, which today is further accelerated due to The Great Resignation.

An augmented workforce is one thing; completely replacing your workforce is different. In the coming years, we will see an explosion of robots put to work in factories, retail, agriculture, the travel industry, and service-oriented industries. For example, in early 2022, the agricultural equipment maker John Deere announced the world's first fully autonomous tractor for large-scale use, promising set-and-forget farming and changing the way how we can grow our crops.[200] For years already, automation and robotics have changed a variety of industries, including manufacturing, processing, energy and mining to just name a few, but this crisis will be a catalyst for more automation as the lockdowns forced organizations to find different ways to keep their businesses open.

Only a few months into the pandemic, companies in China, for example, were already looking for ways to re-open their business with robots instead of employees.[201] Robots cannot become sick, they work 24 hours, and they do not require social distancing. As digital transformation is brought to the extreme, we will see more and more fully automated factories. These factories are equipped with fully automated systems and do not require lights as humans are no longer part of the manufacturing process, which is why they are also referred to as dark factories. The factories will be expensive to build, but once operational will see huge financial returns due to the lack of expensive human workers.[202] For a dark factory to operate, it needs an advanced digital twin, which means they are also part of the metaverse, albeit the closed and secure part of it.

While dark factories are part of the future of work, the metaverse offers the most opportunities when collaborating between humans (and AI), including brainstorming, meeting, designing, and co-creating, which in the near future will comprise mostly meetings in virtual reality with cartoony avatars without legs. Despite some companies moving to a hybrid form of remote work after the pandemic (e.g., 3 days in the office,

2 days at home), once the technologies become powerful enough to enable hyper-realistic, hybrid, digital experiences, more knowledge workers will likely be interested in working from anywhere full-time.

A company that has already switched to virtual reality is the Australian marketing agency *In Marketing We Trust*. The fully remote company has employees living in 14 different countries. In 2021, when Covid canceled their annual get-together for the second time in a row, they decided to give all employees a VR headset and organize their conference in VR. As Paul Hewett, founder of the company, explained, their conferences always have three goals: to create a learning experience, to give people a cultural experience, and to entertain, all with the objective to get to know each other and work better. They replicated all three objectives in virtual reality. To learn from each other, they used Facebook's Horizon Worlds for their meetings and presentations, and they went into Rec Room to relax and play games together in VR. Altogether, they spent three full days in virtual reality, which was a unique cultural experience. All employees had their own avatar, and using spatial audio, the various activities worked out as well as they would normally happen in the physical world. According to Paul, it was a deeply immersive and engaging experience, without any Zoom fatigue common in online meetings.

One of the learnings of the three-day virtual conference was the ability that you can feel really connected as a human, as an avatar, in virtual reality. The only thing they missed was the human aspect of eating together. Although they ordered everyone dinner and drinks, sharing a meal together is better done physically than virtually, until the technology becomes so advanced and enables holographic restaurants as described in the fictional story. Overall, the event was such a success that they have now moved their strategy sessions into virtual reality as well.

While the metaverse is very much still under construction, companies such as Paul's marketing agency show the potential these immersive technologies have for organizations to collaborate and deeply connect with each other, regardless of where employees reside. According to a 2018 Capgemini report, 8 out of 10 companies implementing AR/VR have indicated that the operational benefits of using these technologies exceed their expectations. Early adopters of these technologies showed, on average, a 57 percent increase in efficiency, a 55 percent increase in safety, a 52 percent productivity increase, and a 47 percent reduction in complexity.[203] This is a few years before the pandemic, and since then, the technologies have improved significantly.

For example, it is now possible to bring brainstorming to another level using virtual reality. NeosVR built a virtual reality mind mapping tool, where users are actually inside the mind map they are creating. Traditional mind mapping can already improve learning and retention by up to 15 percent.[204] Now imagine being inside the actual mind map, where you can bring in all kinds of things like videos, audio files, photos, and presentations, and you can scale up the virtual mind map. It is a completely new way of working and collaborating when you operate in a digital, collaborative 3D space. Such immersive tools enable you to do smarter brainstorming and problem solving, albeit it comes with a steep learning curve to use a whiteboard in Horizon Workrooms or Glue. It is a new skill we need to learn, but once mastered, it is much more intuitive than using, for example, a 2D Miro board, especially when colleagues are geographically apart.

An immersive mind map can be beneficial to brainstorming sessions, but the endless space available in virtual reality is a huge advantage in general. With the remote work trend here to stay, large organizations worldwide are closing or downsizing their expensive offices at A-locations, which could have a direct impact on the livelihood of central business districts of the world's biggest cities. With VR headsets and AR glasses quickly improving in capability and comfort, in the not too distant future, employees can spin up a virtual workplace or teleport into their virtual office. People can be together while being apart, and in case you need to focus for a while, with the push of a button, you enable a *Do Not Disturb* field that would prevent your colleagues from interrupting you while you can still see each other.

In the virtual office of tomorrow, instead of a laptop or a physical desk with two screens, employees can have an unlimited number of monitors or whiteboards as they are working in a limitless virtual space. Before the end of this decade, VR headsets will have a far higher resolution than today, be easy to wear, and not tire you out prematurely. We will then no longer need our laptops and can simply launch our workstation in VR or AR and start working anywhere. In the beginning, it will, most likely, look very strange when you see someone staring into the nothingness, feverishly typing on a keyboard that you cannot see while swiping in midair to organize their work. Then again, we also got used to everyone staring and scrolling mindlessness on their smartphones, often even when together with others out for drinks, so I am sure it won't be long before the cafés are full of people doing exactly that.

In the metaverse, employees can be anywhere, and be either digitally or physically in the same office, meeting room, conference, or even water cooler for some much-needed office gossip. The future of work is immersive, and since the metaverse is persistent, the digital office is just there, similar to the physical office. You can just pop in to do your work. Of course, hiring those employees will drastically change as well, as will the type of jobs that will be available.

The Metaverse Job Market

When the Roblox and Minecraft builders of today enter university or the workforce tomorrow, they will have a fundamentally different mindset and skillset than the Millennials, who were part of the transition from analog to digital. Not only will they expect to work whenever from wherever, but thanks to years of exploring, playing, and creating new digital worlds together, many will have strong collaborative, problem-solving, and creative skills. Fortunately for them, how we work will change as the convergence of technologies will enable humans to focus on what they are good at: solving problems together in creative ways, while AI will focus on the mundane and repetitive tasks. Metaverse-natives, those who have grown up with virtual worlds and augmented experiences, are fully aware of the potential of the immersive internet, and they want to be treated as such, including flexibility where and how to do the work.

So if you need to hire Gen Z talent, why not meet them in the virtual worlds they are familiar with? That is exactly what the likes of Samsung and Hyundai are already doing. In the summer of 2021, Hyundai organized a job fair on a platform called Gather Town, a top-down video game that doubles as a web-conferencing platform. They also organized the induction for new employees in Zepeto, a virtual world accessible via mobile devices with around 150 million users and predominantly active in Asia. Designed to develop mutual intimacy and bond new employees, the induction program was well received by new employees who had to start their first job remotely due to Covid.[205] Samsung Electronics brought potential job applicants and human resource (HR) managers together on the Gather Town platform, to have their avatars meet and mingle and learn about what it is like to work for the company.[206]

Virtual job fairs and induction programs are not the only HR activities in the metaverse. Hiring your future employees on the platforms you will actively use can be very beneficial. Art director Richard Chen, whose Space Bugs art project of 3000 NFTs sold out in six hours in November 2021, found his 25 community managers on platforms such as Discord, Telegram, and Clubhouse.[207] Hiring using virtual platforms can also be a lot more inclusive. After all, in the metaverse, you can be anyone you want to be with your avatar, resulting in hiring managers having less opportunity to be biased and judge you by your background, religion, race, or how you appear at the interview.

Hired employees also require training, and as discussed in Chapter 4, trainings are one of the killer applications for virtual reality. Virtual reality trainings are an effective solution, whether teaching new employees the safety standards and requirements by exposing them virtually to dangerous or stressful situations or explaining how complex equipment works. Of course, this is nothing new as airline companies have been using flight simulators already for years, but with prices of headsets dropping, this has now become accessible to all companies. For example, the fast-food chain KFC uses virtual reality to teach new staff the chicken-frying basics in just 10 minutes using a VR escape room, reducing the time to master this task by 50 percent while providing a fun experience.[208] Apart from these simple use cases, virtual reality training can also be used to help employees learn how to deal with sensitive equipment or during delicate operations. Using haptic feedback, proper grip and motion data can be incorporated into very precise VR or AR training to help surgeons become better at their job.[209]

In the short run, the enterprise metaverse offers companies new ways to attract, hire, and train employees, but in the long run, the convergence of the physical and digital worlds will result in many new jobs. Similar to how the internet and social media resulted in new job opportunities, many we did not anticipate at the start of the internet, the metaverse will create a plethora of new jobs. Here are some examples:

- Virtual travel agents or digital tour guides can help you find and explore unique virtual worlds or digital twins of real-world cities that you can explore.
- Virtual shopping assistants that help you find the best outfits for you and your avatar in a 2D or 3D virtual world.
- Digital customer service agents to help you find anything you need in the metaverse. They might even be able to help you get access to virtual events.
- Avatar fashion designers designing the latest dynamic digital fashion items for your avatar.
- Metaverse security officers to stop people from misbehaving in the metaverse, as we will explore in Chapter 8.
- 3D virtual architects to develop buildings for the various virtual worlds or to help you design and build your house in the physical world.
- Spatial audio engineers to ensure the massive interactive live events offer a unique audio experience.
- Immersive storytellers and metaverse journalists, reporting from inside the metaverse.
- 3D virtual entertainers, similar to the famous Disney characters, but exclusively in the virtual world.

Of course, these are just some of the most obvious jobs we can expect, with many others to come that we cannot yet anticipate, as they have during other transformational times. Many of these jobs will exist only in the virtual realm, allowing people to work remotely and simply commute to work by putting on their headsets. While this offers many benefits, it also puts employees at a disadvantage as organizing unions, or being considered an employee instead of a freelancer will be challenging, similar to what happened to Uber drivers or food delivery workers. Especially, if you work for a cross-border organization that exists only in the metaverse and has only a shell company as their administrative head office in a country where the rules are not so stringent.

How to Get Started

Although it might take several years before a fully immersive, seamless, and digital work environment is possible, not starting today to explore the opportunities of a hybrid working environment can have detrimental effects in the long run. Just as most big brands are exploring the metaverse and undoubtedly making mistakes, it is wise to start exploring how the enterprise metaverse can benefit your business.

Those organizations that want to explore the metaverse should start with small experiments, such as a virtual job fair, re-creating your head office for people to virtually explore, or meetings or events in virtual reality using Horizon Worlds, Microsoft Teams, AltspaceVR, or any of the other available virtual platforms. This will enable organizations to quickly learn what works for them and what does not. In the end, the metaverse will require a culture change, embracing the use of immersive technologies to enable anyone to work from anywhere, whenever they want. The metaverse offers a unique opportunity to make work more flexible, inclusive, and accessible to people all over the world, which generally results in higher job satisfaction and increased output, but it will take time and require a significant effort from those employees involved.

In the years to come, when the digital tools will become more immersive and take full advantage of the capabilities of the next generation of VR headsets and AR glasses, we will look back at today's 2D collaborative tools and virtual worlds and view them as primitive, a bit like how we laugh today at the first websites in the 1990s or the first apps in 2008.

Digital Twins

While Zuckerberg's announcement to refocus the company on the metaverse brought the metaverse into the limelight of the general public, it also caused industrial companies to become wary of talking about the metaverse because they don't want to be associated with Facebook. However, the metaverse is not only a platform to connect with consumers, to play your favorite game, or to do business and collaborate. It is also all about simulating the physical world inside the digital world, which can then be experienced using VR or AR to optimize the physical world. In fact, digital twins can be considered one of the building blocks of the metaverse, augmenting the physical world and making it accessible from the digital realm.

IBM describes a digital twin as "a virtual representation of an object or system that spans its lifecycle, is updated from real-time data, and uses simulation, machine learning, and reasoning to help decision-making."[210] Digital twins enable us to take our physical world and re-create it in the digital realm, down to the most microscopic detail. With the help of advanced sensors, AI, and communication tech, these replicas will mimic physical objects, including people, devices, objects, systems, and even places, in a digital space. The virtual model accurately reflects the real object or system through sensors that actively relay data linked to its functionality and environment to its digital counterpart in real time.[211] Any change in the physical object or system will lead to a change in the digital representation and vice versa.[212] All this data will enable all kinds of new processes and services such as predictive maintenance, which uses data analytics to predict when a machine is about to break down, so it can be fixed before it actually breaks down.

If the physical world can be considered as Tier 0 of the metaverse, digital twins are Tier 1, which some would consider the (Industrial) Internet of Things. All the protocols running on top of that are Tier 2. Above that, there can be many layers of applications, either in the 2D virtual world (e.g., mobile apps), virtual reality, or using augmented reality, that interact with either of these layers, which can be considered Tier 3. This might sound counterintuitive (why place digital twins as a tier prior to protocols and applications?), but the sensors of digital twins collecting the raw data are what enable the applications, and to have universal interaction with those applications we would require open standards and protocols. The (raw) data moves between these layers; being analyzed by the applications and fed back to the digital twin for additional insights. Combined, this would deliver the value to the physical and digital worlds; see Figure 6.1. Data is what makes digital twins dynamic digital twins. The more protocols, as in global standards, that exist, the more value the applications can deliver to the global economy. For example, a city can be made smart by using digital twins. By ensuring that the data of those various digital twins are easily accessible using

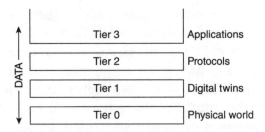

Figure 6.1: Four tiers of the metaverse

universal standards, anyone can create applications that would deliver value to cities, businesses, and inhabitants.

All the applications in tier 3 delivering value can be perceived as lenses, where each lens provides the user with a different perspective or experience of reality. It can be an entertainment lens that offers the user digital art linked to a certain physical location. It can be a monitoring application of a solar farm that allows the user to trade its energy using crypto. It can be a communications lens for users to join a hybrid meeting using VR. It can be a predictive maintenance lens of an airplane's jet engines or an electrical lens for city officials to manage their smart city. There can be countless applications and capabilities, or lenses. Some will be accessible to all, others only after payment, and others only with the right credentials, ideally all secured on the blockchain.

When it comes to tier 1, there are different levels of complexity for digital twins, each increasing in data generated and insights delivered. The simplest variant of a digital twin is the digital representation of a single object, for example, a connected wearable, a simple robot, or a machine in a factory. These product digital twins can be used to design new products by analyzing how a product performs and by enabling digital prototyping. One level up are production digital twins that simulate a process, e.g., a manufacturing process, and that consist of multiple product digital twins. The more complex performance digital twins capture data from a system of objects, for example, an airplane, or more advanced, an entire (dark) factory.[213] The next level comprises entire systems of systems, such as supply chains that cover the globe or city-scale digital twins. The most complex of them is the digital twin of the earth, as developed by the European Space Agency (ESA), which aims to build a dynamic digital replica of our planet.

First and foremost, digital twins enable the optimization of processes through their synchronized systems in the digital and real world. The various applications of tier 3 can be used to monitor and analyze a process or system, run simulations to optimize its physical counterpart, or collaborate with multiple people to prototype and create new physical products. A simple example would be the digital twin of a self-driving car. All car companies use simulations to optimize the development of self-driving cars, even before production. These digital cars have already driven billions of kilometers. They could even collaborate remotely using virtual reality to optimize the car's design, as Volvo does.

Volvo Cars uses mixed reality to completely design and prototype their cars and even test-drive their cars using mixed reality. Since 2018, Volvo Cars has used high-end mixed-reality, prototype headsets developed by Varjo, the Finnish manufacturer of advanced mixed reality headsets, to research designs of future cars before they are even built. The mixed-reality headset allows engineers to drive the real car on real roads wearing the headset while photorealistic virtual elements are added to the car's interior. This enables designers to iterate their designs within days instead of weeks.[214] Volvo Cars also uses mixed reality to test entire new designs of future cars before they have been built, replacing the need for expensive clay modeling. According to Christian Braun, Volvo's VP of Visual Art Design, mixed reality is "the future of creativity" as it enables the car manufacturer to quickly add or change design elements, review all the car's details and materials in different lighting conditions, and find possible surface mistakes very early on in the design process.[215]

Tesla goes one step further and creates a digital twin of every car they sell. The sensors in the car constantly monitor how the car performs in real time, and this data is sent back to the car's digital twin in the factory, which analyzes the data and determines whether the car works as intended and if maintenance will be required soon.[216]

No matter how simple or complex, each digital twin offers value and benefits to its users. The value and level of collaboration possible depend on the digital twin's visualization level. This can be simple visualizations—descriptive, predictive, or prescriptive analytics—that provide the user insights into the status of the digital twin and give the ability to change levers to adjust its behavior. The simplest visualizations consist of 2D analytical insights such as graphs. These can provide valuable information about the past or future performance of the digital twin, but apart from discussing what that means and potentially changing some of the variables, not much interaction with the graphs is possible.

Visualization can also be more advanced 2D visual representations of the digital object or system, such as AutoCAD models used by architects or engineers. These advanced 2D representations enable users to view the digital twin from different angles and collaborate remotely, to further improve or develop either the digital twin or the physical counterpart. Such 2D visual representations have enabled the engineers of Sydney's tallest, 271.3 meters, US$ 1.6 billion skyscraper to complete the building from the kitchen table amid the pandemic.[217]

The most advanced visual representation is a detailed 3D digital replica that can be explored or interacted with within virtual reality or using augmented reality. 3D digital representations enable users to explore the digital twin from different perspectives, drill deep into its inner workings, see real-time insights from its sensors collecting data, make changes that reflect in real time in the physical world, or collaborate with others to design and create a digital prototype of a future physical object, such as a car, or fix a physical problem remotely. In general, the more advanced the visual representation, the more value can be achieved. The Dutch design studio UNSTUDIO used Epic's game engine Unreal Engine to create a virtual mock-up of the new national South Korean football park. The immersive, realistic renders of the park allowed the Dutch architects and the South Korean Career Football Association to collaborate on the project across any device, despite being geographically apart, going into the buildings and getting a good understanding of what the park would look like before it is built.[218]

While digital twins can be used for factories or designs, they can also improve collaboration among dispersed teams. In March 2022, the International Security Alliance—an international working group of Interior Ministries to enhance cooperation, knowledge sharing, and partnerships on global security issues—organized ISALEX 2.0. Hosted by the Dubai World Expo, it was the first law enforcement exercise in the metaverse.[219]

The event took place in VR, and the objective was to prevent a terrorist attack in the fictional country of Brinia. There were witnesses to be interviewed and the Brinia social media channel to be followed (for which they used the decentralized platform Mastodon, a free and open-source social media tool). The 10 law enforcement organizations were presented with digital crime scenes and physical evidence, ensuring a phygital experience.

The exercise was a success. According to Major Hamad Khatir, director of the International Operations Department at the Ministry of Interior of the United Arab Emirates, the dynamics in virtual reality were much better than on Zoom. Moreover, acting in VR removed any barriers and hierarchy as the participants' avatars were all donned in standard uniforms, without any ranks shown. This informal environment helped break the ice faster and resulted in a successful collaboration, despite the exercise taking place across cultures and involving team members from various ranks.

In the years to come, the metaverse can significantly impact law enforcement. As Major Hamad Khatir stated, it will enable investigators from around the world to capture crime or accident scenes immediately after they have happened in volumetric data—creating a digital twin, so to speak, and enabling dispersed teams to have access to a scene as it was, using virtual reality, long after the scene has been cleaned. This could significantly improve capacity and help prevent future (terrorist) attacks.[220]

One of the main benefits of using virtual, augmented, or mixed reality in combination with digital twins is the significant sustainability benefits. As we have seen with ISALEX 2.0, law enforcers from around the globe collaborated seamlessly. Also, designers and engineers no longer have to fly across the world to fix a machine or collaborate to design a future version of a product. Especially when language barriers between designers and engineers used to require staff to fly across the globe to explain something in detail, they can now hop into virtual reality and visually explain what needs to be done. In addition, designers and engineers no longer have to create numerous real prototypes, as these can be created and analyzed virtually.

The next step after a digital replica of a factory would be to create a digital twin of an entire supply chain. Global supply chains are complex processes. Different companies, with distinctive objectives, are working together to achieve a common goal, to bring something from A to B. For a supply chain to work, partners have to trust each other. To do so, there are multiple checks and balances, extensive documents, and different checkpoints all interacting in a web of bureaucratic processes. Knowing the amount of paperwork required to send a product from farm to plate, it is remarkable that we have managed to develop global supply chains and keep them up and running—until they no longer did during the pandemic. Supply chains worldwide came to a grinding halt as the complex web of companies interacting with each other was disrupted by lockdowns. As a result, transportation prices exploded, and a global shortage in AI chips caused further havoc across the globe. Digital twins, combined with blockchain technology, will create more resilient and efficient supply chains by creating a shared understanding of the system of systems and allowing disparate parties to monitor, analyze, and optimize the supply chain asynchronously. Blockchain can become the golden standard for supply chains by enabling secure sharing of proprietary digital twin data across all stakeholders within a given supply chain and using smart contracts to replace bureaucratic, paper processes.[221]

This can be best explained by a simple example. Many processes within supply chains are still done on papers, and it is a common joke that when you want to send a bouquet of flowers, you need a stack of papers as high as the flowers, which significantly slows down the process. Of course, when you send flowers across the world, the buyer would like to make sure that the flowers arrive in optimal quality and, if they don't, that the buyer receives a discount. This can be solved by creating a simple product digital twin of the containers by installing sensors inside them to constantly monitor the temperature and humidity and storing that data on the blockchain to make sure that the seller cannot tamper with the data. If the buyer and seller used a smart contract, which would take into account the data from the sensors, the buyer would automatically receive a discount if the temperature and/or humidity would come outside pre-agreed boundaries.

Another system of systems that stands to benefit from the convergence of technologies is the city. Smart cities around the world are exploring how they can benefit from the metaverse to offer their citizens a more pleasant living experience. Local governments in cities like Seoul, Singapore, or Shanghai are rushing to optimize their cities using digital technologies and real-time data as part of the smart cities movement.[222] A smart city uses data from installed sensors across the city to automate and optimize the various processes within the city to make a city more livable. Integrating the various digital twins of a city and making the real-time data generated from those digital twins publicly available would enable the market to create endless applications, or lenses, to offer city officials, business, and consumers unique ways to interact with their city.

As these hyper-realistic and accurate city-scale digital twins come to life, it will enable users to explore real-world and fictional locations in ways never possible before. Imagine using your avatar and exploring a perfect digital version of New York, Paris, or the moon from the comfort of your own home. Taking this further, users could even move around the real-world version of the city by controlling a drone in the digital realm that flies in the real world and using the area's digital twin as a map to navigate. So, imagine controlling a drone in the digital clone of Paris that is flying around in the real-world Paris.

One of the most complex digital twins of them all is the digital replica of our planet as being constructed by the ESA. The organization plans to replicate the entire physical world in all its detail into its digital twin that would allow us to apply AI and learn, predict, optimize, and protect the earth, deeply understanding the consequences of human activity, now and in the future.[223] The digital twin of the earth will help visualize, monitor, and forecast economic, social, and industrial activities and their impact on the various biological ecosystems of the planet. Thanks to a user-friendly, open source, and secure cloud-based simulation and modeling platform, labeled Destination Earth, researchers will be able to simulate the different systems interconnected with human behavior to develop plans for a sustainable future of our planet.

Whether building factory-scale, city-scale, or planetary-scale digital twins, this is where NVIDIA's Omniverse platform comes in, as it enables all stakeholders to aggregate and interact with the live data feeds of industrial digital twins. The end-to-end collaboration and simulation platform allows organizations to bring in full-fidelity real-time data from physical and virtual sources to transform complex design processes and enable immersive real-time collaboration between humans or AI agents. As Richard Kerris, VP of the NVIDIA Omniverse platform, explained, complex virtual systems can result in significant cost savings. "You can train an infinite number of virtual robots inside the virtual world of a digital city. By the time that knowledge is transferred into the physical robot operating in a physical city, it will be >1000 times smarter and be able to navigate the complex physical world. You can use it to train digital humans driven by AI or digital self-driving cars to figure out what's the best way for them to move around a city, constantly tweaking the layout of the virtual world to optimize it, or better understand the impact of, for example, climate change on the livability of their city, before building the infrastructure in the physical world."[224]

ESA's objective is to launch the full digital replica of earth systems by 2030,[225] and ideally, by then, all other digital twins of factories, supply chains, and cities can be integrated with earth's digital replica to create a more sustainable future.

The Role of Governments

Of course, governments and international organizations are involved in creating and managing digital twins, but they play an additional role in the metaverse, which requires policymakers to step up their game when it comes to digital technologies.

In many countries around the world, government officials have a hard time keeping up with the fast pace of innovation in the digital realm. They generally lack a proper understanding of new (digital) technologies resulting in regulation and laws that take too long to make them relevant to the digital space and often stifle instead of enable innovation. Once new laws are announced eventually, the market has moved on already. It is likely that this won't be any different with the metaverse, and lawmakers either misunderstand the potential of the metaverse or don't understand how emerging technologies are converging into the next version of the internet.

This problem will be amplified in the metaverse as geographical boundaries become increasingly irrelevant, making it harder to develop and enforce the required regulations to create a safe and inclusive metaverse. This is a problem, as the metaverse requires regulation to prevent many of the dangers lurking in the dark corners, as we will explore in Chapter 8.

Moreover, governments will most likely have to operate in a competitive, rapidly changing, and uncertain environment, where companies are attracted by efficiency and cost reductions. Attracting these companies requires a different attitude and a good understanding of applying digital technologies to make a government more attractive to organizations. With the upcoming global minimum corporate tax rate of 15 percent, those governments that apply the latest technology to offer innovative services for companies operating around the globe, such as Estonia with their e-residency program, will develop a competitive advantage worth billions of dollars, especially if a metaverse-native organization can be established anywhere globally to be operational only in the metaverse. Where will it register its business? Most likely, it will be in the country where it will have the most benefits, be it from a tax perspective or an administrative burden perspective. We see this already happening, as in 2021, Wyoming, USA, passed legislation that allows decentralized autonomous organizations (DAOs). As a result, in the coming years, we will likely see governments competing for the best companies based on tax benefits and efficiency gains that can be achieved when launching and managing a metaverse-native organization.

Something else might happen when the metaverse becomes a reality. The more we move into the metaverse and the more truly immersive virtual worlds become the norm, the more they will pose a threat to governments and the concept of nation-states.[226] If *work from anywhere* becomes mainstream and you can earn a living in crypto while residing wherever you want, the loyalty to a country might become less. Over the long run, this could change how we identify ourselves, and at some point in the future, we might identify more with a particular virtual world than with a physical nation-state. Already, digital-only governments have launched, such as Asgardia, although no country has recognized them. Why would they after all? They can be considered more like an online (niche) community, which will be a dime a dozen in the metaverse.

If that is the case and people can live anywhere, be constantly on the move while earning a living in crypto, and identify more with a virtual world than a physical state, how will that impact taxation, and what will it do to the GDP in the real world versus the GDP in the metaverse? Not only that, if people move to low-cost parts of the world, to developing countries, say, we could expect a redistribution of wealth across the world. Suppose there will be indeed one billion digital nomads by 2035 and the metaverse becomes as real as we all expect. In that case, it will fundamentally change how we organize ourselves as humanity and society, thereby directly impacting the role of the nation-state and national government.

Until we reach that stage, which is probably at least 15 to 20 years away, it brings up the question: what should the role of governments be? How should they regulate the metaverse and the virtual worlds that will call the metaverse home? For example, if the metaverse is built on top of a digital replica of the physical world, would governments around the world also be responsible for creating the equivalent of public squares and parks in the digital realm, accessible and inclusive to all and banned from commercial activities trying to lure in the consumer? If all virtual worlds in the metaverse are controlled by commercial entities or decentralized (niche) communities, how would that impact our society, and would it leave some people excluded? Centralized entities can easily decide to limit freedom of speech, while decentralized entities will face challenges to prevent harmful content, such as misinformation, from being published. How would it affect our right to own and control our data or our right to digitally demonstrate against certain policies or actions taken by the leaders of the virtual worlds, and how can governments enforce or abuse this? Plenty of questions still need to be answered, and academic research can contribute in obtaining these answers.

Will governments ensure human rights also in the metaverse or only in the physical world, and how would that work? For many, virtual reality is reality too, as philosopher David Chalmers writes in his new book *Reality+*.[227] Should avatars have fundamental rights similar to people? How would governments enforce that, or does that apply only in the physical world? It may be clear; the metaverse is much more than the next iteration of the internet. It could very well result in a complete reorder of our global society, moving away from nation-states to a more nomadic, digital lifestyle, changing the traditional concept of society. Eventually, this leads to the question of what it means to be a real human living in the metaverse.

Chapter 7
The Creator Economy

A Vibrant Metaverse Economy

Decentralization will play a specific and essential role in the metaverse: to enable secure proof of ownership combined with immutable provenance. For the first time in history, we can undoubtedly prove that someone owns a particular digital asset, including the history of that asset thanks to NFTs. NFTs introduce verifiable digital property rights in a world of abundance, which will create a vibrant metaverse economy.

Similar to the real world, property rights are crucial for an economy to grow because once you can prove that you own something, you can then monetize that asset. Digital proof of ownership protects the owner's rights, ensures the automatic execution of all parts of an agreement using smart contracts, enables the instant and correct transfer of the asset, and prevents fraud as the records are verifiable, immutable, and traceable. As the Peruvian economist Hernando de Soto, known for his work on the informal economy and founder of the Institute for Liberty and Democracy, says, "With titles, shares and property laws, people could suddenly go beyond looking at their assets as they are—houses used for shelter—to thinking about what they could be—things like security for credit to start or expand a business."[228] The same applies to the registration of digital assets. Suddenly, a digital artwork, a virtual house, or a song can become a security to improve your financial situation.

With a near endless digital world, the opportunity for humanity to leverage digital assets and create value for themselves and society is enormous—both for individuals and organizations. Imagine a virtual Disneyland versus a physical Disneyland. In the physical park, apart from being closed during the lockdown, there are only so many people who can visit the park, which means there is a finite amount of money they can make on any given day from ticket sales, merchandise, and food and beverage sales. The virtual Disneyland can be open 24 hours, 7 days a week and as such can welcome more people than the physical park, which means increased revenue opportunities when it comes to digital and physical merchandise or ticket sales, for example, to see the latest virtual Harry Potter experience while on a lunch break. The metaverse will be a dream come true for Walt Disney, and we can be confident that they will bring their magic to the immersive internet.

While brands have ample opportunity to connect with consumers and offer a (social) experience, the most significant change comes to the individual content creator. The digital creator economy is an ~$14 billion market consisting of more than 50 million creators,[229] of which around 46.5 million consider themselves an amateur.[230] While there are around 2 million professional creators making six-figure incomes, most of the creators cannot expect to make a living, which is partially due to the high percentage that centralized platforms take. Even Roblox, which can be perceived as a closed pre-metaverse platform, shares only 25 percent of its revenue with its creators.[231]

In an open metaverse, things will be different, and content creators will not have to forfeit 25 percent to 75 percent of their revenues. User-generated content will define the metaverse, and the content will be owned and controlled by the creator, who can monetize it in novel ways. UGC will make the metaverse alive, as the entire metaverse evolves around and changes depending on the input of individuals and organizations. We can expect all kinds of user-generated content, including unique virtual worlds, immersive digital concerts, and augmented experiences that will enrich our physical world. Creatives will be able to create unique, multidimensional experiences in both the digital and physical world, powered by tools that could turn any person into an architect or artist. Most importantly, there is a shift happening toward decentralized platforms that take only a minimal fee from the content creator. For example, in early 2022, the Web 3.0 company Aave launched the Lens Protocol and Earth DAO launched Social.network.[232] Both aim to empower content creators, where digital assets and NFTs can be easily monetized without the exorbitant fees of Web 2.0.

The more the open metaverse empowers the content creator, the more value can be created and experienced together. Even Fortnite understands this, though they took a closed platform approach. If the creativity in Fortnite is any indication of what we can expect in an open, interoperable metaverse, we are in for an exciting ride!

As more creators join the metaverse and the tools to create 3D content get better, we will see an explosion of creativity and unique communities. Whether open but centralized or fully decentralized, users can collaborate on, create, and celebrate unique content within these communities. Especially in decentralized autonomous organizations (DAOs), democratic governance mechanisms using smart contracts will create fair and inclusive social (micro) economies.

Within these communities and in the open metaverse at large, cryptocurrencies can be viewed as the enabler of economic activity and societal value, no matter how small. Although there are concerns by regulators and lawmakers that cryptocurrencies can harm the financial system due to its high volatility and instability (including questions over the backing of the stablecoin Tether), these are just the hiccups of a new system trying to find its place in the existing world. While regulations would certainly help for crypto to find its rightful place in society, these should not prevent the unique characteristics of crypto (such as the programmability and provenance) to come to fruition and have a positive impact on society. Part of these regulations is also driven by the fear of illicit trading that cannot be controlled by the regulators. While criminals enjoy the borderless trading outside the financial system, trading crypto is anything but anonymous. In fact, thanks to the provenance, it has become increasingly difficult to money launder crypto. As a result, the percentage of illicit trades in the global crypto community is decreasing from an already low 0.62 percent in 2020 to 0.15 percent in 2021.[233] With a total transaction volume of $15.8 trillion in 2021, this amounts to $23.7 billion in illegal use, which is nothing compared to the $2 trillion illegal activities involving the US dollar.[234] In addition, the arrest of Ilya Lichtenstein and Heather Morgan in early 2022 for stealing and trying to launder $4.5 billion worth of crypto shows that it has become harder for criminals to hide and cover their tracks. The couple stole the 120,000 bitcoins from the crypto exchange Bitfinex in 2016, and although they managed to take out some of the funds, in the end the US Department of Justice and IRS Criminal Investigations managed to trace them down, despite the couple using a wide variety of techniques known for their obscurity and anonymity.[235]

The other reason why regulators frown upon crypto is because of its excessive energy consumption. It is certainly true that the energy consumption of the existing blockchains such as the Bitcoin blockchain or Ethereum is unsustainable, especially in times of climate change. Even if the mining is done with renewable energy, it is a waste as the computations itself do not contribute any value, apart from verifying the transactions. In 2022, the Bitcoin blockchain will probably consume approximately 200 TWh of energy, which is the equivalent of the energy consumption of Thailand.[236] In addition, the economist Alex de Vries estimates that the computational power of the hardware used for mining doubles every 1.5 years, making older machines obsolete and contributing to significant e-waste, more than many midsize countries.[237, 238] While the problem of energy consumption is real for *proof of work* blockchains, it is significantly less of a problem for *proof of stake* blockchains that do not require solving complicated puzzles and that will become the norm in the coming years.*

Crypto enables any digital community, large or small, to come together and use a common currency to seamlessly exchange value. Every (niche) community could create its own cryptocurrency to create a parallel economic system independent of traditional financial institutions

---

Proof of work refers to participating miners (also called *nodes* or *validators*) solving difficult mathematical problems to validate the blocks with transactions in a blockchain. The node that publishes the solution first "wins" and receives a reward. The more computing power you have, the bigger your chances are to publish the solution first. The mathematical problem works like a crossword puzzle; it is difficult to solve, but once it is completed, you instantly know if it is correct.

Proof of stake takes a different approach, and validators are selected randomly. To become a validator, a large number of tokens need to be staked, which the validator will lose if the validator validates malicious blocks. Since no complex puzzles need to be solved, this consensus mechanism is significantly more sustainable.

and without the high transaction fees currently associated with fiat currency (credit card transaction fees are generally around 3 percent, and PayPal fees are around 6 percent, especially if you take into consideration exchange rates). Moreover, fiat currency does not allow for microtransactions less than 1 cent, which is not a problem at all with crypto. Of course, crypto has some challenges with high transaction costs, notably Ethereum, but there are new blockchains being developed with negligible transaction fees or even no transaction fees.

Already, at the start of 2022, there were more than 17,000 cryptocurrencies,[239] and this is likely to explode in the years to come, with the metaverse becoming home to millions of communities. Most of these cryptocurrencies will exist only in very small communities and will have a limited impact on the real economy. You will be able to trade them, but the vast majority will have low trading volumes and will live in the corners of the metaverse. If a community has built the perfect social economy, it could grow and slowly take over other communities. If the community grows sufficiently big enough, the cryptocurrency will become more liquid and therefore easier to trade, further contributing to the community's growth and growing the impact it will have on the real economy. In other words, cryptocurrencies are a catalyst for innovation, and we have countless opportunities to build something new that is better than what we have, slowly propelling humanity forward.

Why Tokens Matter

Tokens are a vital tool for creating a global, seamless, and interoperable (digital) metaverse economy, enabling instant settlement of transactions. Although tokens have been around for thousands of years, only recently have we seen the rise of digital tokens. A digital token is a digital representation of value (e.g., asset) on a blockchain, and cryptographic tokens offer us an opportunity to redesign value streams and economic systems. A well-designed token has a clear objective, and the golden rule of token design is to focus on solving a simple game, a specific outcome. The more things you want a token to be doing, the more complexity is added to the system, and the more likely it is to fail.

There are four types of tokens: currency tokens, utility tokens, security tokens, and nonfungible tokens.

- **Currency tokens** are the most well-known tokens, simply because the first crypto token ever, bitcoin, is a currency token. The value of the token is determined by supply and demand. Contrary to fiat money, which is backed by gold, currency tokens are backed only by the demand and trust in the market.
- The second type of token is the **utility token**. This is a token that is backed by some sort of digital asset. It is a token that has a use case and has not been developed as an investment. A utility token, therefore, offers future access to a product or service and can best be compared to a gift card or loyalty points. An example of a utility token is ether (ETH), which is used on the Ethereum blockchain and allows you to run smart contracts and transactions. A utility token allows you to do things.
- **A security token** is a token that allows the owner of that token a (future) stake in a company or another asset such as a painting, a car, or a building, whether it be in the form of dividends, revenue share, or a price appreciation. It is the digital alternative to traditional stocks. It constitutes an investment contract and, hence, attracts the attention of the Security and Exchange Commission (SEC).
- **Nonfungible tokens** can represent an asset on the blockchain, but unlike utility or currency tokens, each NFT is unique and cannot be exchanged for another NFT without a difference in value.

Currency, utility, and security tokens are important components of Web 3.0, but for the metaverse, NFTs will be most useful. NFTs first came to the market in 2017 with the rise of CryptoKitties and truly took off in 2021, when a small market became a billion-dollar market practically overnight. Fungibility means interchangeability, which means that a particular asset can be exchanged for any asset of the same type. Money is fungible; a one-dollar bill can always be exchanged for another one-dollar bill, and you still would have the same value anywhere in the world. They are interchangeable. Nonfungible means that two assets are not the same, have different values, and can therefore not be exchanged.

Collectible baseball cards are nonfungible. Although they are the same type of object—a collectible within a particular category—they have different values, and one can be more expensive than the other. Digital real estate is also nonfungible. Two pieces of land in the same virtual world can be the same size, but since they have different X and Y coordinates, they have different values, similar to one-acre of land in Manhattan that is more expensive than a one-acre parcel in Ohio.

Tokens offer us a chance to redesign existing and new ecosystems, and they are vital to developing an open and inclusive metaverse. Tokens have some unique features compared to traditional securities. Fungible tokens are interchangeable and can be divided into smaller token units, enabling micropayments of a few cents or less. The main benefit of digital tokens over traditional financial instruments is that they are programmable. This means you can incorporate specific rules within the token that automatically apply. These rules could be related to dividend release (the longer you hold a token, the more dividend you will get), voting rights (the longer and the more tokens you have, the more voting rights you will get), or other privileges. These rules can then become an effective way to incentivize ownership and ensure price stability.[240]

Tokens will also profoundly affect liquidity in the world's economy as tokens enable fractional ownership.* This means that an asset, whether digital or physical, can be broken up into smaller parts that can be sold individually. This allows small investors anywhere in the world to invest in anything, starting from a few cents. Anyone anywhere can become a shareholder in anything that is tokenized, and as such tokens will democratize finance. Fractional ownership will open up the world's illiquid assets and make real estate, art, or luxury cars (highly) liquid assets. For example, when a real estate investor wants to sell a building, it generally takes a few months, a lot of paperwork, and expensive lawyers. When the building is tokenized, the investor can sell his tokens on a secondary market, and if there is sufficient demand, the sale can be completed in days. This will have a profound effect on the world economy and is one more reason why regulators should embrace tokens.[241]

---

*While this is technically already possible, if done today without crypto tokens, it is a slow process that involves expensive lawyers.

An NFT by itself is not a liquid asset. First, we need the right infrastructure because even an NFT remains illiquid if you cannot easily sell it. Only when an NFT can be easily exchanged on a secondary market, such as OpenSea, Rarible, or Mintable, does it become liquid—and only if there is sufficient demand for the NFT. After all, an NFT that nobody wants to buy is still illiquid. In short, for NFTs to become liquid assets, there needs to be an infrastructure, and there needs to be demand. While the infrastructure is quickly becoming better, the demand is still relatively low since most of the trades are made by a very small group of people.[242]

Suppose you want to monetize your NFTs and potentially fractionalize the NFT to be sold individually on a secondary market. In that case, it is important to consider whether your NFTs can be considered a financial security. We have only just started to explore the possibilities of NFTs, and the current hype of JPGs being sold for millions is definitely not the endgame. For example, it is possible to mint NFTs so that its creator would receive a percentage of the proceeds every time the NFT is sold on a secondary market, potentially for many years. Such a *sell-on clause* is quite common in the traditional world, so it only makes sense that we will see this happen in the metaverse as well. The creator can even package various of these NFTs with other NFTs and sell them or use them as collateral for other assets.[243] This makes creating art a lot more lucrative, and it will be an important business model for the metaverse, but it might also attract the attention of the US Securities and Exchange Commission (SEC).

Finally, cryptographic tokens are fully traceable as they are recorded on the blockchain. It will always be possible to trace a token throughout the years to see who owned it and for how long. This provenance is helpful in tracing criminals—cryptocurrencies are anything but anonymous—but it can also cause a digital wearable to increase in value if it was used during a specific and unique event in the metaverse. For example, if the digital dress of Ariana Grande, the exact one that she wore during her Fortnite tour, were an NFT, it would significantly increase in value simply because Ariana Grande's avatar wore it during her concert.

While NFTs do not have to have utility—Beeple's $69 million *Everydays—The First 5000 Days* NFT did not have any utility and was literally just a JPEG sold for an insane amount of money—they will become more useful, and therefore valuable, if they do have utility. This utility is basically the perks that come with the asset, such as access to events or communities, as is the case with Budverse Cans and the Bored Apes we discussed earlier, access to certain games, increased capabilities within those games, e.g., being able to fly or walk faster as discussed before, earn rewards that are distributed among owners and renters, or anything that you can come up with that adds value to the owner of the NFT. The more NFTs that enter the market, the more utility they should have as they need to differentiate themselves from one another if they want to be perceived as valuable.

In 2021, the hype around NFT was all about scarce and exclusive digital artwork and showing it off to your network. In early 2022, Twitter jumped on this trend and allowed users to connect their crypto wallet and have their NFT as a Twitter profile picture. However, in the long run, I do not believe that scarcity, exclusivity, and showing off are the main drivers of NFTs. Exclusive items in the metaverse are nice, and they will be an important aspect of the metaverse economy, but exclusive NFTs are not the future. After all, only a small group of people can afford a $4,000 digital Gucci bag that is nothing more than a few pixels within the Roblox world. The vast majority cannot and will not do so. NFTs are proof of ownership that you bought or received a digital item, not proof of exclusivity. For the metaverse to become a rich and vibrant economy, we need the equivalent of IKEA for the metaverse, where there are 1 million items available of something, be it a nice sneaker or a bed for your virtual house, with serialized, certifiable ownership. Hence, you know that you own 1 out of 1,000 or out of 10,000, and you can trade it, sell it, rent it out, display it, borrow against it, i.e., monetize it. This way, NFTs become useful, get utility, and become the oil that lubricates the engine of the metaverse.

For the millions of people playing video games, reading books, or listening to music, buying digital items has been a daily practice for years. But never did the purchase of a skin in Fortnite mean true ownership. If you would play a video game for years, spend hundreds of dollars, and invest thousands of hours in it, and at some time you would get bored with it, all that time and money would become useless—a terrible destruction of value. The same applies to many, if not all, of the other digital items that you can buy. For example, your Spotify music is not really yours; you can spend hours creating playlists, but all that work is lost if you stop paying. Your Kindle books are not really yours either; Amazon can delete them from your Kindle without your permission, and you cannot resell them on the secondary market. Now with NFTs, people can actually own a digital asset and monetize it for the first time, which will have a positive impact on our global society.

Challenges of NFTs

Initially, people have been drawn into the NFT collectibles, art, music, real estate, or fashion because they can relate to it. A lot more than with the start of bitcoin. However, a large part of the billions in trading is done only by a very small group, and NFT trading is anything but mainstream. The news about the million-dollar NFTs is, but the actual trading is not yet. So far, there have been three types of people buying NFTs.

- The speculators—the smart people, the insiders—who make all the money, as discussed in Chapter 2
- The show-offs—those who want to show off that they are rich and can afford a Bored Ape
- The people who got in late and are trying to convince you to buy their NFT because they don't want to lose money

This will change as the metaverse comes to life and NFTs hold actual utility.

The 2021 NFT hype is a traditional gold rush, but the hype is different from the ICO hype in 2017, which involved many scams raising funds from consumers who were driven by fear of missing out (FOMO). With NFTs offering real utility, speculation and extreme prices will eventually disappear for most NFTs, simply because NFTs will become ubiquitous. Already, research by artist Kimberly Parker and an anonymous data scientist in March 2021 revealed that almost 65 percent of NFTs sold on OpenSea in March 2021 had a sale price of $300 or less, and only 19 percent sold for $700 or more.[244] This is similar to the $1.7 trillion art world,[245] where the vast majority of artworks are sold for modest prices and only some paintings are exclusive and very expensive.

One of the great things that has come out of the NFT frenzy is that digital artists can get paid for their work and contribution to society for the first time. However, that does not mean NFTs are without challenges. In fact, there are plenty, and if you are interested in starting minting or trading NFTs, it is important to be aware of them.

Currently, NFTs seem to solve digital ownership, but most NFTs do not consider copyright, actual legal ownership, piracy, theft, or other human problems, and scams are commonplace in these early days. Let's discuss these problems.

First, NFTs prove that you own something that is hosted somewhere, but that does not mean that the underlying asset is genuinely yours. What NFTs show is that you made a transaction for a certain digital asset, so it is a verifiable receipt that indicates that you purchased an asset, e.g., a digital artwork. These assets are, ideally, stored on a decentralized file-sharing system such as IPFS, FileCoin, or Storj, but they can also be stored on a central server such as AWS as it is often too expensive to store a large JPG, GIF, video, or MP3 decentralized. Instead, usually just the web address of where the artwork is stored is on the blockchain. If the item is hosted on a centralized location, the entity that runs that server can delete the item, even if you paid millions of dollars for it. If that happens, what you are left with is a worthless NFT.

The token is basically a smart contract pointing to the location of that web address on the blockchain (that points to the server that stores your asset), which is stored in a digital wallet. As the web address is on the blockchain, that cannot be changed, but someone can remove the asset from the server making your immutable and expensive web address return a "404 not found." Unless your expensive artwork is actually stored on a decentralized storage system, you might own a receipt of a certain asset, but you certainly do not possess it, and the owner of the server where it is stored actually controls it and can delete it if it wanted to.[246] Therefore, it would be wise to use a well-known marketplace such as OpenSea, but even that is no guarantee for success.

While OpenSea uses the IPFS, since it is a centralized exchange, they also control the keys, similar to any centralized crypto exchange. If OpenSea decides to remove or freeze the digital asset because of a copyright infringement or other reason, your NFT becomes worthless, and this has already happened more than once.[247] For example, at the end of 2021, OpenSea stepped in to block the sale of stolen, expensive NFTs from collector Todd Kramer, a well-known art gallery owner, reportedly worth $2.2 million. Using a phishing attack, the NFTs were stolen from his hot wallet—a wallet connected to the internet. While it might be nice for Todd that the thief cannot resell his NFTs, it raises important questions about the decentralization of these NFTs.[248] In addition, if the thief had been able to resell the stolen NFTs, an innocent and unaware buyer might end up with an expensive but worthless NFT.

If it is stored on decentralized storage, only the user who holds the NFT should be able to access and control the digital asset on that decentralized storage. To make matters worse, these centralized marketplaces store the private keys of the NFTs on a centralized storage, which is similar to your crypto stored on a centralized exchange. This means that if the exchange gets hacked, you can lose your valuable NFTs. If the NFT is on your decentralized wallet and is on a hot wallet connected to the internet, you are responsible for the security. As Todd Kramer discovered, if you are hacked due to a phishing scam, you can still lose your NFTs.

To make matters worse, there are still some downsides to blockchain technology, which need to be solved. NFTs are stored on a blockchain, which can be Ethereum, Solana, EOS, or any of the other few dozen blockchains that enable NFTs. These blockchains are kept secure by decentralized miners or stakes, the administrators, and the more administrators, the more secure a blockchain becomes as it becomes harder to perform a so-called 51 percent attack. This is an attack where a group of miners holds more than 50 percent of the network's hashing rate, and as they control the majority, they can reverse transactions that were completed while the group was in control. Meaning they could double-spend tokens, which is the entire promise that blockchains aim to prevent. Blockchains that become the victim to a 51 percent attack will probably not live very long, and if your NFTs are stored on such a blockchain, your NFTs might become completely worthless. Of course, most NFTs reside on Ethereum, which has a broad adoption and is truly decentralized due to its age. However, this comes at a cost as Ethereum's gas fees, the price that needs to be paid to record a transaction, have gone through the roof, which makes the network prone to inequality. There are also other chains used for NFTs that will be cheaper to use, but these might be more centralized and, therefore, have weaker security. What this all means is that for NFTs to achieve mass adoption, transaction costs need to go down, ideally to zero or close to zero, while decentralization needs to go up to keep NFTs secure.[249]

If you are unlucky, you bought an expensive NFT, and either your wallet can get hacked, the security of the blockchain storing the NFT can be breached, or the centralized database storing your actual artwork can be hacked, and the criminal can delete the actual asset, in which case you are still holding the NFT pointing to a web address pointing to a server, but since there is nothing on that server, you own nothing.

If that does not happen, then you still have your own responsibility to make sure that when you do sell your Bored Ape, you do not sell it for the wrong price, as happened to NFT owner Max who accidentally sold his Bored Ape for 0.75 ETH (around $3,000 at the time of the sale) instead of 75 ETH (around $300,000). Before the owner could fix his mistake, a bot had snapped up the unique collector's item by sending the transaction with 8 ETH (around $34,000 at the time of the purchase) of gas fees to make sure it was instantly processed.[250] These so-called *fat-finger errors* have happened before. While it is annoying for the original owner, it also shows a bigger problem that has been causing many debates around the world in the past years: net neutrality. The objective of net neutrality has always been to give everyone equal access to the internet and that internet service providers (ISPs) must treat all internet communications equally. Obviously, due to the gas fees, this no longer applies in the world of blockchain, which could pose a threat for the future, further increasing the digital divide and inequality.

That is not all, as there are also plenty of scams and copyright infringements, or some call it satire or art in itself, of famous and expensive NFT collectibles such as the Bored Ape Yacht Club. One example is the Phunky Ape Yacht Club (or PAYC) which simply flipped the right-facing Bored Apes to face left and resold them, making around $1.8 million in the process. PAYC has since been banned from centralized markets such as OpenSea, Rarible, and Mintable, which again shows the power these centralized markets have by creating a seamless trading experience for the masses.[251] Another example is the *MetaBirkins*, which is a collection of NFT handbags that mimic the French leather goods giant Hermès. While the creator Mason Rothschild sold the digital assets for $42,000 in December 2021, he was soon sued by Hermès for trademark infringement and dilutive use of the Birkin brand. OpenSea quickly removed the MetaBirkins from its online exchange, but the NFTs remained available on other exchanges.[252]

Unfortunately, similar to the ICO boom in 2017, there are many people misusing a technology for criminal activities. There have been many reports of scams, counterfeits, and "wash trading" (users selling NFTs to themselves multiple times to pretend demand) within the NFT ecosystem. In fact, so many people were minting NFTs of content, including songs or artworks, that did not belong to them, that the NFT marketplace Cent, which executed the sale of Jack Dorsey's first tweet for $2.9 million, halted most transactions in February 2022. Cofounder and CEO of Cent, Cameron Hejazi, called this a "fundamental problem" of NFTs.[253]

Suppose you are lucky, and all works fine. In that case, you are still not yet out of the woods because it might very well be that the NFT you bought may include a representation of the artwork but does not include the actual intellectual property or copyrights, potentially preventing you from monetizing it and only using it as a nice image to view in your wallet or virtual home, which everyone else can do as well. This can result in costly mistakes. For example, a group of crypto enthusiasts bought a rare copy of the book *Dune* using a DAO—the *Spice DAO*—with the intention to make the book public, create an animated series of it, and support derivative projects. They paid $3.04 million for it, but obviously, all they bought was the physical copy of the book and definitely not the copyright and IP that would have allowed them to do the things they intended to do.[254] In fact, most NFTs sold in 2021 did not come with any copyright or IP, meaning that you cannot monetize the NFT, which is a crucial component for a vibrant economy. The collection of the Bored Ape Yacht Club does come with all IP and copyrights, as we discussed, resulting in a vibrant community and steep prices, but most collectibles don't, and all you have is a pointer toward an item stored somewhere, which is not a sustainable solution if NFTs are meant to achieve mass adoption.

If you buy something, you want to know if you have exclusive use of the underlying file and how you can use it. Similar to in the real world: if I buy a Gucci bag, I can be sure it is mine, and I can use it. I can give it to someone, lend it to someone for money, exchange it for something else, or sell it, but I am certain that nobody can simply take or destroy it as that would be a criminal activity. The same we need in the virtual world.

If this section shows anything, it is crucial always to do your own research before diving in, as is the case with trading cryptocurrencies.

Of course, this all looks pretty depressing, and it is, but it is not the end of the world. After all, it is still early days. As the legal system catches up, plagiarism can be curbed, and as the blockchain ecosystem continues to evolve and develop, i.e., truly decentralized storage of your digital assets, interoperable blockchains, and minimum to no transaction fees become feasible (which some blockchains already offer), all of the previous problems will likely disappear.

Despite these challenges, in its essence, NFTs are still a much better system than the current centralized approach, where you never truly own your digital assets and a company can simply delete years of your work and all your assets with a click of a button. If we overcome the mentioned challenges, NFTs will define the metaverse economy.

Digital Real Estate

In addition to digital arts, another well-known NFT use case is digital real estate. In 2021, there were multiple million-dollar digital real estate deals in, for example, Decentraland, Axie Infinity, or The Sandbox, and that is just the beginning. With an endless supply of digital land across various virtual worlds, you would expect low prices, but that is not what is happening. Prices are at an all-time high, and the more the metaverse is in the news, the more this will probably continue. Also, digital real estate brokers are jumping on the bandwagon as there is an opportunity because plenty of people have no idea how to purchase digital real estate but still fear missing out. Whether that is a good thing remains to be seen. There will also likely be a few scams where people pretend to be brokers but then disappear with the money or the land.

When buying virtual real estate, you are really purchasing a nonfungible token, and according to Jason Cassidy, founder of the Metaverse Group, the company who purchased a piece of land in Decentraland for 618,000 MANA (roughly $3.2 million at the time of purchase), buying digital real estate is like buying real estate in Manhattan in the 1900s. However, it won't take 120 years for it to explode in value, but merely 5 to 10 years. Many people are very bullish when it comes to digital real estate and its importance. While some argue that digital real estate is all about location, location, location, similar to the real world, and that you want to be in an area with a lot of foot traffic, celebrity neighbors, and a prestige area that raises the value of your virtual real estate, I hold a contrarian view.

The current trend is that digital real estate moguls and brands are snapping up digital land for millions of US dollars across the various virtual worlds, either to rent it out to others, to exploit commercial activities on top of it, or to build a virtual shop or head office to connect with (future) consumers. Although this might be a good idea, and I stand by my earlier comment in Chapter 5 that brands should purchase small amounts of land across various virtual worlds for learning purposes to become familiar with the metaverse, it also comes with its challenges. As the founder of Second Life, Philip Rosedale, said in a tweet in 2021: "When virtual land is owned outright (on blockchain), malicious owners will extort each other by putting offensive content on small highly priced plots in popular spaces."[255] He saw this happening 20 years ago in Second Life, and if it happened then, it will likely happen this time again. So you have just spent $2 to $3 million on a plot of land in Decentraland or The Sandbox, and before you know it, someone could buy a small piece of land close by and put up a massive billboard displaying something offending. Since it is decentralized, there is nothing you can do about it.

In addition, the concept of artificial scarcity when it comes to digital real estate does not make sense to me. Why do you have to deal with neighbors in the first place? While land can be useful in virtual worlds to prevent spam or low-quality content,[256] this can also be achieved by using staking (meaning your crypto will be locked in a decentralized wallet for a specific period and will be released at the end of that period) instead of the purchase of artificially scarce land in a grid-lock pattern. Digital real estate is a made-up construct. In itself, there is nothing wrong with that. We have all kinds of made-up constructs in society that work very well, but in the metaverse, you are not bound by physical limitations. There is unlimited digital space, and if you need to go somewhere, you can simply teleport to it.* Why would you want a finite piece of land in an infinite space? The grid layout and scarcity in these virtual worlds are artificial. I might understand it as a fundraising activity, but there is no other reason why you would want to limit yourself in a digital universe where you can just teleport from one experience to another, never having to deal with any bad neighbor.

Another problem with digital real estate being sold for money is that it is pretty common for players to be done with a game and move to the latest shiny virtual world. Soon, the once-thriving virtual world becomes deserted, removing all the fun because the virtual real estate is no longer maintained. The same happened in Second Life, where the earlier users who bought virtual land left, didn't maintain their digital property (as in keep it alive and up-to-date, similar to how you would maintain a real property or a website), and new users had to buy on the outskirts, far away from where the action happened. As Robert Rice, an early AR/VR pioneer and entrepreneur, shared with me, the better option would be to lease out virtual land by requiring interested parties to stake their crypto, which is automatically returned at the end of the lease period if they decide not to renew it. This way, the owner gets the money back while the land becomes available again to new users to build something nice on top of it and maintain a thriving virtual economy.

The platform Spatial.io takes a different approach altogether. Instead of buying land, creators can buy premade virtual environments designed by artists or create their own virtual environment. Most of these spaces come with some kind of utility, and once owned, you can use them as often as you want, creating all kinds of spaces. For example, you could purchase a digital gallery to display your NFTs and then create as many

---

*The platform Somnium Space tries to benefit from both scarce land and teleportation, allowing users to purchase Somnium land as well as charging for teleportation hubs. Limited Edition of Somnium Space Teleportation Hub, https://opensea.io/assets/0x595f279de4b5df1e47ca55b65175d8a9 a935a0fa/80.

different galleries as you want.[257] This approach is more focused on rewarding the creators instead of the digital real estate moguls or the platforms, which I think is a more sustainable approach.

Moreover, the platforms of today will not be the platforms of tomorrow. The next version, more advanced, with better features and capabilities, is undoubtedly already being developed, so unless these platforms selling digital real estate can continuously reinvent themselves, which is not only a technical challenge but for decentralized platforms also a community challenge to make sure a majority is aligned, a million-dollar investment could be losing its value quickly.

Economic Mechanisms

Similar to how real estate found its way into the metaverse, every business model existing in the real world will be copied into the metaverse. This would include the two most prominent business models: the ad-driven model, which means you are the product, and the freemium subscription model. Although the subscription model is problematic as customers no longer own any of the digital assets, the freemium model could work in the metaverse. The ad-driven model, on the other hand, would be more problematic. This model incentivizes platforms to keep you as long as possible on a platform, as the longer you are online, the more data can be collected, the more ads they can serve, and the more money they make. As a result, recommendation engines are optimized to keep you watching, reading, or scrolling, with devastating consequences to our society, as is clear by now. A metaverse optimized for the ad-driven model would be a terrible idea.

Fortunately, in the metaverse we can expect a wide variety of new business models, driven by the creator economy, that could become an alternative to the ad-driven model. Whether a DAO or a centralized company, an organization optimized for the creator economy could incorporate new economic mechanisms using crypto to ensure instant and seamless exchange of value instead of relying on advertising. Creators could increase their income because the organization would take only a minimal percentage, i.e., 5 or 10 percent, instead of 30 percent (Apple),

45 percent (Google), or even 75 percent (Roblox). At the launch of Meta, Zuckerberg announced that they won't be taking a cut of creators on their platform until 2023, but who knows what will happen afterward once creators have become tied to their platform.

Incorporating new economic crypto mechanisms is complex and requires a thorough understanding of how tokens can be used to incentivize players, especially when it comes to DAOs.

DAOs are like cooperatives, which have been around for years. In fact, one of The Netherlands' biggest banks, the Rabobank, is a cooperative with nearly two million members.[258] In the real world, setting up a cooperative takes a very long time and is expensive due to the involvement of notaries and lawyers. Setting up a DAO can be done a lot faster with the help of smart contracts. There will likely be DAOs-as-a-service, decentralized services where you can instantly spin up a DAO, pool funds, and do whatever you have in mind (most of which will be legal, but of course, some will be illegal).

Using a DAO, you can have ad hoc collectives, either collecting your own stuff or collectively pooling capital to buy, trade, or build stuff together. An example of this was the Constitution DAO, an ad hoc DAO formed in November 2021 to purchase an original copy of the United States Constitution. Within weeks, they raised $47 million in Ether from the community to participate in the Sotheby's auction but lost to a bid by billionaire Ken Griffin. The DAO failed in its objective and subsequently returned the funds to all who contributed. Unfortunately, due to the high gas fees in the Ethereum network, some saw their entire input used up by gas fees, and they received nothing when the funds were returned. Although the Constitution DAO failed in its objective, it is an excellent example of how 17,000 people can come together as an internet collective and raise millions of dollars in a short period. Interestingly, more than one-third of the people contributing to the DAO were first-time crypto buyers, showing the power of this new form of organizing activity.[259]

DAOs can potentially also be used for enterprises if they want to bring together disparate digital twins and share proprietary data using data vaults, thereby increasing the economic value of the data at hand, similar to the example of wind turbine data shared by energy companies mentioned in Chapter 2. In this case, the DAOs members would be the various digital twins, and no human would need to be involved. Furthermore, you can have mini-DAOs, which live inside only a specific virtual world and not across virtual worlds. Regardless of the different types of DAOs that will exist, it is important to know that DAOs are still in the experimental phase, and it might take a while before mass adoption happens. Some will be successful, but most will take time.

While DAOs would reward its community members, both decentralized and centralized platforms or brands can add additional value by rewarding the consumers of a product or service. By rewarding users for their attention with unique perks, we can move away from a subscription society where digital assets are not owned to once again truly owning the (digital) assets that we purchase. Thanks to NFTs, we are at the dawn of a wide variety of new economic mechanisms that could deliver significant value to users and platforms, ranging from *read to earn, stream to earn, wear to earn, attend to earn, play to earn,* to *whatever to earn.* Rewarding users for their attention and purchases creates loyalty and a strong community, which results in significant value for all stakeholders. Using gamification mechanisms, NFTs with utility, and various reward systems, these economic mechanisms can become the standard model in the metaverse.

The most interesting economic mechanism is *play to earn.* In 2021, it exploded in popularity together with the game Axie Infinity. The model is relatively straightforward: it rewards users for playing a game, and the more time and effort a user invests, the higher the rewards, not only for the user itself but also for the other gamers in the ecosystem.[260] Within Axie Infinity this means that players receive Small Love Potion (SLP) tokens when the Axie critters battle against each other. Axies that win more battles become more valuable as they deliver mor SLP tokens. These SLP tokens can be used to breed new Axie critters, or players can swap them for ETH using the decentralized exchange Uniswap. While token engineering—the practice of using tokens as the foundation for designing value flows and ultimately economic systems[261]—can be quite complicated, the result is straightforward: earn more if you play more. This is the exact opposite of what has always been the case in games. Traditionally, if gamers would spend more time and money on and in a game, that value would be grabbed by the company who created the game. *Play to earn* breaks that open and distributes the value back to the participants. Of course, it is not all positive because starting to play the game can be quite complicated, as even Axie Infinity's cofounder Jeff Zirlin acknowledged.[262] Even more, there is a catch as to start playing the game: users need to purchase three Axie critters, which sold at around $100 a pop at the start of 2022 and even around $350 in August 2021.[263] Since most poor people looking into playing this game cannot afford such a large up-front investment, it has resulted in the Axie Scholarship Program, which gives users the ability to loan out their digital monsters to new players to also benefit from the game. While this seems notable, the new players get to keep only 70 percent of the profits they make using the borrowed monsters, and since they never own them, they will never benefit from the real money maker in the game: selling the digital monsters.[264]

The business model relies on the inflow of new players who buy the Axie critters from existing players using the in-game currency as Axie Infinity charges a transaction fee for each purchase. A constant inflow of new players is also required for existing users to extract most of the value generated.[265] The moment the demand for Axie critters would drop, the *play to earn* mechanism would stop working.

Despite the challenges, *play to earn* rewards the player for being the most important stakeholder. As a result, this has created significant societal and economic value for the stakeholders of the game, as we saw in Chapter 2. Consequently, we can expect more games that will embrace the *play to earn* mechanism, one of them being the French game company Ubisoft who announced that they are working on *play to earn* blockchain games.[266] If Microsoft is serious about embracing the metaverse, which they seem to be as the purchase of the gaming studio Activision Blizzard for $68.7 billion in early 2022 indicates, they have a chance to significantly increase the value of their purchase by embracing the economic model of sharing and giving back instead of sticking to the old economic model of value extraction.

This positive economic model of value creation instead of value extraction, where game developers, publishers, and gamers can all benefit from a great experience, shows what could lie ahead in the metaverse.

Unfortunately, as with any disruptive change, the incumbents, in this case governments, are already trying to take advantage of or even block this economic model. The Philippines is exploring taxing the gamers and the publisher,[267] while at the end of 2021, South Korea was pushing Apple and Google to ban *play to earn* games altogether. In South Korea, the money gained in these games would be qualified as prizes, which are legally limited to only $8.50.[268] An example of a short-sighted government that ignores the obvious benefits these games can bring to an entire economy and prefers to ban innovation instead of adapting the rules.

The *play to earn* economic model looks promising, although the economic model is yet to be proven. Of course, there are challenges, but as more brands and startups embrace new economic mechanisms, these will be resolved. Nevertheless, earning money while doing what you love is incredibly important and a breakthrough in economics. Since you are generally good at what you love, it could add a lot of value to the global economy.

As *play to earn* shows, the long-term value of NFTs is not in the scarcity of digital assets but in the ability to truly own a digital asset, prove ownership, and take it with you wherever you go in the metaverse. Whereas in the current platforms, users have their data extracted and exploited, and time and energy result in nothing but value for the shareholder, an open metaverse driven by NFTs enables people to be rewarded for their time spent creating more value to society at large.

From DeFi to MetaFi

Creators can significantly benefit from an open and decentralized metaverse, but that would require moving away from the traditional financial system. Unfortunately, the existing payment systems are too expensive and too slow to enable the real-time flow of economic activity that an open metaverse would enable. That is why the use of crypto is vital for an open metaverse. It would also allow users to easily monetize their assets by embracing the mechanisms of *decentralized finance (DeFi)*.

DeFi is all about creating a global, decentralized alternative to every financial service that exists today, including insurance, savings, loans, etc.; peer-to-peer, using blockchain technology, so without the existing financial institutions. The objective of DeFi is to bring financial tools to anyone with a smartphone and an internet connection, bring financial services to the 1.7 billion unbanked,[269] and catapult them into the global economic system.[270] Crypto will lower the cost of doing business, and tokenization will offer new investment opportunities for anyone across the globe. Moreover, it will empower individuals and organizations and make them less reliant on the "too big to fail" financial institutions that brought chaos during the Great Recession.[271]

Though DeFi can redefine the global financial system, in early 2022, only ~4.3 million users were interacting with DeFi applications.[272] This low number can likely be attributed to the technical expertise required to deal with existing DeFi applications and the risks involved, such as no protection against fraud or mistakes. With all the hard work happening in this space, it may become more accessible for creators and fans to apply DeFi mechanisms and monetize their assets in the coming years.

With the open metaverse embracing these mechanisms, monetizing NFTs and the underlying (digital) assets can become easier and eventually deliver a seamless experience accessible to the masses, thereby unlocking tremendous value for society. Outlier Ventures has coined this *MetaFi*, or *Metaverse Finance*, which includes all the protocols, platforms, and products that enable financial activity between nonfungible tokens and fungible-tokens (cryptocurrencies) to the benefit of the consumer.[273] Although DeFi currently works only with fungible tokens, in the coming years (and it is very early days for MetaFi), it will become available to NFTs and be easier and more accessible for consumers to monetize their NFTs.

Monetization can be achieved by enabling fractional ownership of their NFTs (dividing a nonfungible token into many fungible tokens) or by trading them, lending them, or borrowing against it as collateral on the open market. Once we have achieved this kind of true economic interoperability, the metaverse could increase the income for many people. While at first this will be available only to the more tech-savvy creators and collectors, we should strive to make MetaFi as seamless and accessible as using a credit card and enable anyone to put their digital assets to work.

Imagine a few years from now, when a creator, be it a singer, 3D artist, writer, or gamer, has created a unique piece of content and uploaded it to any of the available decentralized platforms. The creator has decided to ask a small fee, in crypto, for people to consume their content. Whenever a user accesses the content, the creator will instantly receive the funds paid in their wallet, potentially minus a small fee to the platform hosting the content. It is possible to allow users to trial the content, and if they close or leave the experience within a certain timeframe, they will be instantly refunded. Depending on the historical revenues of the creator, which are all transparent on the blockchain, she can decide to put her content to work and submit it as collateral for a loan to develop her next work. Any interest will depend on her historic revenues and reputation. Suppose she fails to repay the loan on time. In that case, the work will automatically transfer to the user, community, or organization providing the loan, including any IP or copyright if that had been agreed upon. If she repays on time, she can use the next work to do the same all over again, further increasing her profile and reputation as a creator and continuing to create (economic) value for society. Of course, an interoperable metaverse would also enable gamers to transfer assets out of the platform where it was earned or bought, use it in other platforms, sell it on the open market, rent it out, or borrow against it using the same MetaFi protocols.

Moreover, NFTs can also be linked to real-world assets, for example, your house. The NFT will prove ownership of a contract that states that you own the house. You can then drop the NFT in some sort of DeFi protocol and use it to refinance your house and have additional funds available within hours or even minutes. While these mechanisms do already exist in the physical world, generally they involve long processes and expensive notaries or lawyers to be organized. Of course, using DeFi to refinance your house will not be without risks as people could lose their assets due to hasty or unwise decisions as well as potential scams, since the checks and balances that are in place to protect people do not exist in a decentralized world.

The metaverse can be a destination of significant value creation by and for the world's millions of creatives, artists, and gamers, enabling everyone to become a micro-entrepreneur; create, earn, and monetize content; build a community; and contribute value to the metaverse and society.

If we build the metaverse correctly, it will give humanity a chance to create new worlds that are informed by our most modern understandings of how to create a rich, fair, and fun society. In 2020, the NFT market was around $232 million, exploding to $22 billion in 2021.[274] If the open metaverse becomes a reality and economic interoperability and monetization of digital assets will become commonplace, this could turn into a trillion-dollar market before the end of the decade where creators and their fans build social communities, create unique experiences, and contribute to the creator economy.

Chapter 8
Digitalism in the Metaverse

Technology Is Neutral

Technology is neutral. It can bring prosperity to humanity or bring pain and destruction to society. The metaverse will not be any different. We can expect any of the crimes committed in the real world to take place, and potentially explode, in the immersive internet. After all, criminals will be active anywhere there is money to be made, and the metaverse will be a blue ocean full of countless opportunities for consumers, creators, and organizations to make money. Unfortunately, online security is challenging. Many organizations fail to protect their (customer) data correctly, resulting in numerous examples of organizations going bankrupt due to a cyber hack. At the same time, there are examples of people taking their own lives because of online harassment or cyberbullying. Digital criminal activities are already causing havoc worldwide, but with society moving into a multidimensional digital experience, cybercrime is expected to grow to $10.5 trillion in 2025.[275] That is trillion, not billion, and more than the GDP of Germany, France, and the United Kingdom combined[276] and more than the entire global eCommerce or commercial real estate industry.[277]

Moreover, emerging technologies such as big data analytics and artificial intelligence, combined with the constant data harvesting thanks to the Internet of Things and social media, have created a surveillance society managed either by private companies or by the state. Add to this mix the extreme data collection from AR and VR headsets, and we could soon be living in a dystopian future where our data define our freedom, for better or for worse. The metaverse could enable endless capture and control of data and identity, all in the pursuit of shareholder value. If it is up to the cybercriminals, the metaverse is an ever-growing playground to make money.

When Zuckerberg announced Meta in October 2021, he also announced that privacy and security should be built into the metaverse from day one. While it is 100 percent correct what he said and privacy, security, and ethics need to be central to the metaverse, Meta defining the ethics of the metaverse sounds a lot like a wolf in sheep's clothing, especially since Frances Haugen's testimony in the US Congress where she said that the social network fuels polarization, hurts kids, and weakens democracy.[278]

An always-on, immersive internet can be a blessing or a curse. Unfortunately, limiting the dangers of the metaverse will require a lot of hard work from regulators, lawmakers, and the companies building the metaverse. It is not a free pass, and we should not expect this to be sorted out by itself. If we wait to build the safety measures after the metaverse is fully operational, we will be too late. So, let's first explore what can go wrong with the metaverse, before we discuss the solutions to prevent some of the dangers awaiting us. Ensuring a safe and inclusive metaverse will require solving serious technical issues, enforcing strict regulations, and ensuring education starts early on, but it is certainly not impossible.

Dangers of the Metaverse

The challenges in the metaverse will be plentiful, ranging from unlimited data harvesting impacting our privacy, constant abuse and harassment, imposter avatars trying to steal sensitive information, widespread security breaches, biased AI, bots and trolls going rampant, a further polarized society, increased inequality, and physical and mental health issues. When we consider the metaverse from this perspective, we should be cautious about how we wish to proceed. Unfortunately, that won't happen as startups, organizations, individuals, and criminals will race to try to get a slice of the pie. As a species, we have gotten very good at moving fast and breaking things but less capable at going slow and thinking first, or even fixing what is broken. Just like the current internet has caused a flood of problems, will the metaverse be the same or solve some of the issues? Will users become addicted to an immersive world and prefer it above reality due to the constant streams of dopamine? Is it the opiate for the masses currently hooked on something far less exotic? Or is it merely fat/sugar, which we need in moderation, or do we need strict regulation and education to counter the risks involved? Let's have a look.

The Datafication of Everything

Datafication refers to turning analog processes and customer touchpoints into digital processes and digital customer touchpoints,[279] and in the metaverse, datafication will reach new heights. Most of the headsets of today are capable of tracking your hands, your environments, and, with some help of a few additional sensors, also your movements. These data points are useful to copy your movements from the physical world into the digital world, but they also collect vast amounts of data about you and your surroundings, including what your hands look like, what stuff you have in your house, the people in your home and whether you have a tremor indicating a possible disease. While these data points are very private, they are not as intimate as the data from your eyes.

Most headsets today also incorporate eye-tracking and face-tracking capabilities; this is a helpful feature because it will give your avatar a more realistic appearance if it mimics your facial expressions. Since most of our communication is done nonverbally, it will make communicating in the metaverse more natural and fun. Primarily these nonverbal, micro-movements tell a unique story about who you are, what you think, your emotions, what you like or dislike, and much more.[280] According to the XR Safety Initiative, the data that can be collected includes the frequency and duration of your blinks, eye movements, eye status (watery, dry, or reddened), pupil properties, iris characteristics, and facial attributes. It's extremely personal information that can tell something about your personality traits, your mental health, your skills and abilities, your level of sleepiness, your cognitive processes, any possible drug use, your age, your cultural background, your physical health, your geographical origin, your gender, and the mental workload you are experiencing.[281] All this in the blink of an eye. And this information is only from analyzing your eyes. That data can then be linked to all your internet browsing history as well as what you are looking at in virtual or augmented reality and for how long, which can tell about your emotions, what gets you excited or scared, your sexuality, and much more—even things you are not aware of yourself. All this data is considered sensitive personal information, which often requires informed consent from the individual to which the data pertains, but the question is to what extent any consent given is really informed consent.

Privacy Is an Illusion

Now suppose you are a large social network with a few billion users, with a strong focus on the metaverse and the owner of a hardware division that makes VR headsets with these capabilities. All that data is precious to you. Thanks to the data from millions of users, you will be able to create sophisticated machine learning models and sell ever-more hyper-personalized advertising. What could possibly go wrong? Keiichi Matsuda explores this dystopian reality in the video *Hyper-Reality*, providing a glimpse of a future where personalized advertising has taken over the physical and digital world.[282]

As more of our lives take place in the metaverse, privacy can increasingly become an illusion, especially if our lives take place in a closed metaverse controlled by Big Tech. Apart from Big Tech controlling and abusing our data, increasingly also governments abuse data if they can get their hands on it. In early 2022 it was revealed that the German police unlawfully abused data from the German Covid-tracing app to find witnesses to a crime. As with many Covid-contact tracing apps used around the world, users had to enter personal data such as phone numbers and email addresses, which were then linked to sensitive personal geolocation data. The police subsequently got access to this sensitive data and traced down 21 potential witnesses.[283] I think it was to be expected that these apps would be abused, but that it was abused in one of the most privacy-sensitive countries is a worrying surprise.

Abuse, Harassment, and Illegal Content

As we discussed in Chapter 4, sexual harassment has been happening in virtual worlds pretty much since virtual worlds first appeared. Unfortunately, some people have twisted minds. All the problems we have on the current Web, including harassment, abuse, and cyberbullying, will be amplified in an immersive environment, especially if users can be anonymous and such activities do not have any consequences. According to the nonprofit Center for Countering Digital Hate, a violating incident such as harassment, assaults, or abuse happens once every seven minutes in the VR game VRChat.[284] That is just one game, at the dawn of the metaverse. Imagine five years from now, when the metaverse has become commonplace.

Even worse is that with virtual reality, tracking and rendering can be done so effectively that the brain treats it as an authentic experience. A sexual assault in a shooter game feels very real for the victims of the virtual abuse and can leave the victim traumatized.[285] Unfortunately, tracking the perpetrator and proving the attack is difficult because the incidents are generally not recorded. It gets worse when kids get involved because abusers could target children through in-game chats by showing sexually explicit content to minors in the game, or they could talk directly to them using the headsets without any oversight or monitoring. These in-game chats can also be used by criminals or terrorists to discuss or recruit. It is nearly impossible to track and ban this behavior. Obviously, all of this behavior violates the terms and conditions of the games and the headset manufacturers, but that does not stop people from doing it, simply because the chance of getting caught is practically zero. Even if you do get reported and banned, spinning up another account takes only a few minutes.

Finally, content moderation has been a challenge in Web 2.0, and the problem has not yet been solved, despite many companies spending large amounts of money on the problem, developing advanced AI, and hiring armies of content moderators. If centralized platforms cannot solve this issue, it could become worse with decentralized platforms that enable persistent content to be uploaded in virtual reality or as augmented reality. Referring to the terrorist recruitment poster from

Chapter 1 and the racial slur about McDonald's that now lives on Ethereum forever, if terrorists or criminals publish defamatory, offensive, or illegal content on a decentralized platform, it will be impossible to remove. Since we have seen from the centralized platforms that artificial intelligence is not an all-encompassing solution to this problem, a massive challenge awaits us.

Imposter Avatars

If seeing is no longer believing, can we still trust what we are part of? In the past years, deepfakes have generated a lot of media attention. We have seen pretty realistic deepfakes of Obama or Queen Elizabeth, and while these were created with good intentions, deepfakes can have real-life consequences. They have been used for online shaming, and TikTok stars and many ex-girlfriends are appearing in pornographic deepfake videos without their consent.[286] The technology to create deepfakes is improving rapidly, including deepfake audio that sounds like the original person as used in the Anthony Bourdain documentary.

While these deepfakes are created with real video images, creating hyper-realistic digital videos is now possible and could lead to real-time, hyper-realistic deepfakes. As discussed, Warner Bros created a video game using Unreal Engine 5 for the promotion for the new *The Matrix Resurrections* movie, including a hyper-realistic Keanu Reeves, created using Unreal Engine's MetaHuman creator tool.

Of course, if Warner Bros can create a digital human of Keanu Reeves, anyone with access to and expertise of MetaHuman can re-create any person they want. It is not unlikely that in the coming years, we will see videos with celebrities, politicians, or business leaders who are digitally re-created against their will, saying or doing things they did not say or do. Unfortunately, it does not stop there. Once the metaverse has become a reality, those same imposter avatars can go about their business in the metaverse, directly harming the reputation of that person or their company and the individuals interacting with them. The problem is that people have a tendency to be gullible, and if an avatar looks and sounds like someone they know, or think they know, they can be easily fooled.

Already, we have seen AI-generated voices convincing business leaders to transfer money to fake suppliers or people sending Bitcoin to a fake address because "Elon Musk" was giving away free money on Twitter. Now imagine you are in a hybrid strategy meeting and the CEO appearing as an avatar is, in fact, a criminal who sounds and looks like the CEO or a fake family member of a politician trying to steal sensitive information as shown in the fictional start of this book. That could have devastating consequences. Unfortunately, it is only a matter of time before this will happen.

Data Security

That leads us to data security. Every company that can be hacked will be hacked, and if you have not yet been hacked, you are simply not important enough.[287] There is no way that companies can win the battle against hackers, as for hackers, it is their core business, and for organizations, it is only a side business. It is not unlikely that in the metaverse, hackers will use (autonomous) artificial agents to attack organizations at unbelievable speed and agility, trying to steal the data of consumers and organizations. Of course, you can fight AI hackers with AI security personnel, and you should, but there is always the problem that security is preventive and, by necessity, also reactive, always trying to keep up, but more importantly that there will always be human mistakes that no AI security can counter.

But that is not all. We will have a wide range of new hacks that could bring damage and destruction in virtual and augmented reality. These attacks include the Human Joystick Attack (controlling the movement of an avatar without the knowledge or consent or guiding/tricking a user into the virtual room they cannot leave unless they pay a ransom); the Man in the Room Attack (snooping in on private rooms without people knowing); the Chaperone Attack (modifying the boundaries within a virtual reality room, so people run into walls or trip over); the Overlay Attack (displaying unwanted images or videos inside VR without the ability to remove that content); or the Disorientation Attack (creating confusion or switching lights on and off to invoke an epileptic seizure).[288] It may be clear that in the metaverse, even if you write the rules, the rules don't protect everything.

There are also NFT hacks, where criminals drop free NFTs into your wallet, even without asking for it, and then try to convince you to sell it. As soon as you click the pop-up, you authorize the hacker to access your wallet, and all your NFTs will disappear before your eyes.[289]

Increased Inequality

With the vast amounts of data generated in the metaverse, Big Tech will become bigger and more powerful, especially if switching costs remain high and the open metaverse remains an illusion. During the pandemic, the 10 richest men doubled their fortune, while the income of 99 percent of humanity fell. The 10 billionaires increased their wealth at a rate of US$15,000 per second during the first two years of the pandemic.[290] With the amount of data to be collected, abused, and monetized in the metaverse likely to be 100x, it won't be long before the first trillionaire is a fact.

Moreover, there are still almost 2.9 billion people who have never been on the internet, and they might have a hard time catching up if the rest of the world has moved on into the metaverse, further increasing the digital divide that already exists today.

Apart from economic inequality, the metaverse could also "thrive" in physical inequality and exclude many people with disabilities. A virtual world or an augmented experience will be difficult to explore if you are blind, and making yourself heard if you are deaf will be challenging. Moreover, not many virtual worlds cater to disabled people to bring their identity to the metaverse. The metaverse is not made for avatars in wheelchairs.

Bad Bots Controlling the Web

Bad bots currently account for 20 percent of all internet traffic, and they are continuously evolving and expanding.[291] It has become easy and financially feasible to hire an army of bots to bring damage to your commercial competitor, political opponent, or any player on the internet. In addition, bots and trolls dominate the online (political) discourse with misinformation. Whether global or local, any major event will see bots and trolls popping up in droves spreading misinformation.

Anything related to the metaverse is, of course, not any different. In January 2022, OpenSea had a brief outage, and as a result, people did not see their NFTs showing up in their MetaMask wallets. When users reached out to MetaMask on Twitter, bots immediately jumped in trying to redirect users to fake websites to steal their NFTs.[292] In addition, bots are trying to snap up as many NFT airdrops as possible to sell for a profit, leaving honest users with empty hands.

Increased Polarization

Apart from bots, trolls have become the norm on the internet too. The sole objective of trolls is to create disagreement on the internet by starting arguments or upsetting people through the placement of inflammatory or off-topic messages in an online community. A troll on social media is someone (or something) who deliberately says something controversial to feed latent emotions or thoughts to ignite anger and frustration to influence specific political or commercial issues.[293] Often this involves misinformation. During the pandemic, there was a flood of misinformation spreading over the internet like the virus itself, which the WHO coined an *infodemic*.[294] The examples of the 2020 Presidential campaign in the United States and the 2016 Brexit campaign no longer require explanation. Misinformation is a threat to the internet and, as such, to our society. In 2019, large-scale, intentional disinformation campaigns occurred in more than 48 countries.[295] Even commercial companies are hiring virtual influencers to change the behavior of (future) customers.[296] It seems fake has become more powerful on the internet than integrity and truth, and citizens find it increasingly difficult to know what and who to trust online.

To make matters worse, filter bubbles and toxic recommendation engines feed the polarization. Recommendation algorithms already run the world, and they are rapidly limiting an individual's freedom, although many might not perceive it that way.[297] Due to the unconstrained data harvesting, AI will know better what you want than yourself and reinforce existing attitudes and beliefs, tipping internet users more into extreme directions. Whether free will exists has been debated for ages, but with the rise of such unrestricted, ever-more advanced recommendation engines hacking consciousness, free will could disappear and be replaced by an illusion, ending the debate for good.

These algorithms base their recommendations on data collected and often only provide recommendations that match a user's profile, resulting in a feedback loop that limits freedom and serendipity. They do not serve the individual, but the company that created them, intending to sell more or have users stay around longer so they can sell more ads. Recommendation engines are toxic, but they are everywhere. Unfortunately, also governments increasingly lean on such algorithms to make decisions.[298]

An immersive internet with synthetic avatars sharing misinformation and disrupting discussions with inflammatory comments, as well as niche communities living in their filter bubbles, would result in a pretty dystopic metaverse, and an internet far worse than portrayed in the Netflix movie *The Social Dilemma*, or the books *Snow Crash* and *Ready Player One*.

Biased AI

Artificial intelligence will be vital to keep the metaverse running and accessible, but, unfortunately, algorithms are black boxes. Often, we don't know why an algorithm comes to a specific decision. They can make great predictions, on a wide range of topics, but how much are these predictions worth if we don't understand the reasoning behind them?[299] Thanks to neural networks, it will become difficult to understand why certain decisions were made. How we run our society will become increasingly opaque, known only to the elite owning the data and AI.

Moreover, biased AI is more the norm than the exception. Too often, AI is trained with biased data and created by biased developers, further reinforcing existing harmful stereotypes and putting women, minorities, and other disadvantaged social groups at risk. Potentially harmful gender stereotypes are rampant among public-facing chatbots.[300] Biased AI could lead to adverse outcomes in numerous settings, including healthcare, education, and hiring practice. Amazon abandoned a machine learning algorithm designed to source talent after discovering a clear bias against female applicants.[301] The algorithm proposed candidates based on historical data, which caused a preference for male applicants since past hires were predominantly men.

With AI expected to run the show, biased AI could certainly ruin the fun for many individuals and extend or worsen group inequities in the metaverse, especially if an appeal against an AI-driven decision is not possible.

Health Issues

Video games can be great entertainment and an excellent educational tool, but they can also cause many physical and mental health issues. Excessive video gaming can result in similar symptoms as a drug addiction[302] and result in serious brain or health issues and even death. In addition, people spend hours per day on social media, showing off their "perfect" lives, which for many results in anxiety, stress, or depression.

If the current design of games and social media are destroying and deteriorating mental health, doing more of the same but on steroids in a highly addictive, immersive environment will have significant physical and psychological health issues. Especially if people will spend more time in virtual reality than in the physical reality, the consequences could be devastating.

The dangers and ethical challenges of the metaverse are genuine, and it does not seem very promising for the metaverse. However, the metaverse is not here yet. We still have a chance to fix these issues before they get worse, but how do we ensure that the metaverse does not turn out like a bad version of Web 2.0? How do we create an inclusive metaverse where users have complete control over their data, privacy, and identity and feel safe and welcome?

Verification, Education, and Regulation

While we will not prevent all the potential dangers and ethical dilemmas discussed, we should make every effort to mitigate as much as we can and certainly try to prevent a dystopian reality as portrayed in *Ready Player One* or *Snow Crash*. Web 2.0 and social media sort of happened to us. This time, we are still at the drawing board.

We can still make conscious decisions to steer the metaverse in the right direction and avoid a dystopic future. However, it means we need to act now and remain vigilant. It means that we should develop the standards to enable an inclusive and interoperable metaverse. It means we should solve the issue of online identity and reputation. It means we should educate our children, and parents, on how to behave in the metaverse. And it means we need regulation now, not tomorrow when it is too late. This means there is work to be done for developers, educators, and regulators. But of course, we cannot shift our responsibility onto others. As citizens and consumers, we also have an obligation to do the right thing, read the terms and conditions, limit our time in the metaverse, educate ourselves, think before we act, and vote with our data and wallets.

The dangers and ethical challenges of the metaverse are numerous, and I do not hold all the answers on how to deal with these issues. However, based on my research, I believe three important pillars can contribute to keeping the metaverse safe: verification, education, and regulation.

Verification

Trust is a fundamental good that, while largely intangible, will be crucial to the functioning of practically every meaningful interaction in the metaverse. We tend to think of trust concerning business, banking, relationships, and finance, since the necessity of trust in these areas is clear and undeniable. In fact, without trust, no transaction can go forward. Indeed, the very idea of even the simplest negotiations becomes implausible without it. Without trust, the law becomes tyranny, and business becomes piracy.[303]

The first pillar is all about verifying that a user is human and providing the trust that a user is who they say they are while at the same time ensuring that negative behavior has consequences.

Blockchain technology has the potential to change the nature of trust, not only in digitally rendered transactions but also in everyday life of the metaverse. However, trust also has a victim, called privacy. To trust one another, we have to give away some of our privacy, though maybe not for much longer. I have been thinking a lot about this problem in the past decade. The best possible solution is to enable *anonymous account-ability*, which has now become possible thanks to blockchain and *zero-knowledge proof* (ZKP). ZKP is a method used in cryptography to prove ownership of a specific piece of knowledge without revealing the content of that knowledge. It ensures that data can be shared without sharing personal information. One party can prove a particular fact without revealing that information, thereby creating the required trust to perform a transaction.

Anonymous accountability can contribute to preventing bad bots, trolls, and bad actors from continuing to reign freely in the metaverse. While this will allow people to continue to be anonymous if wanted—a fundamental human right—harmful actions will start to have consequences, similar to the real world. It would require an open standard and a self-sovereign identity to enter the metaverse so users can begin to build up their reputation anonymously. By linking a verified identity from a trusted source—a bank or government institute—using ZKP to your self-sovereign identity, platforms will be able to confirm whether a user is a real person or not, without knowing who the person is behind an account. If subsequently the reputation of the anonymous user on a particular platform is connected cryptographically to their self-sovereign identity, we can start to build up a self-sovereign reputation.

Whenever a user wants to open a new account, the platform can see how many reputations are linked to the user and the average reputation score, without revealing anything about the user, their profiles, interests, or backgrounds. It is then up to the platform to decide whether to grant access to the user or not and, if access is granted, the level of access and possibilities the user receives. For example, a user can have a very high reputation score from 10 accounts, which would indicate a trustworthy user, or the user could have a low reputation score created from 250 accounts, which could indicate a user that uses bots to act on their behalf. Of course, at any time, a user could spin up a new self-sovereign identity and start all over again, but since such a new user would not have a lot of historical data, platforms could opt to limit access to such new users until they have proven to be a trustworthy user. Interestingly, we use the same approach in the real world; if you join a new organization as a member or employee, you first have to prove yourself as trustworthy before getting more perks, access, or responsibility. Note that no platform would receive any personally identifiable data at any time, but that negative behavior would start to have consequences, which I believe is vital if we want to create a safe metaverse.

Of course, if we want to take this a step further, we can use crypto-graphically secured biometric data as additional *proof of human* in case a user's self-sovereign identity has been breached. This could be useful in particularly sensitive situations when a hyper-realistic avatar joining a hybrid meeting must be who she says she is but also must be con-trolled by that person. After all, as we have discussed, eye tracking and motion capture data can be used to uniquely identify a person, and if that data would not match the hashed data on file, it could indi-cate a breach.

Verification is both a technical and a cultural challenge that we need to overcome. Developing an *anonymous accountability* open standard will be challenging, but ensuring it can be implemented by all websites, social networks, and metaverse platforms is a different ballgame as it would require all of them to change their processes and platforms, espe-cially because we should not exclude the one billion people who do not have a bank account or a government-verified identity and would not be able to become verified by a trusted source.[304]

Education

The second pillar is all about teaching the metaverse-natives, and the metaverse illiterates, of today and tomorrow how to deal with the dan-gers and ethical challenges of the immersive internet. This would include teaching children a variety of programming languages to ensure they become native in the languages that will define their future. After all, if you understand how something works, you will be better at navigating the (digital) world, similar to the benefits of a second or third language when traveling. Understanding how the technology that controls society is built will help children become less dependent on the technology and not simply accept the status quo. If we educate them early on, they could develop new ideas and bring them to life independently. It will help them understand the inherent technical dangers.

Apart from teaching programming skills, we should also educate children and parents how to behave in the metaverse. Unfortunately, not all parents will teach their children this, simply because they do not know or understand the platforms and their rules of engagement themselves. I am sure many parents have little clue how Roblox, Minecraft, or Fortnite work and what can happen within these platforms. Therefore, schools have a responsibility to teach children the dos and don'ts of the metaverse—ideally, not simply by telling them what to do or not to do, but by using the tools of the metaverse itself. As we saw in Chapter 4, learning by doing increases the memory retention rate by 75 percent, so using virtual and augmented reality tools to show and discuss the dangers of the metaverse could contribute to a generation that is better capable of dealing with these technologies.

Finally, we should increase the focus on privacy, security, and ethics at schools and university. I only vaguely remember my ethics classes at university, simply because they were not very engaging and didn't provide examples that I could relate to. We should ensure that our children will obtain a deep ethical understanding of the metaverse to ensure that these considerations become standard practice as early on as possible.

Regulation

The third pillar toward a safe and inclusive metaverse is regulation. Even with today's internet, policymakers often have little understanding of the latest technologies, and it generally takes a long time before regulations are created, accepted, and implemented. As a result, most regulations are out-of-date by the time they come into effect. If we want to build the regulations for the metaverse, we have to start today, and we have to do so at a global level. After all, borders don't really matter in the metaverse, so we should avoid that criminals can hide behind an entity in a country with weak regulations.

There are a variety of regulations that come to mind that we should try to get into effect as soon as possible. A first step could be to require organizations to create visual and easy-to-read terms and conditions and privacy statements, especially for large tech companies with millions of users. Facebook's Terms and Policies that apply to its users are longer than the US Constitution, and the fine-print legal documents are more difficult to read and understand. We should not accept this, and regulators should require companies to make sure that anyone can read and understand their terms and conditions, for example, using infographics that explain in clear terms how data is used and what rights you grant to a platform. Ideally, this should apply to all companies, though that might be too much, so it should at least apply to public companies and companies having more than 1 million users.

Moreover, the burden of responsibility for sound and ethical use of information should not be with the individual ensuring they inform themselves of the potential dodginess of an organization, but organizations must design their environment to ensure such standards are adhered to. The imbalance of power and information between users and organizations is too big to trust companies on their terms and conditions and privacy policies. Organizations could simplify this process by ensuring industry standards when it comes to the terms and conditions and privacy policies, since the practice of data collection and data usage is pretty similar across many platforms. Standardization could prevent that users constantly have to figure out how their data is being (mis)used. This could be driven by either the standard organizations or the regulators.

Second, regulations around AI and how to avoid biased AI, black boxes, and unethical research come to mind. We should require public companies to have their algorithms scrutinized by AI auditors, who are responsible for making sure that the AI does what is intended and preventing AI from becoming black boxes that even the organization itself no longer understands. These AI auditors should be held accountable for their audits, similar to how accountants can be held responsible for their financial audits. Moreover, public companies should be required to install an independent AI ethics oversight board that requires organizations to run large AI (research) projects past an ethics committee, similar to university researchers who are required to get any research project approved by an independent ethics committee. Of course, these AI ethics boards should have the power to stop any research or project, and any outcome should be published in the annual reports to ensure transparency for society.

Other recommendations for governance include encouraging companies to hire a chief trust and safety officer, accountable for driving user safety, as suggested by Tiffany Xingyu Wang, president and cofounder of the Oasis Consortium, since "user safety is foundational in building inclusive communities and digitally sustainable growth."[305] Other regulations could involve requiring games to implement measures to try to limit the number of hours that children can play in the metaverse. For example, regulations could require platforms to proactively warn parents and children when spending too much time (as determined by health scientists) in the metaverse. Finally, platforms could be required to implement safety measures to limit online abuse, bullying, or sexual harassment.

I recognize that these types of regulations can seem extreme, and many would argue that it is the market's responsibility to do this. Unfortunately, as Web 2.0 has shown, the market has not taken its responsibility in ensuring a safe online environment, so perhaps it is time to involve the regulators to do so. As Dan Turchin, CEO of People-Reign, told me during one of my podcasts, "data rights are the new civil rights," so if we protect the individual citizen's basic rights in the constitution, maybe we should do the same for an individual citizen's data rights.[306] Of course, there will always be a responsibility of the consumer as well to read the terms and conditions, vote with our data, and stop using those platforms that breach our rights.

In the coming 10 to 15 years, we will develop the next iteration of the internet. This immersive internet will fundamentally change how we live, work, and play. It will likely change how we perceive being human, so we need to ensure a safe, inclusive metaverse, and we need to have a healthy metaverse-reality balance. Verification, education, and regulation can contribute to this, but we need to start now.

Surveillance or Empowerment

Corporations and governments have an important say in how the metaverse will turn out. Good governments and sustainable corporations will find ways to make sure people are safe, don't get digitally or physically hurt, and can make an honest living in the metaverse, which will contribute to a more equal and richer society. On the other hand, authoritarian regimes and a continued focus on the shareholder model can result incorporate or state surveillance and a metaverse that delivers most of the value to a tiny elite.

Since the exponential growth of the internet and the explosive growth of data harvesting, a new story has slowly developed. It is the story that I like to call *Digitalism*. The story of *Digitalism* is about the struggle and control for data by organizations and governments trying to collect as much data as possible and citizens trying to protect their data and privacy.[307] Where there is data, this data can be collected and exploited, and in the metaverse, there will be brontobytes of data. *Digitalism* envisions a world where data is the most crucial resource in society.

Due to the ever-increasing hunger for data, corporations consistently and deliberately breach consumers' rights, trust, privacy, and freedom as governments fail to control them. Ever-intelligent AI, combined with constant data harvesting enabled by AR and VR, means we are sleepwalking into a surveillance society.

Digitalism will require humans to adapt as machines will increasingly play an important role in society. What will start with human-to-machine collaboration and an augmented workforce will quickly result in predominantly machine-to-machine collaboration across all levels of society and the metaverse, significantly limiting the number of jobs available.

Unless we can create an open metaverse, a society organized based on *Digitalism* will result in a tiny elite controlling the digital tools while the vast majority will be subservient to them. Although many citizens will experience the benefits of these digital tools, if *Digitalism* isn't well managed and regulated, these same citizens will also feel increasingly irrelevant as their lives, jobs, and futures become uncertain.

Governments around the world, from every ideological sphere, are starting to recognize the power of digitalization. Depending on the country, this results in either a reduction of rights, protections, and digital freedom or empowered and free citizens. What we will see in the coming decades as the metaverse comes online is a division across the world in three streams of *Digitalism* depending on how governments and organizations deal with data and how citizens can respond to it.

- **State Digitalism** will result in state surveillance at an unprecedented level. We can already see the first signs in China, especially in the Xinjiang province, where an AI-powered panopticon limits the Uyghurs' movements. A society organized according to state surveillance gives full accountability to the state, stripping citizens of their privacy and limiting or blocking the internet. The state knows everything about its citizens to a level that would make the Stasi or KGB blush. Any misstep, mistake, or lapse in loyalty in the metaverse, is caught by the mass surveillance system and has immediate consequences.

- **Neo Digitalism** will result in extreme company surveillance far beyond what we see today. It will be characterized by a closed metaverse, an extreme free-market, unlimited data harvesting, and raging capitalism. Within a Neo Digital society, the likes of which we see slowly unfolding in the United States, there is limited online accountability. The state has little to say about, nor has any control over, people's digital lives as this power lies entirely with the tech titans. A citizen's privacy depends on a corporation's interest to sell their personal data for profit. Driven by libertarians, it results in unregulated companies enacting extreme data harvesting. The result is a small group of elites gaining wealth at unprecedented levels, causing extreme inequality.

- **Modern Digitalism** would be the best option for citizens as it combines the advantages of digital tools with strict privacy, security regulations, and an open metaverse. Citizen empowerment will give citizens more control over their data. Here, a self-sovereign identity and an open, interoperable metaverse are the way forward. This allows citizens to track and control their data by defining who they want to expose their data to and under which terms. Online anonymous accountability will become the norm, securing citizens' privacy, and encouraging real-world ethics in the online sphere. Modern Digitalism likely stands the best chance to succeed in Europe. With its General Data Protection Regulation (GDPR), its ethical AI guidelines, and its upcoming Digital Markets Act (DMA) and Digital Services Act (DSA), the EU is offering at least some protection to its citizens.

Digitalism will be the story of the metaverse. If you live in a country organized according to State Digitalism or Neo Digitalism, it is not something to look forward to. But *Digitalism* done right can help us solve some of today's pressing issues. After all, technology is, in essence, neutral. What can be used for creating AI hackers or fake news can in reverse also be used to combat these or create beautiful, immersive experiences. Blockchain can empower citizens to own their own data and adopt a self-sovereign identity to remain in control at all times. We can empower citizens and give them control over recommendation engines so that users are not pulled into a rabbit hole every time they open YouTube. If *Digitalism* is constrained, its adverse effects can be limited or bent positively. Regulating and fighting today's monopolies, breaking them up, and preventing them from becoming the new world dictators will be crucial going forward.

While the rise of *Digitalism* is unstoppable, as citizens, we still stand a chance to build a metaverse for us, for the citizens, the creators, and creatives, not for corporations or the state. We can not kid ourselves, though; it will require hard work, dedication, and need the involvement of all stakeholders, but it is certainly worth the effort.

Chapter 9
The Future of the Metaverse

•

BCI: The Future of Immersive Experiences

The future of the metaverse might very well be one without computers and headsets. Ever since Elon Musk's Neuralink showcased the monkey Pager controlling a game with its mind, Brain-Computer Interfaces (BCIs) came into the spotlight. Using a BCI, people can make what they want to happen, happen without needing to move a muscle. Brain-computer interfaces hold tremendous promises for the metaverse.[308]

BCIs, also known as brain-machine interfaces, mind-machine interfaces, or neural-control interfaces, have been around for a while. The research on BCIs started already in the 1970s at the University of California, initially focused on restoring damaged sight, hearing, and movements. Thanks to AI and machine learning, researchers have become very good at this. BCIs can detect minuscule changes in the energy radiated by the brain when you think, recognizing patterns in the brain.[309] Magnetic Resonance Imaging (MRI) enables us to understand in extreme detail which parts of the brain light up when thinking about something. This has allowed scientists to read our dreams, read our thoughts, and know our feelings.[310] However, an MRI machine is not very portable, is very expensive—an entry-level machine starts at $250,000—and requires a team of researchers or doctors to operate. Therefore, the race is on to create brain-computer interfaces that are cheap, small, and can be operated by anyone. Within this category, there are two types of BCI: internal BCI using delicate cybernetic implants such as developed by Neuralink or wearable BCI devices such as developed by NextMind or OpenMind.

The vision of Neuralink is to develop ultra-high bandwidth brain-machine interfaces to connect humans and computers to survive the upcoming age of AI and explore the metaverse in novel ways. Elon Musk believes that our only way to stand a chance when super-intelligent AI arrives is to merge with AI, hence Neuralink's mission statement: "If you can't beat 'em, join 'em."[311]

They have made remarkable progress. In the summer of 2020, they demonstrated three pigs with a surgically implanted Neuralink, recording their everyday brain activities like smelling and moving. Only a year later, they showed the monkey Pager playing games with its mind. Enabling a monkey to play games just with its thoughts, and being very good at it, is an amazing engineering feat.[312]

Pager had the coin-sized link disc installed in its brain via a surgical robot, connecting thousands of micro threads from the chip to specific neurons to record the brain patterns. After a lot of training, it could play ping-pong simply by thinking about its actions. If this is what a monkey can achieve with an internal BCI, imagine what humans can do when our brains are connected to computers or VR headsets.

Implanting a tiny computer in your brain is not everyone's idea of connecting with computers, albeit the cyborgs and transhumanists of this world will probably think differently. Fortunately, there are also wearable BCIs on the market that do not require a robot operating on our most precious organ.

These less invasive options for a brain-computer interface use an external device that records your brainwaves. They have been around for a long time as well, in the form of EEG caps. Electroencephalography, or EEG, is probably the second-best known technique for recording neural activity, next to the use of an MRI machine.[313] Using electrodes placed on the scalp, it can record the brain's electrical activity. While they are cheap to buy—you can find them on Alibaba for just $20—they are not the most comfortable, or fashionable, to wear. In addition, it requires a lot of software development to make them useful.

New wearable BCIs are being developed, allowing anyone to hook up their brain to the metaverse. For example, the French company NextMind has developed a portable, easy-to-use, plug-and-play device that can measure brain activity using EEG sensors that are comfortable and easy to wear. All of a sudden, controlling a computer with your brain, and using it as a mouse, has become a possibility. According to neuroscientist and founder of NextMind, Sid Kouider, this is just the beginning. Within a few decades, wearable BCIs will enable us to transmit thoughts telepathically to each other across the metaverse.[314] Already it is possible to control your car with your mind, and in a world's first, a BCI enabled a paralyzed man to communicate again. The BrainGate Consortium implanted a sensor in the brain of Nathan Copeland, a man who broke his spine in a car accident and is paralyzed from the chest down, enabling a locked-in patient to write at a rate of 90 characters per minute, which is a lot faster than using your old Nokia.[315] In the years to come, many more applications will follow.[316]

As discussed, digital twins will be an important aspect of the metaverse, and in 2022, the company Neurotwin wants to create a digital twin of our brain. We can then link up a BCI and stream the metaverse straight into our brains.[317] In 2022, the AR company Snap acquired NextMind, bringing this vision a lot closer to reality. You will be able to communicate with your friends in the virtual world simply by thinking. You can experience Ariana Grande's next concert in the metaverse and convey your thoughts directly to your friends without having to talk. They will be able to see what you are seeing, hear what you are hearing, and be part of a completely new experience. According to Gabe Newell, founder of Valve, brain-computer interfaces are the future of gaming.[318] Valve works with wearable BCI developer OpenBCI to develop open source software to help game developers better understand what responses they are stimulating in a player's brain. OpenBCI has developed a headset called Galea, specifically designed to work in unison with Valve's own VR headset, the Valve Index.[319]

According to Newell, "if you're a software developer in 2022 who doesn't have one of these in your test lab, you're making a silly mistake."[320] In the (near) future, not only will game developers use BCIs to fine-tune their games, but players will be able to experience games in a whole new way. According to Mike Ambinder, the experimental psychologist at Valve, Valve aims to move away from games with 17 buttons as a standard and more toward something more naturalistic.[321] Newell speaks critically of our natural seeing abilities and instead envisions a future where BCIs would beam visuals directly into our heads.[322] This more direct path would make games much more natural, turning what was once a flat and colorless experience into something richer than we could ever imagine.

Brain-computer interfaces promise us an entirely new way of interacting with computers, machines, and eventually with each other. However, with this new way of communicating also comes a new potential privacy disaster. After all, our thoughts are currently one of the last genuinely private domains, and BCIs will likely change this.

The more we integrate BCIs into our lives, the more it will change our relationship with computers. In the past decades, we have gone from typing to speaking, and soon we might move to thinking to computers. Similar to how Alexa, Siri, or Echo have changed our relationship with computers and brands (they decide what is good for you, instead of you choosing), the same will likely happen when we bring telepathy using BCIs into the metaverse.

Would we still need physical computers, smartphones, or even virtual reality headsets when we can simply send our thoughts to the other side of the world? How would social media change if everyone would "shout" their thoughts on a future version of social media instead of tweeting? How can we block specific messages from entering our brains, and how can we stop certain thoughts from accidentally being sent to our boss?

Exploring the first opportunities with this new technology is undoubtedly cool, but there are many unknowns when it comes to how it will change our relationship with computers and machines. It will require significant research to understand the best way of dealing with BCIs, whether invasive or noninvasive, but the impact of BCIs on the metaverse will be incredible, enabling immersive experiences unlike we have ever imagined.

A Renaissance of Art, Creativity, and Innovation

Before BCIs will dramatically change our perception of reality, we first need to make sure that the future of the metaverse is one that we actually want to be part of. As Sir Tim Berners-Lee said during the Decentralized Web Summit in 2016,[323] "the web was designed to be decentralized so that everybody could participate by having their own domain and having their own web server, and this hasn't worked out." The Web turned out to be a moneymaker for corporations and a platform for unlimited abuse and harassment. In fact, a 2021 Pew Research Center survey found that around 4 in 10 Americans have experienced online harassment.[324] This is a shocking number, which, together with all the issues discussed in the last chapter, clearly indicates a problem with the current internet design.

As we enter the next iteration of the internet, we have an opportunity to start all over again. It's a new beginning to create something better. To create a metaverse where trust, safety, and privacy are embedded in its design, in the code of the metaverse. We shape the metaverse, and we determine what it will look like. Whether we build a similar Web as today or whether we build a different, more open, and inclusive Web, the choice is up to us. Before we dive headfirst into this immersive world, we need to make sure that these crucial components do not become an afterthought again, similar to Web 2.0, but become the de facto standard of the metaverse. This will require regulators and lawmakers to step up their game and standard organizations to deliver the standards required for an open metaverse.

If we do so, the metaverse can become a parallel digital universe that amplifies the things we like with the technologies we have built. To achieve that, we need to bring together the thinkers, experts, and creators of today and evoke a rich debate about what kind of metaverse we want to build and live in and how we will do so. Otherwise, we might be sleepwalking into a closed metaverse controlled by the Zuckerbergs of this world.

Or as Eminem famously said, "If you had one shot, or one opportunity. To seize everything you ever wanted in one moment. Would you capture it or just let it slip?"[325]

We are at the dawn of a new era, and we have one opportunity, one shot, to create a new reality for humanity. We have a chance to rewrite society, change the internet for the better, learn from the mistakes we have made, and build the phygital reality of our dreams. Will we capture it and create an open, interoperable metaverse or let it slip and end up in a dystopian nightmare?

I certainly hope we can get our act together and build a digital universe that is always there for us to interact with, consisting of unique experiences that enable us to explore our inner self, to be who we want to be, to go where we want to go, when we want, while having complete control over our identity, data, and assets.

There will not be a defining moment in the future when we will say *the metaverse has arrived!* but over time, we will gradually step into the immersive internet and embrace a digital experience that will amaze us, surprise us, and entertain us. How the metaverse will look at the end of this decade is impossible to predict. Even Zuckerberg's vision will likely be off by miles as the metaverse is created by unique individuals and creators, especially in an open and interoperable metaverse.

As we set out to build the metaverse, it is unlikely to be designed and created by the Millennials or Generation X. Instead, it will predominantly be crafted by Gen Z and Gen Alpha as these generations are the metaverse-natives who have grown up with an ever-digitalized world. As Douglas Adams, famous author of *The Hitchhiker's Guide to the Galaxy*, wrote in his book *The Salmon of Doubt*[326]:

- Anything that is in the world when you're born is normal and ordinary and is just a natural part of the way the world works.
- Anything that's invented between when you're 15 and 35 is new and exciting and revolutionary, and you can probably get a career in it.
- Anything invented after you're 35 is against the natural order of things.

Imagine what could happen 10 years from now, when the cutting-edge technologies of tomorrow have been adopted by a generation of designers and developers who have been playing with these technologies for years and who have explored the early remnants of the metaverse as a child.

We will see truly creative and immersive experiences that we cannot even begin to imagine today.[327] We will see a Cambrian Explosion of identity and creativity, where everyone can have multiple identities, displayed as different avatars ranging from standard digital humans to out-of-this-world unique creations. We will join hybrid meetings in hyper-realistic fantasy worlds, learn by doing in VR, and experience an augmented reality with unlimited layers on top of the physical world that can be explored as entertainment or for business purposes. Some of these layers will be available to everyone. Some will be available only after payment in crypto, and others will be accessible only with the right credentials.

As augmented reality becomes a more significant part of our lives and surpasses the usage of VR, people will gain unique perspectives on reality, for better or for worse. The metaverse will enable the gamification of humanity, although we should be cautious not to end up in a *Black Mirror* episode. We also should not forget to live life in the real, physical world, instead of 24/7 online, and have some time without digital distractions and with our physical friends and family.

As the technology progresses, we will leave the low-polygon worlds behind us and interact with a unique variety of high-fidelity and high-polygon virtual worlds and augmented experiences before beaming the metaverse straight into our brains. It will become easier to create more immersive worlds, and the most exciting things can happen in an environment that rewards creativity and innovation and lets people seamlessly monetize their work. As emerging technologies further converge, it will result in a global renaissance of art, creativity, and innovation, leading to breakthroughs that will upgrade humanity and define the Imagination Age.

We are only starting to understand what the metaverse might be. The future of the metaverse will be personal, with unlimited choices and creativity. We will experience new levels of human evolutions as we integrate ourselves with technology, ranging from BCI implants to sensors that will give us additional senses. In the metaverse, there are no limits to where we can go. What lies beyond is probably the proactive spatial Web, with personalized AI directly communicating with our brain. The gap between computers and humans will be blurred until we have seamlessly integrated our physical and digital lives. Welcome to the metaverse, it is going to be a wild ride!

Epilogue

While there is a lot of hype around the metaverse, it is still early days. A true interoperable and open metaverse is at least a few years away, which means we still have a say in how we want to construct the next iteration of the internet. If anything, I hope it has become clear from reading this book that we should take this opportunity very seriously. This decade can be a defining moment for humanity while we build the metaverse. To reflect that and to help anyone creating the various components of the metaverse, I would like to finish this book by sharing 10 guidelines, or principles, of the metaverse. I have arrived at these principles based on all the interviews and input I have received from almost 250 stakeholders involved in the metaverse, as well as the 10 Burning Man principles, and hope that these principles can help create a metaverse that will be there to serve humanity instead of a tiny elite.[328]

- **Open**: An open metaverse enables anyone to benefit from the metaverse by creating or sharing unique experiences and to easily move between the various worlds, taking your data, identity, and wearables easily from one platform to another.

- **Inclusive**: Anyone should be able to participate in the metaverse and form their own identity that best reflects their real-world identity. In the metaverse, anything goes, and no one should be excluded based on their physical or digital appearances.
- **Private**: Your life, your privacy. In the metaverse, anyone and anything should have complete custody over their or its data. Whether an individual, organization, or digital twin, data remains with the original creator, and no one should be allowed to collect, analyze, or abuse data without explicit consent.
- **Transparent**: No more legal fine print, but instead anyone should be able to understand the rules of engagement of any platform, virtual world, or augmented experience in easy-to-read terms.
- **Fair**: No exorbitant fees by platform owners, but a fair reward for fair work. No extraction of value but value creation. Those contributing most of the value should receive most rewards, ideally enabled by cryptocurrencies.
- **Secure**: Security should be part of the DNA of the metaverse, embedded in the code—secure by design. Data should be secure and encrypted, especially when it comes to sensitive biometrics data.
- **Safe**: The metaverse should be a safe environment, where nobody should be afraid to be harassed, bullied, or insulted. Safety measures should be built into the platforms and turned on by default to protect. Offenders should not be able to get away with their actions.
- **Consensual**: Similar to the physical world, consent should be common practice. Platforms should prevent that anyone can contact anyone, without asking for permission, and consent should be embedded in the code.
- **Creative**: The metaverse thrives on creativity and creators, and artists should be able to express themselves in whatever way they want as long as it does not harm others. Since the law of physics do not apply in the digital realm, out-of-the-box thinking should be rewarded.

- **Community-centric**: The metaverse is social, and the immersive internet can best be experienced together. From tiny niche communities to global communities exploring, playing, and working together, the metaverse should be built around creative collaboration.

Ideally, anyone creating anything for the metaverse should check to what extent their platform, virtual world, or augmented experience complies with these guidelines. If we are able to create a metaverse for all, everyone will benefit, and humanity will thrive.

Acknowledgments

Writing a book about the metaverse has been an incredible journey, one that I would not have been able to do without the many people who helped me, shared their insights, and provided their feedback. After all, I might have had a lot of ideas at the start, but I certainly did not have all the answers. It has become a true communal effort as almost 250 people involved in building the metaverse have contributed their opinion and insights, resulting in a book that I hope can help people build an open metaverse.

First, I would like to thank my partner, Louise, for allowing me to practically "disappear" for three months. Without that, it would not have been possible to write this book in such a short timeframe. I also would like to thank my editor Chris Nelson and publishers Jim Minatel and Pete Gaughan as well as Melissa Burlock for supporting me during this time and providing valuable feedback while writing the book. I also would like to thank Jamie Burke for providing the foreword.

Next, I would like to thank all the people who I have been able to interview and who also provided their valuable feedback on the draft manuscript by doing a proofread of the book. In alphabetical order,

I would like to thank Alec Lazarescu, Avinash Kaushik, Benjamin Bertram Goldman, Christiaan Eisberg, Daniel Sisson, George Visniuc, John Gaeta, Justin Hochberg, Kevin O'Donovan, Lindsey McInerney, Michaela Larosse, Neil Trevett, Paul Hamilton, Rabindra Ratan, Raghu Bala, Robert Long, and Tiffany Xingyu Wang.

I also would like to thank Cathalijn van Rijmenam, Pieter Bos, Sam Johnston, and Kathryn Bruce for doing a friendly review of the book.

Thanks also to all the people who shared their insights in one of the many great interviews that I did. In alphabetical order, I would like to thank Adil Bougamza, Adonis Zachariades, Alex Lee, Anna Gandrabura, Antony Tran, Athena Demos, Avonne Darren, Bayan Towfiq, Belal Miah, Blake Lezenski, Cai Felip, Celeste Lear, Charles Markette, Chavy Goh, Christian Ulstrup, Clement Oh, David Francis, Delz Erinle, Doug Jacobson, Douglas Park, Edmund Lu, Edwin Mata, Eric Korn, Eve Logunova-Parker, Evelyn Mora, Evo Heyning, Ezra Dey, Francesca Tabor, Gabriel Rene, Georgina Wellman, Hannah Glass, Imran Sheikh, Jamie Burke, Jason Cassidy, Jay Es, Jerry Heinz, Jimi Daodu, Jimmy Chan, Joey Dunne, Jon Radoff, Julian Voll, Justin Lacche, Kavya Pearlman, Konrad Gill, Lily Li, Lisa Kolb, Lukę Gniwecki, Matias Calzada, Matthew Brewbaker, Matthew Scott Jones, Max Koenig, Michael Patrick Potts, Mila Bessmann, Nathan Grotticelli, Nathan Nasseri, Neil Haran, Paul Hewett, Ralph Kalsi, Ray Lu, Richard Kerris, Robert Long, Robert Rice, Ryan Gill, Ryan Kieffer, Sandra Escobedo, Shauna Lee Lang, Shidan Gouran, Sidsel Rytter Loschenkohl, Slavica Bogdanov, Stuart Hall, Tamer Garip, Tamer Garip, Timmu Tõke, Vijay Dhanasekaran, Vincent Hunt, and Xavier Egan.

Next, I would like to thank all the people who shared their insights using the survey I put online. Although I would have wanted to talk to all of you individually, it was impossible due to the short timeframe. Hence, completing my long survey has been much appreciated. Based on everyone who provided their LinkedIn details, in alphabetical order, I would like to thank Abiodun Victoria, Akhil Gupta, Alan Rodriguez, Alexey Shmatok, Amit Kolambikar, Amy Peck, An Coppens, Andreas Fauler, Andrii Gorbenko, Andy Wood, Anshuman Tripathi, Arian Koster, Ashraf AL-Tayeb, Astir Mayers, Axel Schumacher, Ben Maloney, Bryan Bu, Cameron Stubbs, Charles L. Perkins, Charles V., Cliff Baldridge, Darren Teh, Dave Sampson, Denis Santelli, Dima Lylyk, Dima Schott, Dixon

Melitt James, Dominique Wu, Dr Jane Thomason, Dr. Rich Melheim, Dustin Wish, Dwayne Mithoe, Eugenio Galioto, Fatemeh Monfared, Fernando Carrión, Florian Couret, Francisco Asensi Viana, Franjo Maretic, Gabriele Cavargna Bontosi, Gianluca Rosania, Guy Purdy, Hank Kalinowski, Henry Chan, Horacio Torrendell, Ilana Milkes, Janine Yorio, Jarno Eerola, Jehan-Michel Bernard, Jehan-Michel Bernard, Jesus G. Bonilla, Joe Swaty, Jonathan Wade, Juliane Demuth, Justin Cheu, Karen Jouve, Kelly Martin, Kenneth Mayfield, Kerry F. Smith, Kevin Russell, Kishore Dharmarajan, Kristina Podnar, Lee Yee, Lily Snyder, Lisa Laxton, Luca Lisci, Mao Lin Liao, Marcus Arnet, Marina Bottinelli, Mark Dando, Martin Petkov, Marty M. Weiss, Massimo Buonomo, Mattia Crespi, May Mahboob, Mees Rutten, Michael D Polak, Michael Luby, Michael Weymans, Murugan Velsamy, Nathanael Girard, Nelson Inno, Nick Dehadray, Nick Merritt, Nicolas Waern, Pascal Niggli, Paula Marie Kilgarriff, Peter Trapasso, Philip Mostert, Pushpak Kypuram, Raj A. Kapoor, Ralph Benko, Rob Chong, Rod Vowell, Ron van Rijswijk, Ruslan Mogilevets, Sam Johnston, Sanjay Ojha, Sean Low, Sekayi Mutambirwa, Shravan Rajpurohit, Shrawan Banerjee, Simon Graff, Stefan Hackländer, Stefano Sandri, Stephanie Bretonniere, Sven Van de Perre, Tamsin O'Hanlon, Therkel Sand Therkelsen, Thijs Pepping, Tim Wild, Tom Sargent, Tomasz Figarskit, Tristan Schroeder, Valentin Valle, Vincent Tessier, Wan Wei, Wendy Diamond, William Burns III, Wladimir Baranoff-Rossine, Xyras To, Yurii Filipchuk, and Zeynep Balkan.

Last but not least, I want to thank all the creators and creatives building the metaverse. You hold the power to create a unique experience for humanity, and I am grateful for all the work that you do!

References

1. Mike Proulx and Jessica Liu, "The Metaverse Won't Fix Facebook," October 25, 2021, www.forrester.com/blogs/the-metaverse-wont-fix-facebook

2. Dr Mark van Rijmenam, LinkedIn poll, www.linkedin.com/posts/mark vanrijmenam_book-metaverse-trust-activity-68697426145 35557121-N7oX, December 2021

3. Lil Nas X's Roblox concert was attended 33 million times, by Jacob Kastrenakes, The Verge, www.theverge.com/2020/11/16/21570454/lil-nas-x-roblox-concert-33-million-views, November 16, 2020, visited January 27, 2022

4. Merch sales from Lil Nas X Roblox gig near 'eight figures,' by Stuart Dredge, Musically, https://musically.com/2021/07/06/merch-sales-from-lil-nas-x-roblox-gig-near-eight-figures, July 6, 2021, visited January 27, 2022

5. "Metaverse Festival" website, https://themetaversefestival.io

6. Decentraland announces the Metaverse Festival, by Kristin Houser, Freethink, www.freethink.com/culture/metaverse-festival, October 20, 2021, visited January 27, 2022

7. The first Metaverse Festival in Decentraland!, Besancia, Non Fungible, https://nonfungible.com/blog/first-metaverse-festival-decentraland, October 25, 2021, visited January 27, 2022

8. "A Magazine Is an iPad That Does Not Work," UserExperiencesWorks, *YouTube*, Oct 25, 2011, accessed November 10, 2021, www.youtube.com/watch?v=aXV-yaFmQNk

9. Ernest Cline, *Ready Player One* (Crown Publishing Group, 2011)

10. Keynote Address: Tim Berners-Lee, Re-decentralizing the web, some strategic questions, https://archive.org/details/DWebSummit2016_Keynote_Tim_Berners_Lee, 08-06-2016, accessed November 10, 2021

11. Cybercrime To Cost The World $10.5 Trillion Annually By 2025, by Steve Morgan, Cybercrime Magazine, https://cybersecurityventures.com/cybercrime-damage-costs-10-trillion-by-2025, November 13, 2020, visited January 24, 2022

12. As discussed by Matthew Ball in the 'Building the Open Metaverse' Podcast, Episode 1, https://open.spotify.com/episode/5Vo1a5EPxDWI5quQOSf9wy

13. "The First Mainframes," *Computer History Museum*, www.computerhistory.org/revolution/mainframe-computers/7/166, visited November 14, 2021

14. Shen, PC., Su, C., Lin, Y., et al., Ultralow contact resistance between semimetal and monolayer semiconductors, Nature 593, 211–217 (2021), https://doi.org/10.1038/s41586-021-03472-9

15. www.nano.gov/nanotech-101/what/nano-size, National Nanotechnology Initiative, visited November 14, 2021

16. Ada Lovelace, "Notes" to a "Sketch of the Analytical Engine Invented by Charles Babbage," by L.F. Menabrea, in Scientific Memoirs (London, 1843), vol. 3

17. "BASIC," *Wikipedia*, last modified on February 6, 2022, https://en.wikipedia.org/wiki/BASIC

18. Cerf, V. G. & Leiner, B. M. (1997), Brief history of the internet, internet Society

19. The New Yorker cartoon by Peter Steiner, 1993

20. The Biggest Companies in the world, Visual Capitalist, Jenna Ross, www.visualcapitalist.com/the-biggest-companies-in-the-world-in-2021, visited November 14, 2021

21. Bailenson, J. (2018), Protecting nonverbal data tracked in virtual reality, JAMA pediatrics, 172(10), 905–906

22. Zuckerberg's Meta Endgame Is Monetizing All Human Behavior, The Verge, Janus Rose, www.vice.com/en/article/88g9vv/zuckerbergs-meta-endgame-is-monetizing-all-human-behavior, visited December 13, 2021

23. Zuckerberg and team consider shutting down Facebook and Instagram in Europe if Meta can not process Europeans' data on US servers, by Michiel Willem, City A.M., www.cityam.com/mark-zuckerberg-and-team-consider-shutting-down-facebook-and-instagram-in-europe-if-meta-can-not-process-europeans-data-on-us-servers, February 6, 2022, visited February 7, 2022

24. Maddison Connaughton, "Her Instagram Handle Was 'Metaverse.' Last Month, It Vanished." www.nytimes.com/2021/12/13/technology/instagram-

handle-metaverse.html By Maddison Connaughton, The New York Times, December 13, 2021, visited December 17, 2021

25. Nakamoto, S. (2008), Bitcoin: A peer-to-peer electronic cash system, *Decentralized Business Review*, 21260

26. Harari, Y. N. (2016), *Homo Deus: A Brief History of Tomorrow*, Random House

27. Morton Heilig, "The Cinema of the Future," *Espacios* 23–24, (1955)

28. Morton Heilig, (1962), US Patent #3,050,870

29. Bailenson, J. (2018), Experience on demand: What virtual reality is, how it works, and what it can do, WW Norton & Company

30. Kuo: Apple plans to replace the iPhone with AR in 10 years, 9To5Mac, José Adorno, https://9to5mac.com/2021/11/25/kuo-apple-plans-to-replace-the-iphone-with-ar-in-10-years, November 25, 2021, visited December 13, 2021

31. Why is Occlusion in Augmented Reality So Hard?, by Neil Mathew, Hackernoon, https://hackernoon.com/why-is-occlusion-in-augmented-reality-so-hard-7bc8041607f9, January 28, 2018, visited February 7, 2022

32. Snap Inc. Introduces the Next Generation of Spectacles, Investor Relations Snap, May 20, 2021, https://investor.snap.com/news/news-details/2021/Snap-Inc.-Introduces-the-Next-Generation-of-Spectacles/default.aspx, visited December 14, 2021

33. Kura AR Gallium, by Kura AR, CES Innovation Awards 2022, www.ces.tech/Innovation-Awards/Honorees/2022/Honorees/K/Kura-AR-Gallium.aspx

34. LinkedIn post ARun Prasath, LinkedIn, www.linkedin.com/posts/arunxr_augmentedreality-ar-tourismmarketing-activity-6893046514395029506-173s, February 2, 2022

35. Lik-Hang Lee, Tristan Braud, Pengyuan Zhou, Lin Wang, Dianlei Xu, Zijun Lin, Abhishek Kumar, Carlos Bermejo, Pan Hui, (2021), "All one needs to know about metaverse: A complete survey on technological singularity, virtual ecosystem, and research agenda." arXiv preprint, https://arxiv.org/abs/2110.05352

35a. Clarke, Arthur C. (1968-01-19), "Clarke's Third Law on UFO's". Science. 159 (3812): 255. doi:10.1126/science.159.3812.255-b. ISSN 0036-8075

36. The Age of Imagination, by Charlie Magee, Second International Symposium: National Security & National Competitiveness: Open Source Solutions Proceedings, 1993 Volume I, https://web.archive.org/web/20110727132753/www.oss.net/dynamaster/file_archive/040320/4a32a59dcdc168eced6517b5e6041cda/OSS1993-01-21.pdf

37. internet Statistics 2021: Facts You Need-to-Know, by Artem Minaev, https://firstsiteguide.com/internet-stats, November 30, 2021, visited December 19, 2021

38. Announcement Satya Nadella about the Enterprise Metaverse, November 2, 2021, `www.linkedin.com/feed/update/urn:li:activity:686138859173037260 8`

39. Interview with Bayan Towfiq, CEO of Subspace, December 16, 2021

40. Madden NFL 22 & Nike NRC App Super Bowl Challenge! EARN AARON DONALD!, EA, `https://answers.ea.com/t5/Madden-NFL-Ultimate-Team/Madden-NFL-22-amp-Nike-NRC-App-Super-Bowl-Challenge-EARN-AARON/m-p/11266356`, February 7, 2022, visited February 8, 2022

41. De 'verbeterde mens' is onder ons, by Lex Rietman, FD, December 17, 2021, `https://fd.nl/samenleving/1422461/de-verbeterde-mens-is-onder-ons`, visited December 23, 2021

42. Mark van Rijmenam, & Philippa Ryan, (2018), *Blockchain: Transforming Your Business and Our World*, Routledge

43. The Elephant in the Metaverse, Shannon Low, October 3, 2021, `https://shannonlow.substack.com/p/the-elephant-in-the-metaverse`

44. Interview with Neil Trevett, elected President of The Khronos Group, December 16, 2022

45. Morini, M., From 'Blockchain Hype' to a Real Business Case for Financial Markets. Available at SSRN 2760184, 2016

46. Luu, L., et al., Making smart contracts smarter, 2016, Cryptology ePrint Archive, Report 2016/633, 201 6, `http://eprint/.iacr.org/2016/633`

47. Pascuale Forte, Diego Romano, and Giovanni Schmid, "Beyond Bitcoin-Part I: A critical look at blockchain-based systems," IACR Cryptol. ePrint Arch, 2015

    Melanie Swan, *Blockchain: Blueprint for a new economy*, 2015: O'Reilly Media, Inc.

48. Mark van Rijmenam and Philippa Ryan, (2018), *Blockchain: Transforming Your Business and Our World*, Routledge

49. Andreessen Horowitz, "How to Win the Future: An Agenda for the Third Generation of the Internet," October 2021, `https://a16z.com/wp-content/uploads/2021/10/How-to-Win-the-Future-1.pdf`

50. The Metaverse: What It Is, Where to Find It, and Who Will Build It, Matthew Ball, January 13, 2020, `www.matthewball.vc/all/themetaverse`, visited December 23, 2021

51. *The Spatial Web: How Web 3.0 Will Connect Humans, Machines, and AI to Transform the World,* by Gabriel René and Dan Mapes, 2019, Self-published: Gabriel Rene (27 August 2019)

52. "The Metaverse Takes Shape as Several Themes Converge," by Pedro Palandrani, Global X, `www.globalxetfs.com/content/files/The-Metaverse-Takes-Shape-as-Several-Themes-Converge.pdf`

53. Mark van Rijmenam & Philippa Ryan, (2018), *Blockchain: Transforming Your Business and Our World*, Routledge

54. The 5P's of a Self-Sovereign Identity, by Dr Mark van Rijmenam, TheDigitalSpeaker.com, www.thedigitalspeaker.com/5ps-self-sovereign-identity, September 25, 2018

55. 9 Megatrends Shaping the Metaverse, by Jon Radoff, https://medium.com/building-the-metaverse/9-megatrends-shaping-the-metaverse-93b91c159375, May 20, 2021, visited December 24, 2021

56. "Seeing is believing," PwC, www.pwc.com/gx/en/industries/technology/publications/economic-impact-of-vr-ar.html, November 19, 2019

57. The Metaverse Explained Part 3: Economics, Gene Munster & Pat Bocchicchio, https://loupfunds.com/the-metaverse-explained-part-3-economics/, December 21, 2018, visited December 24, 2021

58. David Grider & Matt Maximo, "The Metaverse, Web 3.0 Virtual Cloud Economies," Grayscale Research, https://grayscale.com/wp-content/uploads/2021/11/Grayscale_Metaverse_Report_Nov2021.pdf, November 2021

59. Mark Zuckerberg's metaverse could fracture the world as we know it — letting people 'reality block' things they disagree with and making polarization even worse, by Katie Canales, Business Insider, www.businessinsider.com.au/facebook-meta-metaverse-splinter-reality-more-2021-11, November 11, 2021, visited February 10, 2022

60. Interview with Jamie Burke, Founder and CEO Outlier Ventures, November 16, 2021

61. Jamie Burke, The Open Metaverse OS, Outlier Ventures, https://outlierventures.io/wp-content/uploads/2021/02/OV-Metaverse-OS-V5.pdf

62. Why Axie Infinity Is at the Forefront Towards a Sustainable P2E Economy, by Jungruethai Songthammakul, Alpha Finance, https://blog.alphafinance.io/why-axie-infinity-is-at-the-forefront-towards-a-sustainable-p2e-economy, December 20, 2021, visited December 24, 2021

63. Axie Infinity facing taxes in the Philippines, Market Business News, by Edward Bishop, https://marketbusinessnews.com/axie-infinity-facing-taxes-in-the-philippines/280528, November 4, 2021, visited January 18, 2022

64. Axie Infinity Raising $150M at $3B Valuation: Report, by James Rubin, CoinDesk, www.coindesk.com/business/2021/10/04/axie-infinity-to-raise-150m-series-b-at-3b-valuation-report, October 5, 2021, visited January 18, 2022

65. CoinMarketCap web site https://coinmarketcap.com, January 18, 2022

66. Earnings for Axie Infinity players drop below Philippines minimum wage, by Lachlan Keller, Forkast, https://forkast.news/headlines/earnings-axie-infinity-below-minimum-wage, November 16, 2021, visited February 12, 2022

67. Mansoor Iqbal, "Fortnite Usage and Revenue Statistics (2022)," *Business of Apps*, January 11, 2022, www.businessofapps.com/data/fortnite-statistics

68. Soulbound, by Vitalik Buterin, https://vitalik.ca/general/2022/01/26/soulbound.html, January 26, 2022, visited February 13, 2022

69. Interview with Lindsey McInerney, November 29, 2021

70. Jamie Burke, The Open Metaverse OS, Outlier Ventures, https://outlierventures.io/wp-content/uploads/2021/02/OV-Metaverse-OS-V5.pdf

71. "Hashrate Distribution," Blockchain.com, https://blockchain.info/pools, as reported on January 18, 2022

72. Bitcoin: Who owns it, who mines it, who's breaking the law, by Betsy Vereckey, MIT Management Sloan School, https://mitsloan.mit.edu/ideas-made-to-matter/bitcoin-who-owns-it-who-mines-it-whos-breaking-law, October 14, 2021, January 18, 2022

73. Report Preview: The 2021 NFT Market Explained [UPDATED 1/13/22], Chainanlysis, https://blog.chainalysis.com/reports/nft-market-report-preview-2021, December 6, 2021, visited January 18, 2022

74. @ryancrucible, *Twitter*, May 10, 2021 https://twitter.com/RyanCrucible/status/1391851471243726851

75. Interview with Neil Trevett, The Khronos Group, December 16, 2021

76. Kellie Patrick, "A Brief History of Avatars," *The Philadelphia Inquirer* (March 18, 2007): www.inquirer.com/philly/entertainment/20070318_A_Brief_History_of_Avatars.html

77. What are some different types of gender identity?, by Veronica Zambon, Medical News Today, www.medicalnewstoday.com/articles/types-of-gender-identity, November 5, 2020, visited January 15, 2022

78. "About NFT Profile Pictures on Twitter," *Twitter*, https://help.twitter.com/en/using-twitter/twitter-blue-fragments-folder/nft

79. Interview with Timmu Tõke, CEO and co-founder of Wolf3D, November 19, 2021

80. VRChat, "Avatar Performance Stats and Rank Blocking," https://medium.com/vrchat/avatar-performance-stats-and-rank-blocking-1ae0feddc775, June 12, 2019, Visited December 29, 2021

81. CA18, "The Matrix Awakens: you have to try this crazy Unreal Engine 5 demo!" California 18, https://california18.com/the-matrix-awakens-you-have-to-try-this-crazy-unreal-engine-5-demo/2021062021, December 10, 2021, visited December 29, 2021

82. Why "Uncanny Valley" Human Look-Alikes Put Us on Edge, by Jeremy Hsu, Scientific American, www.scientificamerican.com/article/why-uncanny-valley-human-look-alikes-put-us-on-edge, April 3, 2012, visited January 2, 2022

83. Ready Player Me, a metaverse avatar platform, raises $13M in funding, by Rachel Kaser, VentureBeat, https://venturebeat.com/2021/12/28/ready-player-me-a-metaverse-avatar-platform-raises-13m-in-funding, December 28, 2021, visited December 29, 2021

84. Rabindra Ratan, David Beyea, Benjamin J. Li, & Luis Graciano Velazquez, (2020). Avatar characteristics induce users' behavioral conformity with small-to-medium effect sizes: A meta-analysis of the proteus effect. Media Psychology, 23(5), 651–675

85. Nick Yee & Jeremy Bailenson, (2007). The proteus effect: The effect of transformed self-representation on behavior. Human Communication Research, 33(3), 271–290. doi:10.1111/hcre.2007.33.issue-3

Rabindra Ratan, David Beyea, Benjamin J. Li, & Luis Graciano Velazquez (2020). Avatar characteristics induce users' behavioral conformity with small-to-medium effect sizes: A meta-analysis of the proteus effect. Media Psychology, 23(5), 651–675

86. Ready Player Me, a metaverse avatar platform, raises $13M in funding, by Rachel Kaser, VentureBeat, https://venturebeat.com/2021/12/28/ready-player-me-a-metaverse-avatar-platform-raises-13m-in-funding, December 28, 2021, visited, January 3, 2022

87. Kim Kardashian's Met Gala Look Rewrote the Red Carpet's Rules, by Janelle Okwodu, Vogue, www.vogue.com/article/kim-kardashian-balenciaga-met-gala-2021-look, September 13, 2021, visited January 2, 2022

88. Twitter search, https://twitter.com/search?q=kim%20kardashian%20unlocked%20character&src=typed_query&f=top

89. Epic's high-fashion collaboration with Balenciaga in Fortnite includes a hoodie for a walking dog, Jay Peters, The Verge, www.theverge.com/2021/9/20/22679754/fortnite-balenciaga-collaboration-epic-games-unreal-engine, September 20, 2021, visited January 2, 2022

90. Balenciaga Brings High Fashion to Fortnite, Epic Games, www.epicgames.com/site/en-US/news/balenciaga-brings-high-fashion-to-fortnite, September 21, 2021, visited January 2, 2022

91. Balenciaga makes phygital haute couture with Fortnite, Robin Driver, Fashion Network, https://ww.fashionnetwork.com/news/Balenciaga-makes-phygital-haute-couture-with-fortnite,1336247.html, September 21, 2021, visited January 2, 2022

92. Gucci Garden by Roblox, www.roblox.com/games/6536060882/Gucci-Garden

93. A digital Gucci bag sold for US$4,000 on gaming platform Roblox – will virtual fashion really become a US$400 billion industry by 2025?, www.scmp.com/magazines/style/news-trends/article/3136325/digital-gucci-bag-sold-us4000-gaming-platform-roblox, June 7, 2021, visited January 2, 2022

94. LOOK: Dolce and Gabbana sells virtual suit for R18m, by Gerry Cupido, IOL, www.iol.co.za/lifestyle/style-beauty/fashion/look-dolce-and-gabbana-sells-virtual-suit-for-r18m-a870a72f-59ba-482b-b2de-a7508fc12ac6, October 6, 2021, visited January 3, 2022

    Dolce & Gabbana's NFT Experiment Is A Million-Dollar Success Story, by Alex Kessler, Vogue, www.vogue.co.uk/news/article/fashion-nft-dolce-and-gabbana, September 30, 2021, visited January 3, 2022

95. Interview with Michaela Larosse, Head of Content & Strategy at The Fabricant, December 8, 2021

96. Digital Fashion House 3.0, The Fabricant, https://the-fab-ric-ant.medium.com/the-fabricant-91e88b5b6b76, October 12, 2021, visited January 3, 2022

97. Unlocking utility is key for fashion brands launching NFTs in 2022, by Rachel Wolfson, Cointelegraph, https://cointelegraph.com/news/unlocking-utility-is-key-for-fashion-brands-launching-nfts-in-2022, January 3, 2022, visited January 3, 2022

98. Interview with Lindsey McInerney, November 29, 2021

99. Fewer Than Half of Returned Goods Are Re-Sold at Full Price: Here's Why, by Jasmine Glasheen, The Robin Report, October 23, 2019, visited January 3, 2022

100. Your brand new returns end up in landfill, by Harriet Constable, BBC, www.bbcearth.com/news/your-brand-new-returns-end-up-in-landfill, visited February 9, 2022

101. CGTN, "'Smart' mirrors delight shoppers in fitting rooms across China," *YouTube*, www.youtube.com/watch?v=GNKa8ZDOnF4, published October 8, 2017

102. How on earth is trading virtual items in video games a $50 billion industry?, WAX.io, https://medium.com/wax-io/how-on-earth-is-trading-virtual-items-in-video-games-a-50-billion-industry-5972c211d621, December 12, 2017, visited January 3, 2022

103. Interview with Konrad Gill, NeosVR, December 15, 2021

104. Richard A. Bartle, (2004). *Designing Virtual Worlds*. New Riders

105. Mulligan, Jessica & Patrovsky, Bridgette (2003), Developing Online Games: An Insider's Guide, New Riders, pp. 444, ISBN 978-1-59273-000-1, 1980 [...] Final version of MUD1 completed by Richard Bartle. Essex goes on the ARPANet, resulting in internet MUDs!

106. Presentation by Benjamin Bertram Goldman, Beyond Games Conference in November 2021, https://benjamin.tv/virtual-worlds

107. Richard Bartle: we invented multiplayer games as a political gesture, Keith Stuart, The Guardian, www.theguardian.com/technology/2014/nov/17/richard-bartle-multiplayer-games-political-gesture, November 17, 2014, visited January 6, 2022

108. Presentation by Benjamin Bertram Goldman, Beyond Games Conference in November 2021, https://benjamin.tv/virtual-worlds

109. Keynote Raph Koster, Still Logged In: What AR and VR Can Learn from MMOs, 2017 Game Developers Conference, www.raphkoster.com/games/presentations/still-logged-in-what-social-vr-and-ar-can-learn-from-mmos

110. Do MUDs still exist?, Board Game Tips, https://boardgamestips.com/wow/do-muds-still-exist/#Do_MUDs_still_exist

111. The Metaverse Explained Part 3: Economics, by Gene Munster & Pat Bocchicchio, Loup, https://loupfunds.com/the-metaverse-explained-part-3-economics, December 21, 2018, visited January 5, 2022

112. Duan, H., Li, J., Fan, S., Lin, Z., Wu, X., & Cai, W. (2021, October 17). Metaverse for Social Good, Proceedings of the 29th ACM International Conference on Multimedia, https://doi.org/10.1145/3474085.3479238

113. First millionaire in Second Life, Guinness World Records, www.guinnessworldrecords.com/world-records/first-millionaire-in-second-life

114. Taking a Second Look at Second Life, by Jonathan Schneider, ORCA Views, https://qrcaviews.org/2020/11/10/taking-a-second-look-at-second-life, November 10, 2020, visited January 5, 2022

115. Black Rock City 2022, https://burningman.org/event

116. Mark W. Bell, (2008), "Toward a Definition of 'Virtual Worlds,'" Virtual worlds research: Past, Present and Future issue, *Journal of Virtual Worlds Research*, 1(1)

117. Presentation by Benjamin Bertram Goldman, Beyond Games Conference in November 2021, https://benjamin.tv/virtual-worlds

118. Elizabeth Reid (1994), *Cultural Formations in Text-Based Virtual Realities*, (master's thesis), University of Melbourne

119. Keynote Raph Koster, Still Logged In: What AR and VR Can Learn from MMOs, 2017 Game Developers Conference, www.raphkoster.com/games/presentations/still-logged-in-what-social-vr-and-ar-can-learn-from-mmos

120. People Are Already Using Pokémon Go as a Real Estate Selling Point, by Cara Giaimo and Sarah Laskow, Atlas Obscura, www.atlasobscura.com/articles/people-are-already-using-pokemon-go-as-a-real-estate-selling-point, July 12, 2016, visited January 6, 2022

121. Criminals Targeting Victims with the Geo-Located Pokémon Go Game, Reyhan Harmonic, Atlas Obscura, www.atlasobscura.com/articles/criminals-targeting-victims-with-the-geolocated-pokemon-go-game, July 10, 2016, visited January 6, 2022

122. Pokemon Go Turns Man's Home into a 'Gym,' Causing Chaos, by Andrew Griffin, Independent, www.independent.co.uk/life-style/gadgets-and-tech/gaming/pokemon-go-man-s-house-accidentally-turned-

into-a-gym-causing-huge-problems-a7129756.html, July 14, 2016, visited January 6, 2022

123. Virtual Pedophilia Report Bad News For Second Life, TechCrunch, https://techcrunch.com/2007/10/30/virtual-pedophilia-report-bad-news-for-second-life, October 31, 2007, visited January 6, 2022

124. Pink penis attack on Second Life chat show, by Paul Kevan, Metro, https://metro.co.uk/2006/12/22/pink-penis-attack-on-second-life-chat-show-3433996, December 22, 2006, visited January 6, 2022

125. My First Virtual Reality Groping, by Jordan Belamire, Athena Talks, https://medium.com/athena-talks/my-first-virtual-reality-sexual-assault-2330410b62ee#.wxqm21s7v, October 21, 2016, visited January 6, 2022

126. Meta opens up access to its VR social platform Horizon Worlds, Alex Heath, The Verge, www.theverge.com/2021/12/9/22825139/meta-horizon-worlds-access-open-metaverse, December 9, 2021, visited January 6, 2022

127. Woman claims she was virtually 'groped' in Meta's VR metaverse, by Hannah Sparks, New York Post, https://nypost.com/2021/12/17/woman-claims-she-was-virtually-groped-in-meta-vr-metaverse, December 17, 2021, visited January 6, 2022

     The State of Online Harassment, Pew Research Center, www.pewresearch.org/internet/2021/01/13/the-state-of-online-harassment, January 13, 2021

128. Dealing With Harassment in VR, by Aaron Stanton, UploadVR, https://uploadvr.com/dealing-with-harassment-in-vr, October 25, 2016, visited January 6, 2022

129. Meta opens up access to its VR social platform Horizon Worlds, Alex Heath, The Verge, www.theverge.com/2021/12/9/22825139/meta-horizon-worlds-access-open-metaverse, December 9, 2021, visited January 6, 2022

130. Meta to bring in mandatory distances between virtual reality avatars, by Dan Milmo, The Guardian, www.theguardian.com/technology/2022/feb/04/meta-to-bring-in-mandatory-distances-between-virtual-reality-avatars, February 5, 2022, visited February 9, 2022

131. My First Virtual Reality Groping, by Jordan Belamire, Athena Talks, https://medium.com/athena-talks/my-first-virtual-reality-sexual-assault-2330410b62ee#.wxqm21s7v, October 21, 2016, visited January 6, 2022

132. Gaming: the new super platform, Accenture, www.accenture.com/us-en/insights/software-platforms/gaming-the-next-super-platform, April 2021

133. Film And Video Global Market Report 2021, The Business Research Group, www.thebusinessresearchcompany.com/report/film-and-video-global-market-report-2020-30-covid-19-impact-and-recovery

134. 35% of the total world's population are gamers, by Justinas Baltrusaitis, Finbold, https://finbold.com/35-of-the-total-worlds-population-are-gamers, August 15, 2020, visited January 7, 2022

135. The Metaverse: What It Is, Where to Find It, and Who Will Build It, by Matthew Ball, www.matthewball.vc/all/themetaverse, January 13, 2020, visited January 7, 2022

136. Fortnite earned $9bn in two years, by Tom Phillips, Eurogamer, www.euro gamer.net/articles/2021-05-04-fortnite-earned-usd9bn-in-two-years, May 18, 2021, visited January 7, 2022

137. Fortnite Usage and Revenue Statistics (2021), by Mansoor Iqbal, Business of Apps, www.businessofapps.com/data/fortnite-statistics, November 12, 2021, visited January 7, 2022

138. Minecraft boasts over 141 million monthly active users and other impressive numbers, by Zachary Boddy, Windows Central, www.windowscentral.com/minecraft-live-2021-numbers-update, October 16, 2021, visited January 7, 2022

139. Roblox User and Growth Stats 2022, by Brian Dean, Backlinko, https://backlinko.com/roblox-users, January 5, 2022, visited January 7, 2022

140. Over half of US kids are playing Roblox, and it's about to host Fortnite-esque virtual parties too, by Taylor Lyles, The Verge, www.theverge.com/2020/7/21/21333431/roblox-over-half-of-us-kids-playing-virtual-parties-fortnite, July 21, 2021, visited January 7, 2022

141. The Metaverse: What It Is, Where to Find It, and Who Will Build It, by Matthew Ball, www.matthewball.vc/all/themetaverse, January 13, 2020, visited January 7, 2022

142. What is Roblox? | An In-Depth Guide To Roblox, by Werner Geyser, Influencer Marketing Hub, https://influencermarketinghub.com/what-is-roblox, August 16, 2021, visited January 7, 2022

143. This 21-year-old is paying for college (and more) off an amateur video game he made in high school, by Tom Huddleston Jr., CNBC, www.cnbc.com/2019/09/23/college-student-video-game-creator-made-millions-from-jailbreak.html, March 9, 2021, visited January 7, 2022

144. The Metaverse Overview: From the Past to the Future (Part 2), by LD Capital, https://ld-capital.medium.com/the-metaverse-overview-from-the-past-to-the-future-part-2-c4e60ce10e00, August 16, 2021, visited January 7, 2022

145. Business models in the blockchain gaming world, by Devin Finzer, https://devinfinzer.com/blockchain-gaming-business-models, December 31, 2018, visited January 7, 2022

146. Beyond Sports, Blocky Nickelodeon NFL Wildcard Game, Beyond Sports, https://vimeo.com/555851612/c8d9a6aaed

147. Nickelodeon aired an NFL game and proved technology can make football way more fun, by Julia Alexander, The Verge, www.theverge.com/2021/1/11/22224770/nickelodon-nfl-wild-card-new-orleans-saints-chicago-bears-spongebob-squarepants-slime, January 11, 2021, visited February 14, 2022

148. How to Explain the 'Metaverse' to Your Grandparents, by Aaron Frank, https://medium.com/@aaronDfrank/how-to-explain-the-metaverse-to-your-grandparents-b6f6acae17ed, January 9, 2022, visited February 14, 2022

149. Intel, "Intel True View, Intel in Sports," www.intel.com/content/www/us/en/sports/technology/true-view.html

150. The Ultimate Echo Arena on the Quest Resource Guide, by Sony Haskins, VR FItness Insider, www.vrfitnessinsider.com/the-ultimate-echo-arena-on-the-quest-resource-guide, May 6, 2020, visited January 7, 2022

151. IOC launches Beijing Olympics-themed mobile game with NFTs, by Ryan Browne, CNBC, www.cnbc.com/2022/02/03/ioc-launches-beijing-olympics-themed-mobile-game-with-nfts.html, February 3, 2022, visited February 14, 2022

152. AO releases exclusive NFT's to celebrate iconic moments in history, Australian Open, https://ausopen.com/articles/news/ao-releases-exclusive-nfts-celebrate-iconic-moments-history, Janiuary 17, 2022, visited February 10, 2022

153. AO launches into Metaverse, serves up world-first NFT art collection linked to live match data, Australian Open, https://ausopen.com/articles/news/ao-launches-metaverse-serves-world-first-nft-art-collection-linked-live-match-data, January 11, 2022, visited February 10, 2022

154. 10m players attended Fortnite's Marshmello concert, by Tom Phillips, Eurogamer, www.eurogamer.net/articles/2019-02-04-10m-players-attended-fortnites-marshmello-concert, February 4, 2019, visited January 7, 2022

155. Fortnite – Twitter, https://twitter.com/FortniteGame/status/1254817584676929537, April 28, 2020

156. How Hip-Hop Superstar Travis Scott Has Become Corporate America's Brand Whisperer, by Abram Brown, Forbes, www.forbes.com/sites/abrambrown/2020/11/30/how-hip-hop-superstar-travis-scott-has-become-corporate-americas-brand-whisperer/?sh=5477095574e7, November 30, 2020, visited January 7, 2022

157. Travis Scott reportedly grossed roughly $20m for Fortnite concert appearance, by Rebekah Valentine, GamesIndustry, www.gamesindustry.biz/articles/2020-12-01-travis-scott-reportedly-grossed-roughly-USD20m-for-fortnite-concert-appearance, December 1, 2020, visited January 7, 2022

158. Ivors Academy, "8 out of 10 music creators earn less than £200 a year from streaming," https://ivorsacademy.com/news/8-out-of-10-music-creators-earn-less-than-200-a-year-from-streaming-finds-survey-ahead-of-songwriters-and-artists-giving-evidence-to-a-select-committee-of-mps, December 7, 2020, visited January 7, 2022

159. Music NFTs: A centre-stage investment?, Raphael Sanis, Currency.com, https://currency.com/music-nft, November 9, 2021, visited January 7, 2022

160. Susan Sonnenschein & Michele L. Stites (2021), The Effects of COVID-19 on Young Children's and Their Parents' Activities at Home, Early Education and Development, 32:6, 789–793, DOI: 10.1080/10409289.2021.1953311

    Stanford researchers identify four causes for 'Zoom fatigue' and their simple fixes, by Vignesh Ramachandran, Stanford News, https://news.stanford.edu/2021/02/23/four-causes-zoom-fatigue-solutions, February 23, 2021, visited January 8, 2022

161. The Learning Pyramid, The Peak Performance Center, https://thepeakperformancecenter.com/educational-learning/learning/principles-of-learning/learning-pyramid

162. The Experiences of the Metaverse, by Jon Radoff, https://medium.com/building-the-metaverse/the-experiences-of-the-metaverse-2126a7899020, May 28, 2021, visited January 8, 2022

163. Public Policy for the Metaverse: Key Takeaways from the 2021 AR/VR Policy Conference, by Ellysse Dick, ITIF, https://itif.org/publications/2021/11/15/public-policy-metaverse-key-takeaways-2021-arvr-policy-conference, November 15, 2021, visited January 8, 2022

164. Example Use Cases of How to Use Virtual Reality (VR) for Training, www.instavr.co/articles/general/example-use-cases-of-how-to-use-virtual-reality-vr-for-training, visited February 10, 2022

165. 7 Mad Men Quotes That Applied Both Then and Now, Glad Works, www.gladworks.com/blog/7-mad-men-quotes-applied-both-then-and-now, visited January 9, 2022

166. Warner Music is determined not to make another Napster mistake as it plots A-list concerts in the metaverse, by Marco Quiroz-Gutierrez, Fortune, https://fortune.com/2022/01/27/warner-music-metaverse-theme-park-concerts-sandbox-napster-cardi-b-dua-lipa, January 28, 2022, visited February 14, 2022

167. JPMorgan's Dimon says bitcoin 'is a fraud', by David Henry, Anna Irrera, Reuters, www.reuters.com/article/legal-us-usa-banks-conference-jpmorgan-idUSKCN1BN2PN, September 21, 2017, visted February 18, 2022

168. JPMorgan opens a Decentraland lounge featuring a tiger as the bank seeks to capitalize on $1 trillion revenue opportunity from the metaverse, by Natasha Dailey, Business Insider, https://markets.businessinsider.com/news/currencies/jpmorgan-decentraland-onyx-lounge-metaverse-virtual-real-estate-crypto-dao-2022-2, visited February 16, 2022, visited February 18, 2022

    Opportunities in the metaverse, by Christine Moy & Adit Gadgil, J.P.Morgan, www.jpmorgan.com/content/dam/jpm/treasury-services/documents/opportunities-in-the-metaverse.pdf, February 2022

169. Visions for 2020: Key trends shaping the digital marketing landscape, by Jacel Booth, Oracle Advertising Blog, https://blogs.oracle.com/advertising/post/visions-for-2020-key-trends-shaping-the-digital-marketing-landscape, January 18, 2020, visited January 9, 2022

170. Are you ready for the metaverse?, The Customer Experience Column, Circlesquare, https://ezine.moodiedavittreport.com/ezine-301/the-customer-experience-column, visited January 10, 2022

171. Stella Artois Gallops Into The Metaverse With Horse Racing NFTs, by Cathy Hackl, Forbes, www.forbes.com/sites/cathyhackl/2021/06/18/stella-artois-gallops-into-the-metaverse-with-horse-racing-nfts, June 18, 2021, visited, February 14, 2022

172. Interview with Lindsey McInerney, November 29, 2021

173. Virtual-world simulator, United States Patent, Coffey, et al., 2021, https://patft.uspto.gov/netacgi/nph-Parser?Sect1=PTO2&Sect2=HITOFF&u=%2Fnetahtml%2FPTO%2Fsearch-adv.htm&r=1&f=G&l=50&d=PTXT&p=1&S1=11210843&OS=11210843&RS=11210843

174. Big Data Meets Walt Disney's Magical Approach, Dr Mark van Rijmenam, The Digital Speaker, www.thedigitalspeaker.com/big-data-meets-walt-disneys-magical-approach, May 21, 2013, visited February 10, 2022

175. Distribution of Roblox games users worldwide as of September 2020, by age, Statista, www.statista.com/statistics/1190869/roblox-games-users-global-distribution-age

176. Wendy's: Keeping Fortnite Fresh by VMLY&R, www.thedrum.com/creative-works/project/vmlyr-wendys-keeping-fortnite-fresh

177. Keeping Fortnite Fresh, Cannes Lions 2019, https://canneslions2019.vmlyrconnect.com/wendys

178. David Robustelli, LinkedIn post, www.linkedin.com/feed/update/urn:li:activity:6884489471849480192, January 16, 2022

179. McDonald's® USA Unveils First-Ever NFT to Celebrate 40th Anniversary of the McRib, https://corporate.mcdonalds.com/corpmcd/en-us/our-stories/article/OurStories.40-anniversary-mcrib.html, Press Release October 28, 2021

180. McDonald's McRib NFT Project Links to Racial Slur Recorded on Blockchain, by Will Gottsegen & Andrew Thurman, www.coindesk.com/business/2021/12/11/mcdonalds-mcrib-nft-project-links-to-racial-slur-recorded-on-blockchain, December 11, 2021, visited January 10, 2022

Etherscan – Transaction details, https://etherscan.io/tx/0xd3a616c65e94f0a78d77a0ef0da699e294043c94b3643bc2c718577f2179b1b1

181. Interview with Justin Hochberg, CEO of the Virtual Brand Group, January 11, 2021

182. The brands are at it again — Taco Bell is hopping on the NFT train, by Mitchell Clark, The Verge, www.theverge.com/2021/3/8/22319868/taco-bell-nfts-gif-tacos-sell, March 8, 2021, visited January 11, 2022

183. Coca-Cola NFT Auction on OpensSea Fetches More than $575,000, Coca-Cola Press Release, www.coca-colacompany.com/news/coca-cola-nft-auction-fetches-more-than-575000, 06 August 2021, visited January 11, 2022

184. What fashion week looks like in the metaverse, Maghan McDowell, Vogue Business, www.voguebusiness.com/technology/what-fashion-week-looks-like-in-the-metaverse, visited April 16, 2022, published February 1, 2022

185. Metaverse Fashion Week Draws Big Brands, Startups, Ann-Marie Alcántara, The Wall Street Journal, www.wsj.com/articles/metaverse-fashion-week-draws-big-brands-startups-11648166916, visited April 16, 2022, published March 24, 2022

186. Metaverse Fashion Week: The hits and misses, Maghan Mcdowel, Vogue Business, www.voguebusiness.com/technology/metaverse-fashion-week-the-hits-and-misses, visited April 16, 2022, published March 29, 2022

187. Mel Slater, et al. (2020), "The Ethics of Realism in Virtual and Augmented Reality," Frontiers in Virtual Reality, 1, 1

188. Rare Bored Ape Yacht Club NFT Sells for Record $3.4 Million, by Rosie Perper, Hyperbeast, https://hypebeast.com/2021/10/bored-ape-yacht-club-nft-3-4-million-record-sothebys-metaverse, October 26, 2021, visited January 12, 2022

189. 10:22 pm Forms Kingship, The First-Ever Group Consisting of NFT Characters from Bored Ape Yacht Club, Press Release, Universal Music Group, www.universalmusic.com/1022pm-forms-kingship-the-first-ever-group-consisting-of-nft-characters-from-bored-ape-yacht-club, November 11, 2021, visited January 12, 2022

190. Adidas to enter the metaverse with first NFT products, by Rima Sabina Aoef, Dezeen, www.dezeen.com/2021/12/19/adidas-enter-metaverse-first-nft-products-design, December 19, 2021, visited January 12, 2022

191. ADIDAS Has Landed On The Ethereum Metaverse with Sandbox, BAYC, and Coinbase!, by Dennis Weldner, Cryptoticker, https://cryptoticker.io/en/adidas-ethereum-metaverse, November 29, 2021, visited January 12, 2022

192. Truly Immersive Retail Experiences: How Brands Like Nike Are Using Augmented Reality in 2021, by Madeleine Streets, Footwear News, https://footwearnews.com/2021/business/retail/nike-hovercraft-studio-augmented-virtual-reality-experience-1203103817, February 4, 2021, visited January 12, 2022

193. Nike Creates NIKELAND on Roblox, Press Release Nike, https://news.nike.com/news/five-things-to-know-roblox, November 18, 2021, visited January 12, 2022

194. What the metaverse will (and won't) be, according to 28 experts, by Mark Sullivan, Fast Company, www.fastcompany.com/90678442/what-is-the-metaverse, October 26, 2021, visited January 12, 2022

195. How to Quit Your Job in the Great Post-Pandemic Resignation Boom, by Arianne Cohen, Bloomberg, www.bloomberg.com/news/articles/2021-05-10/quit-your-job-how-to-resign-after-covid-pandemic, May 10, 2021, visited January 14, 2022

196. Pieter Levels, There will be 1 billion digital nomads by 2035, https://levels.io/future-of-digital-nomads, October 25, 2015, visited January 14, 2022

197. Jeremy N. Bailenson, (2021), Nonverbal Overload: A Theoretical Argument for the Causes of Zoom Fatigue, Technology, Mind, and Behavior, 2(1), https://doi.org/10.1037/tmb0000030

   Vignesh Ramachandran, (2021), Stanford researchers identify four causes for Zoom fatigue and their simple fixes, Retrieved from Stanford News: https://news.Stanford.edu/2021/02/23/four-causes-zoom-fatigue-solutions

198. *Augmenting Your Career*, by David Shrier, Piatkus, 2021

199. Erik Brynjolfsson & Andrew McAfee, (2011), *Race Against the Machine: How the Digital Revolution is Accelerating Innovation, Driving Productivity, and Irreversibly Transforming Employment and the Economy*, Brynjolfsson and McAfee

200. John Deere's self-driving tractor lets farmers leave the cab — and the field, by James Vincent, The Verge, www.theverge.com/2022/1/4/22866699/john-deere-autonomous-farming-ai-machine-vision-kit, January 4, 2022, visited January 14, 2022

201. TECH TRENDS The rush to deploy robots in China amid the coronavirus outbreak, by Rebecca Fannin, CNBC.com, www.cnbc.com/2020/03/02/the-rush-to-deploy-robots-in-china-amid-the-coronavirus-outbreak.html, March 2, 2020, visited January 14, 2022

202. Welcoming our new robots overlords, by Sheela Kolhatkar, The New Yorker, www.newyorker.com/magazine/2017/10/23/welcoming-our-new-robot-overlords, October 16, 2017, visited January 14, 2022

203. Augmented and Virtual Reality in Operations, Capgemini, www.capgemini.com/wp-content/uploads/2018/09/AR-VR-in-Operations1.pdf, September 2018

204. Farrand, P., Hussain, F., & Hennessy, E., (2002), The efficacy of the mind map study technique, Medical education, 36(5), 426–431

205. New Employees, Come to Metaverse!, Hyundai, https://news.hyundaimotorgroup.com/Article/New-Employees-Come-to-Metaverse, August 26, 2021, visited January 15, 2022

206. Big companies thinking out of the box for recruitment, Korea JoongAng Daily, https://koreajoongangdaily.joins.com/2021/09/15/business/industry/metaverse-job-fair-recruitment/20210915180700311.html, September 15, 2021, visited January 15, 2022

207. Looking for a job? You might get hired via the metaverse, experts say, CNBC, www.cnbc.com/2021/11/30/looking-for-a-job-you-might-get-hired-via-the-metaverse-experts-say.html, November 30, 2021, visited January 15, 2022

208. 5 Virtual Reality Training Benefits HR Managers Should Know, by Andrew Hughes, eLearning Industry, https://elearningindustry.com/virtual-reality-training-benefits-hr-managers-know-5, March 5, 2019, visited January 15, 2022

209. Cecilie Våpenstad, Erlend Fagertun Hofstad, Thomas Langø, Ronald Mårvik, Magdalena Karolina Chmarra, Perceiving haptic feedback in virtual reality simulators, Surg Endosc., 2013 Jul;27(7):2391-7, doi: 10.1007/s00464-012-2745-y, Epub 2013 Jan 26, PMID: 23355154

210. How does a digital twin work?, IBM, www.ibm.com/topics/what-is-a-digital-twin

211. How does a digital twin work?, IBM, www.ibm.com/topics/what-is-a-digital-twin

212. Lik-Hang Lee, et al., (2021), All one needs to know about metaverse: A complete survey on technological singularity, virtual ecosystem, and research agenda, arXiv preprint, https://arxiv.org/abs/2110.05352

213. Digital Twin, Siemens, www.plm.automation.siemens.com/global/en/our-story/glossary/digital-twin/24465, visited February 13, 2022

214. Varjo, "The world's first mixed reality test drive" (case study), https://varjo.com/testimonial/xr-test-drive-with-volvo

215. Varjo, "Case Volvo Cars" with Christian Braun, https://varjo.com/testimonial/volvo-cars-on-varjo-mixed-reality-this-is-the-future-of-creativity

216. Taking Digital Twins for a Test Drive with Tesla, Apple, by Jesse Coors-Blankenship, IndustryWeek, www.industryweek.com/technology-and-iiot/article/21130033/how-digital-twins-are-raising-the-stakes-on-product-development, April 30, 2020, visited February 10, 2022

217. The B1M, "Building a $2BN Skyscraper From Home," *YouTube*, www.youtube.com/watch?v=4lnncgMCLKA, October 7, 2020

218. The B1M, "Why This Korean Stadium Will Be a Game Changer for Football," *YouTube*, www.youtube.com/watch?v=88nWMhURPgc, January 26, 2022, watched, February 14, 2022

219. EXPO 2020 Dubai hosts ISALEX 2.0, the world's first law enforcement exercise in the metaverse, by International Security Alliance Secretariat, PR Newswire, www.prnewswire.com/news-releases/expo-2020-dubai-hosts-isalex-2-0--the-worlds-first-law-enforcement-exercise-in-the-metaverse-301508827.html, visited April 16, 2022, published March 23, 2022

220. Interview with Guillaume Alvergnat and Faraz Hashmi, Advisors, International Affairs Bureau, UAE Ministry of Interior, March 25, 2022

221. Why Blockchain is Quickly Becoming the Gold Standard for Supply Chains, by Dr Mark van Rijmenam, Datafloq, https://datafloq.com/read/blockchain-gold-standard-supply-chains, November 22, 2018, visited January 16, 2022

222. Seoul will be the first city government to join the metaverse, by Camille Squires, Quartz, https://qz.com/2086353/seoul-is-developing-a-metaverse-government-platform, November 10, 2021, visited January 16, 2022

223. Working towards a Digital Twin of Earth, ESA, www.esa.int/Applications/Observing_the_Earth/Working_towards_a_Digital_Twin_of_Earth, October 14, 2021, visited January 16, 2022

224. Interview with Richard Kerris, VP of the NVIDIA Omniverse platform, December 15, 2021

225. ESA moves forward with Destination Earth, by European Space Agency, www.esa.int/Applications/Observing_the_Earth/ESA_moves_forward_with_Destination_Earth, October 22, 2021, visited January 16, 2022

226. Edward Castronova, (2008), *Exodus to the Virtual World: How Online Fun Is Changing Reality*, Palgrave Macmillan

227. David J. Chalmers, Reality+: *Virtual Worlds and the Problems of Philosophy*, New York: W. W. Norton, 2022

    Virtual reality is reality, too, by Sean Illing, Vox, www.vox.com/vox-conversations-podcast/2022/1/12/22868445/vox-conversations-david-chalmers-the-matrix-reality, January 12, 2022, visited January 16, 2022

228. Hernando de Soto, "The Power of the Poor," 2009, www.freetochoosenetwork.org/programs/power_poor

229. The Creator Economy Survey by The Influencer Marketing Factory, by Globe Newswire, MarTech Series, https://martechseries.com/social/influencer-marketing/the-creator-economy-survey-by-the-influencer-marketing-factory, September 21, 2021, visited January 21, 2022

230. 22 Creator Economy Statistics That Will Blow You Away, by Werner Geyser, Marketing Hub, https://influencermarketinghub.com/creator-economy-stats, May 15, 2021, visited January 21, 2022

231. MetaFi: DeFi for the Metaverse, Outlier Ventures, https://outlierventures.io/wp-content/uploads/2021/12/OV_MetaFi_Thesis_V1B.pdf

232. What Is Lens?, https://docs.lens.dev/docs, visited February 11, 2022

    A New Decentralized Social Network for Web3 Is Coming, by Tatiana Kochkareva, BeinCrypto, https://beincrypto.com/a-new-decentralized-social-network-for-web3-is-coming, January 3, 2022, visited February 11, 2022

233. Crypto Crime Trends for 2022: Illicit Transaction Activity Reaches All-Time High in Value, All-Time Low in Share of All Cryptocurrency Activity, Chainalysis, https://blog.chainalysis.com/reports/2022-crypto-crime-report-introduction, January 6, 2022, visited January 21, 2022

234. Criminals Use USD More in Illicit Affairs Than Cryptocurrency Says US Treasury, by Osaemezu Emmanuel, ZyCrypto, https://zycrypto.com/criminals-use-usd-illicit-affairs-cryptocurrency-says-us-treasury, January 3, 2018, visited January 21, 2022

235. The DOJ's $3.6B Bitcoin Seizure Shows How Hard It Is to Launder Crypto, by Andy Greenberg, Wired, www.wired.com/story/bitcoin-seizure-record-doj-crypto-tracing-monero, February 9, 2022, visited February 12, 2022

236. Bitcoin Energy Consumption Index, Alex de Vries, Digiconomist, https://digiconomist.net/bitcoin-energy-consumption, visited February 11, 2022

237. Bitcoin Electronic Waste Monitor, Alex de Vries, Digiconomist, https://digiconomist.net/bitcoin-electronic-waste-monitor, visited February 11, 2022

238. Bitcoin Uses More Electricity Than Many Countries. How Is That Possible?, by Hiroko Tabuchi, Claire O'Neill, & Jon Huang, the New York Times, www.nytimes.com/interactive/2021/09/03/climate/bitcoin-carbon-footprint-electricity.html, September 3, 2021, visited February 11, 2022

239. Coin Market Cap website https://coinmarketcap.com, visited January 21, 2022

240. Mark van Rijmenam, (2019), *The Organisation of Tomorrow: How AI, blockchain, and analytics turn your business into a data organisation*, Routledge

241. Clarifying the path to tokenisation, Dr Mark van Rijmenam in combination with the 2Tokens Foundation, www.thedigitalspeaker.com/clarifying-path-tokenisation, December 18, 2019, visited January 20, 2022

242. How Security Tokens Could Change Liquidity and Transform the World's Economy, by Dr Mark van Rijmenam, The Digital Speaker, www.thedigitalspeaker.com/security-tokens-change-liquidity-economy, February 14, 2019, visited January 20, 2022

243. NFTs: But Is It Art (or a Security)?, by Latham & Watkins LLP, www.fintechandpayments.com/2021/03/nfts-but-is-it-art-or-a-security, March 12, 2021, visited January 20, 2022

244. Most artists are not making money off NFTs, and here are some graphs to prove it, Kimberly Parker, https://thatkimparker.medium.com/most-artists-are-not-making-money-off-nfts-and-here-are-some-graphs-to-prove-it-c65718d4a1b8, April 20, 2021, visited January 22, 2022

245. Investing in the Art Market: A $1.7 Trillion Asset Class, by Mike Parsons, CAIA Association, https://caia.org/blog/2021/07/22/investing-art-market-17-trillion-asset-class, July 22, 2021, visited January 20, 2022

246. NFTexplained.info, "Where Is an NFT Stored? – A Simple and Comprehensive Breakdown", https://nftexplained.info/where-is-an-nft-stored-a-simple-and-comprehensive-breakdown

247. "My first impressions of web3," Jan 07, 2022, https://moxie.org/2022/01/07/web3-first-impressions.html

248. OpenSea Steps in After NFT Art Theft Raising Questions About Decentralization, by Bob Mason, FX Empire, www.fxempire.com/news/article/opensea-steps-in-after-nft-art-theft-raising-questions-about-decentralization-853408, December 31, 2021, visited January 20, 2022

249. Are your NFTs on the wrong blockchain?, by David Z. Morris, Fortune, https://fortune.com/2021/03/10/are-your-nfts-on-the-wrong-blockchain, March 11, 2021, visited January 20, 2022

250. $300,000 Bored Ape NFT sold for $3,000 because of the misplaced decimal point, by James Vincent, The Verge, www.theverge.com/2021/12/13/22832146/bored-ape-nft-accidentally-sold-300000-fat-finger, December 13, 2021, January 20, 2022

251. Two NFT copycats are fighting over which is the real fake Bored Ape Yacht Club, by Adi Robertson, The Verge, www.theverge.com/2021/12/30/22860010/bored-ape-yacht-club-payc-phayc-copycat-nft, December 30, 2021, January 20, 2022

252. Hermès Sues NFT Creator Over 'MetaBirkin' Sales, by Robert Williams, BusinessofFashion, www.businessoffashion.com/news/luxury/hermes-sues-nft-creator-over-metabirkin-sales, January 17, 2022, visited February 14, 2022

253. Marketplace suspends most NFT sales, citing 'rampant' fakes and plagiarism, by Elizabeth Howcroft, Reuters, www.reuters.com/business/finance/nft-marketplace-shuts-citing-rampant-fakes-plagiarism-problem-2022-02-11, February 11, 2022, visited February 13, 2022

254. James Felton, "NFT Group Buys Copy of Dune for €2.66 Million, Believing It Gives Them Copyright," IFL Science, www.iflscience.com/technology/nft-group-buys-copy-of-dune-for-266-million-believing-it-gives-them-copyright, January 2022, visited February 11, 2022

255. @philiprosedale – Twitter, https://twitter.com/philiprosedale/status/1467640781494095877, December 6, 2021

256. taetaehoho and ryanshon.xyz, "Economic Primitives of the Metaverse 2: Mortgages," Blockchain@Colombia, https://blockchain.mirror.xyz/MZmMEDUckY5Vo3QMwZPHcgcSr_FTpg1X025VUad_s9o, December 2, 2021, visited January 21, 2022

257. NFT Real Estate: Why Buying Land in the Metaverse Is Not It, Spatial, https://spatial.io/blog/nft-real-estate-why-buying-land-in-the-metaverse-is-not-it, February 9, 2022, visited February 14, 2022

258. Rabobank website, www.rabobank.com/en/about-rabobank/cooperative/index.html

259. ConstitutionDAO: Paving the Future of Web3, Identity Review, https://identityreview.com/constitutiondao-paving-the-future-of-web3, January 19, 2022, visited January 21, 2022

260. Pieter Bergstrom on LinkedIn, www.linkedin.com/posts/peterberg strom_blockchain-gaming-economics-play-to-earn-activity-6890574350089637888-TDpx, January 22, 2022

261. How Purpose-Driven Tokenisation Will Enable Innovative Ecosystems, Dr Mark van Rijmenam, The Digital Speaker, www.thedigitalspeaker.com/purpose-driven-tokenisation-innovative-ecosystems, January 29, 2020, visited January 22, 2022

262. Web3 Is Not a Scam, But It Can Feel Like One, by Jeff John Roberts, Decrypt, https://decrypt.co/90480/web-3-nft-game-axie-infinity-hard-to-use, January 16, 2022, visited January 22, 2022

263. 3 problems that might hinder Axie Infinity's quest for game immortality, by Derek Lim -Tech in Asia, www.techinasia.com/3-problems-hinder-axie-infinitys-quest-game-immortality, August 2, 2021, visited January 22, 2022

264. 3 problems that might hinder Axie Infinity's quest for game immortality, by Derek Lim -Tech in Asia, www.techinasia.com/3-problems-hinder-axie-infinitys-quest-game-immortality, August 2, 2021, visited January 22, 2022

265. Play-to-earn crypto games have exploded onto the scene and are shaking up gaming business models. Here's how they work, and where the value comes from for investors, by Shalini Nagarajan, Market Insider, https://markets.businessinsider.com/news/currencies/play-to-earn-crypto-axie-infinity-business-model-gaming-value-2022-1, January 23, 2022, visited February 13, 2022

266. Ubisoft Reveals Plans to Step into Play-to-Earn Gaming, by Robert Hoogendoorn, Dapp Radar, https://dappradar.com/blog/ubisoft-reveals-plans-to-step-into-play-to-earn-gaming, November 1, 2021, visited January 22, 2022

267. Philippines Looks to Tax Hit Blockchain Game Axie Infinity: Report, by Eliza Gkritsi, CoinDesk, www.coindesk.com/markets/2021/08/25/philippines-looks-to-tax-hit-blockchain-game-axie-infinity-report, August 25, 2021, visited January 22, 2022

268. Korea pushes Google, Apple to pull play-to-earn games from stores, by Miguel Cordon, TechinAsia, www.techinasia.com/korea-pushes-google-apple-pull-playtoearn-games-stores, December 29, 2021, visited January 22, 2022

269. Financial Inclusion on the Rise, But Gaps Remain, Global Findex Database Shows, The World Bank, Press Release, www.worldbank.org/en/news/press-release/2018/04/19/financial-inclusion-on-the-rise-but-gaps-remain-global-findex-database-shows, April 19, 2018, visited January 20, 2022

270. How Decentralised Finance Will Change the World's Economy, by Dr Mark van Rijmenam, The Digital Speaker, www.thedigitalspeaker.com/decentralised-finance-change-world-economy, February 13, 2020, visited January 22, 2022

271. How Decentralised Finance Will Change the World's Economy, Dr Mark van Rijmenam, The Digital Speaker, www.thedigitalspeaker.com/decentralised-finance-change-world-economy, February 13, 2020, visited January 20, 2022

272. @rchen8, "DeFi users over time," Dune Analytics, https://dune.xyz/rchen8/defi-users-over-time, visited January 23, 2022

273. MetaFi: DeFi for the Metaverse, Outlier Ventures, https://outlierventures.io/wp-content/uploads/2021/12/OV_MetaFi_Thesis_V1B.pdf

274. NFT Market Size Statistics and Forecast Report, 2022–2031, www.marketdecipher.com/report/nft-market

275. Cybercrime to Cost The World $10.5 Trillion Annually by 2025, by Steve Morgan, Cybercrime Magazine, https://cybersecurityventures.com/cybercrime-damage-costs-10-trillion-by-2025, November 13, 2020, visited January 24, 2022

276. The Top 25 Economies in the World, by Caleb Silver, Investopedia, www.investopedia.com/insights/worlds-top-economies, February 3, 2022, visited February 17, 2022

277. Trish Novicio, "5 Biggest Industries in the World in 2021," www.insidermonkey.com/blog/5-biggest-industries-in-the-world-in-2021-925230/3, March 24, 2021, visited January 24, 2022

278. Statement of Frances Haugen, October 4, 2021, www.commerce.senate.gov/services/files/FC8A558E-824E-4914-BEDB-3A7B1190BD49

279. Mark van Rijmenam, (2019), *The Organisation of Tomorrow: How AI, blockchain, and analytics turn your business into a data organisation*, Routledge

280. Kavya Pearlman, Marco Magnano, Ryan Cameron, Sam Visner, (2021), "Securing the Metaverse, Virtual Worlds Need REAL Governance," Simulation Interoperability Standards Organization, www.academia.edu/66984560/Securing_the_Metaverse_Virtual_Worlds_Need_REAL_Governance

281. Kavya Pearlman, Marco Magnano, Ryan Cameron, Sam Visner, S. (2021), "Securing the Metaverse, Virtual Worlds Need REAL Governance," Simulation Interoperability Standards Organization, www.academia.edu/66984560/Securing_the_Metaverse_Virtual_Worlds_Need_REAL_Governance

282. Hyper-Reality, by Keiichi Matsuda, www.youtube.com/watch?v=YJg02ivYzSs, May 20, 2016, visited February 11, 2022

283. German police used a tracking app to scout crime witnesses. Some fear that's fuel for covid conspiracists, by Rache Pannett, The Washington Post, www.washingtonpost.com/world/2022/01/13/german-covid-contact-tracing-app-luca, January 13, 2022, visited January 24, 2022

284. Sheera Frenkel and Kellen Browning, "The Metaverse's Dark Side: Here Come Harassment and Assaults," The New York Times, www.nytimes.com/2021/12/30/technology/metaverse-harassment-assaults.html, December 30, 2021, visited January 24, 2022

285. The Metaverse Has a Sexual Harassment Problem and It's Not Going Away, by Kishalaya Kundu, Screenrant, https://screenrant.com/vr-harassment-sexual-assault-metaverse, December 16, 2021, visited January 25, 2022

286. TikTok Stars Are Being Turned into Deepfake Porn Without Their Consent, by Geordie Gray, RollingStone, https://au.rollingstone.com/culture/culture-features/tiktok-creators-deepfake-pornography-discord-pornhub-18511, October 27, 2020, visited January 24, 2022

287. Mark van Rijmenam, (2014), Think Bigger: Developing a Successful Big Data Strategy for Your Business, AMACOM

288. Peter Casey, Ibrahim Baggili, and Ananya Yarramreddy, "Immersive Virtual Reality Attacks and the Human Joystick," in IEEE Transactions on Dependable and Secure Computing, vol. 18, no. 2, pp. 550–562, 1 March-April 2021, doi: 10.1109/TDSC.2019.2907942

289. Found a random NFT in your wallet? Interacting with it could be a big mistake, by Morgan Linton, www.morganlinton.com/found-a-random-nft-in-your-wallet-interacting-with-it-could-be-a-big-mistake, September 21, 2021, visited January 24, 2022

290. Ten richest men double their fortunes in pandemic while incomes of 99 percent of humanity fall, Oxfam International, www.oxfam.org/en/press-releases/ten-richest-men-double-their-fortunes-pandemic-while-incomes-99-percent-humanity, January 17, 2022, visited January 24, 2022

291. Imperva, "Bad Bot Report 2021: The Pandemic of the internet," www.imperva.com/resources/resource-library/reports/bad-bot-report

292. Scammers are impersonating MetaMask tech support on Twitter, by Will Gendron, Input, www.inputmag.com/tech/beware-of-scammers-impersonating-metamask-support-on-twitter, January 22, 2022, visited January 24, 2022

293. The Problem of Misinformation, Bad Bots and Online Trolls, Especially during the Coronavirus Crisis, Dr Mark van Rijmenam, The Digital Speaker, www.thedigitalspeaker.com/problem-misinformation-bad-bots-online-trolls-coronavirus, March 19, 2020, visited January 25, 2022

294. Managing the COVID-19 infodemic: Promoting healthy behaviours and mitigating the harm from misinformation and disinformation, WHO, www.who.int/news/item/23-09-2020-managing-the-covid-19-infodemic-promoting-healthy-behaviours-and-mitigating-the-harm-from-misinformation-and-disinformation, September 23, 2020, visited February 11, 2022

295. Samantha Bradshaw and Philip N. Howard, "Challenging Truth and Trust: A Global Inventory of Organized Social Media Manipulation," Computational Propaganda Research Project, Oxford internet Institute, https://demtech.oii.ox.ac.uk/wp-content/uploads/sites/93/2018/07/ct2018.pdf

296. Brands Are Building Their Own Virtual Influencers. Are Their Posts Legal?, by Jesselyn Cook, Huffington Post, www.huffpost.com/entry/virtual-

instagram-influencers-sponcon_n_5e31cbefc5b6328af2ef97fd, January 29, 2020, visited January 24, 2022

297. How Recommendation Algorithms Run the World, by Zeynep Tufekci, Wired, www.wired.com/story/how-recommendation-algorithms-run-the-world, April 22, 2019, visited January 24, 2022

298. AI Experts Want to End 'Black Box' Algorithms in Government, by Tom Simonite, Wired, www.wired.com/story/ai-experts-want-to-end-black-box-algorithms-in-government, October 10, 2017, visited January 24, 2022

299. Algorithms Are Black Boxes, That Is Why We Need Explainable AI, Dr Mark van Rijmenam, The Digital Speaker, www.thedigitalspeaker.com/algorithms-black-boxes-explainable-ai, March 1, 2017, January 24, 2022

300. "I'd Blush If I Could," EQUALS Global Partnership and UNESCO, https://en.unesco.org/Id-blush-if-I-could

301. Amazon scraps secret AI recruiting tool that showed bias against women, by Jeffrey Dastin, Reuters, www.reuters.com/article/us-amazon-com-jobs-automation-insight/amazon-scraps-secret-ai-recruiting-tool-that-showed-bias-against-women-idUSKCN1MK08G, October 11, 2018, visited January 24, 2022

302. Aviv Weinstein and Michel Lejoyeux (March 2015), "New developments on the neurobiological and pharmaco-genetic mechanisms underlying internet and videogame addiction." The American Journal on Addictions (Review), 24 (2): 117–25. doi:10.1111/ajad.12110. PMID 25864599

303. How Zero-Knowledge Proof Enables Trustless Transactions and Increases Your Privacy, Dr Mark van Rijmenam, The Digital Speaker, www.thedigitalspeaker.com/zero-knowledge-proof-enables-trustless-transactions-increases-privacy, December 20, 2017, visited January 25, 2022

304. Vyjayanti T. Desai, Anna Diofasi, and Jing Lu, "The global identification challenge: Who are the 1 billion people without proof of identity?", The World Bank, https://blogs.worldbank.org/voices/global-identification-challenge-who-are-1-billion-people-without-proof-identity, April 25, 2018, visited January 25, 2022

305. Oasis Consortium, www.oasisconsortium.com/usersafetystandards and interview with Tiffany Xingyu Wang on January 26, 2022

306. Why Data Rights Will Be The New Civil Rights, Dr Mark van Rijmenam, The Digital Speaker, www.thedigitalspeaker.com/why-data-rights-new-civil-rights-the-digital-speaker-series-ep12, June 24, 2021, visited February 11, 2022

307. The Rise of Digitalism: Will the Coronavirus Trigger the End of Liberalism?, Dr Mark van Rijmenam, The Digital Speaker, www.thedigitalspeaker.com/rise-digitalism-coronavirus-trigger-end-liberalism, April 2, 2020, visited January 24, 2022

308. The Future of Computing: How Brain-Computer Interfaces Will Change Our Relationship with Computers, Dr Mark van Rijmenam, The Digital Speaker,

www.thedigitalspeaker.com/brain-computer-interfaces-change-relationship-computers, October 21, 2021, visited January 26, 2022

309. The Brief History of Brain-Computer Interfaces, Brain Vision UK, www.brainvision.co.uk/blog/2014/04/the-brief-history-of-brain-computer-interfaces, April 30, 2014, January 26, 2022

310. Scientists Can Now Read Your Thoughts with a Brain Scan, by Avery Thompson, Popular Mechanics, www.popularmechanics.com/science/health/a27102/read-thoughts-with-brain-scan, June 17, 2017, visited January 26, 2022

    Scientists 'read dreams' using brain scans, by Rebecca Morelle, BBC, www.bbc.com/news/science-environment-22031074, April 4, 2013, visited January 26, 2022

    Scientists are using MRI scans to reveal the physical makeup of our thoughts and feelings, by Lesley Stahl, CBS News, www.cbsnews.com/news/functional-magnetic-resonance-imaging-computer-analysis-read-thoughts-60-minutes-2019-11-24, November 24, 2019, visited January 26, 2022

311. @elonmusk – Twitter, https://twitter.com/elonmusk/status/1281121339584114691, July 9, 2020

312. Monkey MindPong, by Neuralink, www.youtube.com/watch?v=rsCul1sp4hQ, April 9, 2021

313. How to measure brain activity in people, Queensland Brain Institute, The University of Queensland, https://qbi.uq.edu.au/brain/brain-functions/how-measure-brain-activity-people

314. Sid Kouider interviewed by Marques Browniee, https://youtu.be/MhKiMPiZOdE, April 16, 2021, visited January 26, 2022

315. Dr Mark van Rijmenam, The Future of Computing: How Brain-Computer Interfaces Will Change Our Relationship with Computers, The Digital Speaker, www.thedigitalspeaker.com/brain-computer-interfaces-change-relationship-computers, October 21, 2021, visited February 17, 2022

316. NextMind brings Brain-Computer Interface wearable to IAA Mobility, Business Wire, www.businesswire.com/news/home/20210909005669/en/NextMind-brings-Brain-Computer-Interface-wearable-to-IAA-Mobility, September 21, 2021, visited January 26, 2022

317. The Quest to Make a Digital Replica of Your Brain, by Grace Browne, Wired, www.wired.com/story/the-quest-to-make-a-digital-replica-of-your-brain, February 15, 2022, visited February 17, 2022

318. Gabe Newell says brain-computer interface tech will allow video games far beyond what human 'meat peripherals' can comprehend, by Luke Appleby, 1News, www.1news.co.nz/2021/01/25/gabe-newell-says-brain-computer-interface-tech-will-allow-video-games-far-beyond-what-human-meat-peripherals-can-comprehend, January 25, 2021, visited January 26, 2022

319. Tobii, Valve & OpenBCI Collaborate on 'Galea' VR Brain-Computer Interface, by Peter Graham, GMW3, www.gmw3.com/2021/02/tobii-valve-openbci-collaborate-on-galea-vr-brain-computer-interface, February 5, 2021, visited January 26, 2022

320. Gabe Newell says brain-computer interface tech will allow video games far beyond what human 'meat peripherals' can comprehend, by Luke Appleby, 1News, www.1news.co.nz/2021/01/25/gabe-newell-says-brain-computer-interface-tech-will-allow-video-games-far-beyond-what-human-meat-peripherals-can-comprehend, January 25, 2021, visited January 26, 2022

321. Valve psychologist explores controlling games directly with your brain, by Dean Takahashi, VentureBeat, https://venturebeat.com/2019/03/24/valve-psychologist-explores-controlling-games-directly-with-your-brain, March 24, 2019, visited January 26, 2022

322. Valve Founder Says Brain-Computer Interfaces Could One Day Replace Our 'Meat Peripherals', by Mike Fahey, Kotaku, https://kotaku.com/valve-founder-says-brain-computer-interfaces-could-one-1846124830, January 25, 2021, visited January 26, 2022

323. Tim Berners-Lee, Re-decentralizing the web: Some strategic questions, 2016. Available from: https://archive.org/details/DWebSummit2016_Keynote_Tim_Berners_Lee

324. The State of Online Harassment, Pew Research Center, www.pewresearch.org/internet/2021/01/13/the-state-of-online-harassment, January 13, 2021, visited January 26, 2022

325. Eminem – Lose Yourself. Album: 8 Mile – Music from and Inspired by the Motion Picture, 2002

326. Douglas Adams, (2002). *The Salmon of Doubt: Hitchhiking the Galaxy One Last Time* (Vol. 3). Harmony

327. Metaverse Marketing Podcast, EP08 as discussed by Jonathan Glick, www.adweek.com/category/metaverse-marketing-podcast

328. The 10 Principles of Burning Man, https://burningman.org/about/10-principles, visited January 28, 2022

Index

A

Aave, 131
abuse, in virtual worlds, 159–160
Activision Blizzard, 2, 149
Adams, Douglas, 180
Adidas, 60, 103–104
Alexa, 50, 178
Altberg, Ebbe, 68
AltspaceVR, 69, 70, 117
Amazon Web Services (AWS),
        42–43, 139
Ambinder, Mike, 177–178
Anheuser Busch InBev, 39–40, 93
Animaze, 55
anonymity, level of, 4
anonymous accountability, 29,
        167–168
AO Decades Collection, 79–80
Apple, 10, 96, 150
application programming interfaces
        (APIs), 19

AR glasses, 81–82, 113, 117
ARKit, 96, 150
ARPANET, 2–3, 47, 67
artificial intelligence (AI), biased,
        164–165, 170
augmented reality (AR), xxx, 1–2,
        10–12, 32–33, 36, 112–113
Australian Open, 79–80
AutoCAD models, 121
avatars, 47–55, 116, 160–161
Axie Infinity, 11, 25–26, 38–39, 71, 76,
        143, 148–149
Axie Scholarship Program, 149

B

Baby Boomers, xxvi
backward compatibility, 42
bad bots, 162–163
Bailenson, Jeremey, 8, 52, 85–86
Balenciaga, 55–58, 95
Ball, Matthew, 74

Banksy, 23–24
Bardeen, John, 1
Bartle, Richard, 67
Battle Royale, 79
Baumann, Thea-Mai, 5, 26
Beane, Billy, 78
Beeple, 136–137
Beginner's All-purpose Symbolic
    Instruction Code (BASIC), 2
Belamire, Jordan, 72
Berners-Lee, Tim, 3, 179
Beyond Sports, 78
biased AI, 164–165, 170
Big Tech, xxix, 3–4, 6, 16, 20, 21, 26, 36,
    39, 40, 42–43, 44–45, 53,
    76, 158, 162
Bitcoin blockchain, 21, 132
Bitcoin whitepaper, 6
Bitfinex, 132
black box, 28
Blender, 44, 73
blockchain, 6, 21, 75–76, 123, 140–141,
    166–167
*Blockchain: Transforming Your Business
    and Our World* (van Rijmenam
    and Ryan), 6
Bored Ape, 48, 65, 141
Bored Ape Yacht Club (BAYC), 47,
    103–104, 141–142
Boson Protocol, 58
bots, bad, 162–163
Brain-Computer Interfaces
    (BCIs), 175–178
BrainGate Consortium, 177
brand creativity
   beyond flash, 89–92
    creativity, community, and
       co-creation, 102–105
    experience marketing, 98–102
    power of immersive community,
       92–97
Brattain, Walter Houser, 1

Braun, Christian, 120
Burke, Jamie, 38, 39
Burning Man, 69–70
business-to-commerce (B2C) business
    models, 33

C
Cambrian Explosion, 65–66, 180
Cambridge Analytica, 4
Cassidy, Jason, 144
Cent, 142
Center for Countering Digital Hate, 159
Chalmers, David (author), *Reality+,* 127
Chaperone Attack, 161
Chen, Richard, 115
Chinese metaverse, 33
"The Cinema of the Future" (Heilig), 8
Clarke, Arthur C., 12
Cline, Ernest (author), *Ready Player
    One,* xxviii, 14
closed metaverse, open metaverse
    vs., 35–41
Clubhouse, 115
Coca-Cola, 100, 102
co-creation, creativity, community
    and, 102–105
Coinbase, 103–104
Colley, Steve, 47
community, 92–97, 102–105
community-driven data, 17, 25–26
Constitution DAO, 147
content moderation, 159–160
continuous insights, 95–96
Copeland, Nathan, 177
Cortana, 50
Covid-19 pandemic. *See* The Great
    Resignation
creativity, community, co-creation
    and, 102–105
cryptocurrency, 131–133, 151
cryptographic tokens, 136
CryptoKitties, 76, 134

CryptoPunks, 47, 48
CryptoVoxels, 70, 76
currency tokens, importance
        of, 133–138

D
data collection, 5
data security, 161–162
datafication, 157–158
datafying processes, xxvii
de Soto, Hernando, 129
de Vries, Alex, 132
Deadmau5, xxiv
Decentraland, 11, 14, 30, 43, 70, 75, 76,
        80, 92, 143, 144
decentralization, 17, 20–22, 129
decentralized application (dApp), 30
decentralized autonomous organization
        (DAO), xxiv, 22, 43, 126,
        131, 147–148
decentralized finance (DeFi), 150–153
Decentralized Web Summit, 179
Defense Advanced Research Projects
        Agency (DARPA), 2
Deliveroo, 63
Demos, Athena, 69
designing avatars, 50–51
digital assistants, 50
digital creator economy
    challenges of NFTs, 138–143
    from DeFi to MetaFi, 150–153
    digital real estate, 143–146
    economic mechanisms, 146–150
    importance of tokens, 133–138
    vibrancy of metaverse
        economy, 129–133
digital customer service agents, 116
digital fashion, 55–61, 62–63
digital humans. *See* avatars
Digital Markets Act (DMA), 3, 173
digital real estate, 143–146
Digital Services Act (DSA), 173

digital twins, 33, 117–125
digital wallets, 29, 40–41
digitalism
    dangers of the metaverse, 156–165
    neutrality of technology, 155–156
    surveillance or empowerment,
        171–174
    types of, 172–174
    verification, education, and regula-
        tion, 165–171
digital-to-physical (D2P) model, 62
Dimonn, Jamie, 91
direct-to-avatar (D2A) business
        models, 33, 62
Discord, 3, 115
Disorientation Attack, 161
Dolce, Domenico, 58
Dolce & Gabbana, 95
Dota2 Counterstrike, 79
Draper, Don, 89, 102
Dreem, 70
Dune, 142
Durr Burger, 95

E
Earth DAO, 131
Echo, 178
Echo Arena, 79
eCommerce, brands and, 90
economic system, 12, 38–39,
        44–46, 146–150
education, 83–86, 165–171
electroencephalography (EEG), 176
emerging technologies, 155–156
empowerment, surveillance or, 171–174
entertainment, in the metaverse, 80–83
Epic Games, 12, 56, 68, 121
Epyllion Industries, 74
eSports, 79
Estonia, 126
ether (ETH), 134
Ethereum blockchain, 21, 132, 133

European Space Agency (ESA), 119, 124–125
experience marketing, 98–102
Experience Theater, 8
exponential enterprise connectivity
   changing worlds, 107–109
   digital twins, 117–125
   future of immersive work, 110–117
   role of governments, 125–127
extended reality (XR), origins of, 11

F

The Fabricant, 58–59, 61, 104
Facebook, xii, 5, 8, 18, 36, 42–43, 74, 112, 117, 169–170
fan economy games, 76
fear of missing out (FOMO), 138
fiat currency, 133, 134
field of view (FOV), 8, 10
FileCoin, 42, 139
The First 5000 Days NFT, 136–137
5G, 15
flash, 89–92
Forever 21, 99–100, 104
Fortnite, xxiv, 11, 12, 14, 16, 19, 25–26, 38, 39, 47, 55–57, 70, 74–75, 76, 81, 95, 107, 137, 169
The Freedom Platform, 30–31, 32

G

Gabbana, Stefano, 58
Galea, 177
gaming, in the metaverse, 74–77
Gather Town platform, 114–115
General Data Protection Regulation (GDPR), 173
Generation Alpha, xxv–xxvi, xxviii, 62, 74, 91, 99, 104, 107, 180
Generation Z, xxv, xxviii, 62, 91, 99, 107, 108, 114, 180
Gill, Konrad, 65
Gill, Ryan, 44

Glass Suit, 58, 61
Glue, 113
Goldman, Benjamin Bertram, 68, 70
Google, 25, 36, 42–43, 150
Google ARCore, 10
Google Glasses, 9
governments, role of, 125–127
Graef, Ailin, 68, 71
Graphics Language Transmission Format (.g1TF) standard, 20
The Great Resignation, 108–109, 111
Griffin, Ken, 147
Grimes, 82
GrooveUp, 83
Gucci, 57–58, 94, 95, 98, 102, 137, 143

H

harassment, in virtual worlds, 159–160
health issues, 165
Heilig, Morton, "The Cinema of the Future," 8
Hejazi, Cameron, 142
Hewett, Paul, 112
Hewlett-Packard, 2
high-poly, 19
Hill, Montero Lamar (aka Lil Nas X), xxiii–xxiv
Hilton, Paris, xxiv
The Hitchhiker's Guide to the Galaxy (Adams), 180
H&M, 60
Hochberg, Justin, 98, 99
Homo Digitalis, 13
Horizon Workrooms, 113, 117
Horizon Worlds, 12, 70, 71–73, 112
Human Joystick Attack, 161
hybrid Web, 41–44
hyper-realistic avatars, 49–50
Hyper-Reality, 158

HyperText Markup
     Language (HTML), 3
Hypertext Transfer Protocol (HTTP), 3
Hyundai, 114

I
IBM, 118
identity, 27–28, 65–66
IKEA, 96, 137
illegal content, in virtual
     worlds, 159–160
Imagination Age, 12, 32, 87
immersive commerce (iCom-
     merce), 33, 62–64
immersive community, power of, 92–97
immersive experiences, future
     of, 175–178
immersive future
  about, 110–117
  as an ocean of opportunity, 31–34
  from AR to VR to XR, 8–12
  characteristics of metaverse, 17–31
  future of the metaverse, 12–17
  from Web 1.0 to Web 3.0, 1–7
immersive mind map, 113
immersive storytellers, 116
imposter avatars, 160–161
In Marketing We Trust, 112
inequality, increased, 162
Infinite Marketing Loop, 99
infodemic, 163
Information Age, 1
initial coin offering (ICO), 17
insights, continuous and real-
     time, 95–96
Institute for Liberty and
     Democracy, 129
Intel's True View technology, 78, 109
International Standards Organization
     (ISO), 19–20, 45
Internet of Things (IoT), 7, 32
internet service providers (ISPs), 141

interoperability, xii, 3, 17,
     18–20, 38–39, 45
InterPlanetary File System (IPFS),
     42, 139–140
Into the Metaverse campaign, 103–104

J
Jacobson, Doug, 69
job market, in the metaverse,
     114–116
John Deere, 111
JPMorgan Chase, 91

K
Kardashian, Kim, 55–56
Kentucky Derby, 92–93
Kerris, Richard, 125
KFC, 115
The Khronos Group, 19–20, 45–46
Kickstarter, 8
Kindle, 138
Klotz, Anthony, 108
know your customer (KYC), 29
Koster, Raph, 68
Kouider, Sid, 177
Kramer, Todd, 140
Kuo, Ming-Chi, 9
Kura, 10
Kura Gallium, 10

L
Larosse, Michaela, 59
League of Legends, 79
Lens Protocol, 131
Levels, Pieter, 109
Lichtenstein, Ilya, 132
Lil Nas X (aka Montero Lamar Hill),
     xxiii–xxiv
Linden Lab, 68
Listen to Earn concept, 82
Lovelace, Ada, 2

low-poly, 19
Luckey, Palmer, 8

M
Mad Men, 89–90
Magee, Charlie (designer and
       writer), 12
MagicLeap, 9, 10
Magnetic Resonance Imaging
       (MRI), 175–176
Man in the Room Attack, 161
Marshmello, 80–81
massive interactive live events (MILEs),
       xxv–xxvi
massive multiplayer online games
       (MMOs), xxv
massively multiplayer online role-
       playing games
       (MMPORGs), 25–26, 44
MazeWar, 47
McDonald's, 98, 102, 160
McInerney, Lindsey, 39–40, 63, 93
media, in the metaverse, 80–83
Medium, 40
Mesh, 14
Meta, xii, 5, 6, 12, 16, 26, 49, 70, 71–73,
       74, 147, 156
Meta Quest, 73
MetaBirkins, 142
MetaHuman, 28, 49, 160
MetaMask, 163
Metaverse
    about, x, xxv–xxxii
    characteristics of, 17–31
    dangers of the, 156–165
    digitalism in the, 155–174
    education in the, 83–86
    freedom of open, 30–31
    future of, 12–17
    future of the, 175–181
    gaming in the, 74–77

hybrid Web, 41–44
job market in, 114–116
journalists, 116
media and entertainment in, 80–83
open economic system, 44–46
open *vs.* closed, 35–41
security officers, 116
sports in the, 77–80
Metaverse Festival, xxiv
Metaverse Finance (MetaFi), 150–153
Metaverse Group, 144
Michele, Alessandro, 57
Microsoft, 2, 14, 49, 69, 70, 110, 149
Microsoft Azure, 42
Microsoft HoloLens, 9, 10
Microsoft Mesh, 61
Microsoft Teams, 108–109, 110, 117
Millennials, xxvi, 108, 114, 180
mind map, immersive, 113
Minecraft, 11, 19, 25–26, 47, 70, 74–75,
       76, 107, 114, 169
Mintable, 136, 141–142
Miro, 110, 113
Modern Digitalism, 173
monetization, 151
Morgan, Heather, 132
motion capture (mocap), 55
multiuser dungeon (MUD), 67–68
Musk, Elon, 14, 176

N
Nadella, Satya, 14
Nakamoto, Satoshi, 6
Napster, 90
NBA Top Shot, 76
Neo Digitalism, 173
NeosVR, 65, 113
Neuralink, 176
Neurotwin, 177
neutrality, of technology, 155–156
Newell, Gabe, 177–178

NextMind, 176, 177
Niantic, 70–71
Nickelodeon, 78
Nike, 15, 60–61, 102, 104
nonfungible tokens (NFTs)
    about, xxiv, xxvii
    Adidas, 103–104
    avatars and, 54
    Bored Ape Yacht Club
        (BAYC), 103–104
    challenges of, 138–143
    Coca-Cola, 100
    digital fashion and, 59
    fractional ownership of, 151
    importance of, 133–138
    linked to real-world assets, 152
    McDonald's, 98
    in media and entertainment,
        82–83
    proof of ownership and, 20
    smart contracts and, 22
    in sports, 79–80
    Taco Bell, 100
    transferability of, 39–40
    transformative power of, 12
nonplayer characters (NPCs).
        See avatars
North Korea, 40
NVIDIA, 124

O
Oasis Consortium, 171
occlusion, 9–10
Oculus, 8
Oculus Rift headset, 8
Olympic Games Jam: Beijing 2022, 79
Omniverse platform, 124
One Laptop per Child project, 85
open economic system, 44–46
open metaverse, closed metaverse
        vs., 35–41

Open Metaverse Association, 44
OpenBCI, 177
OpenMind, 176
OpenSea marketplace, 100, 136, 138,
        139–140, 141–142, 163
Outlier Ventures, x, 38, 151
Overlay Attack, 161

P
Palmer, Howard, 47
Parker, Kimberly, 138
People-Reign, 171
permissioned and public virtual
        worlds, 37
permissionless and public virtual
        worlds, 37
persistency, of data, 16, 17, 22–24
personal nature, of data and identity, 16
pet games, 76
Phunky Ape Yacht Club
        (PAYC), 141–142
phygital experiences, 15, 59, 179
physical-to-digital (P2D) model, 62
Pizza Pit, 95
Place app (IKEA), 96
platform POAP, 40
play to earn model, 148–150
Play-to-Learn, 86
Pokémon Go, 14, 70–71, 77
polarization, increased, 163–164
polygons, 49
portability, of data and identity, 16
Portal, 83
privacy, 16, 158
private spaces, 37
programming languages, 2
Proof of Attendance (PoA) NFT,
        xxiv, 39–40
proof of human, 168
proof of ownership, 20
proof of stake blockchains, 132

proof of work blockchains, 132
protected nature, of data and
        identity, 16
Proteus effect, 52
protocols and standards, 45–46

Q
Quest, 49
QuiVr, 71–71

R
Rabobank, 147
Rarible, 136, 141–142
Ratan, Rabindra, 50
Ready Player Me platform, 49, 51, 53
Ready Player One, xxviii, 14, 35, 55,
        67, 164, 165
real estate, digital, 143–146
Reality+ (Chalmers), 127
Reallusion, 73
Reallusion Character Creator 4, 28, 49
real-time insights, 95–96
regulation, verification, education
        and, 165–171
remote work, 13, 108–109
Ribas, Moon, 15
Rice, Robert, 145
Roblox, xxiii–xxiv, 11, 49, 57, 61, 65, 70,
        74–75, 94, 95, 99–100, 104, 107,
        114, 130, 147, 169
Rosedale, Philip, 144
Rothschild, Mason, 142
Royal.io, 82
RTFKT, 60–61, 104
Ryan, Philippa (author), *Blockchain:
        Transforming Your Business
        and Our World,* 6

S
The Salmon of Doubt (Adams), 180
Samsung, 92, 114
Samsung Electronics, 115

sandbox games, 76
The Sandbox, 30, 49, 61, 65, 70, 75, 76,
        103–104, 143, 144
Second Life, 68, 71, 144, 145
security tokens, importance of,
        133–138
self-sovereignty, 17, 26–29, 53
sell-on clause, 136
Sensorama, 8
Shockley, William Bradford, 1
show-offs, 138
Signal, 18
Siri, 50, 178
Slack, 110
SLP tokens, 148
smart contracts, 21–22
Snap, 96–97, 177
Snaps Spectacles AR, 10
Snow Crash (Stephenson), xxviii,
        68, 164, 165
social media platforms,
        decentralized, 37
Social.network, 131
The Social Dilemma (film), 164
Solice, 11, 70, 77
Somnium Space, 11, 43, 70, 77, 145
South Korean Career Football
        Association, 121
Space Bugs art project, 115
spatial audio engineers, 116
Spatial.io, 145–146
spatiality, of data, 17, 24–25
speculators, 138
Spice DAO, 142
sports, in the metaverse, 77–80
Spotify, 137–138
Stanford Virtual Human Interaction
        Lab (VHIL), 85–86
Starlink, 14
State Digitalism, 173
Status.im, 40
Steem.it, 40
Stella Artois, 92–93

Stephenson, Neal (author), *Snow Crash,*
 xxviii, 68, 164, 165
Storj, 42, 139
Stream-to-Earn concept, 83
Strivr, 85–86
Subspace, 15
surveillance, empowerment or, 171–174
Sussman, Adam, 56
sustainability, increased, 96–97

T
Taco Bell, 100
technology, neutrality of, 155–156
Telegram, 18, 115
Tesla, 120
TeslaSuit, 55
Thompson, Greg, 47
3D avatars, 48–49
3D computer graphics, 74
3D content, 15
3D virtual entertainers, 116
TikTok, 36, 73
Tõke, Timmu, 49, 53
tokens, importance of, 133–138. *See
 also* nonfungible tokens (NFTs)
Tommy Jeans, 96–97
touchpoints, 94–95
Towfiq, Bayan (CEO), 15
transistor, invention of, 1
Trevett, Neil, 19–20, 46
Trubshaw, Roy, 67
"try-before-you-buy" virtual
 experiences, 96
Turchin, Dan, 171
2032 story, xiv–xxii
Twitch, 95
Twitter, 48, 54, 56, 137, 161
2D avatars, 53
2D content, 15

U
Uber, 116
Uber Eats, 63

uncanny valley of the mind concept, 50
Uniform Resource Identifier (URI), 3
unique selling points (USPs), 94–95
Uniswap, 148
Unity, 9, 44, 73
Unreal Engine, 9, 44, 49, 68,
 73, 121, 160
Unreal Engine's MetaHuman
 Creator, 28
UNSTUDIO, 121
Upland, 75
US Securities and Exchange
 Commission (SEC), 136
user experience (UX), of Web 3.0, 40
user-generated content (UGC), 72,
 130
utility tokens, importance of, 133–138
Utopia, 75

V
Valve, 177–178
Valve Index, 177
van Rijmenam, Mark (author), xi
 *Blockchain: Transforming Your
 Business and Our World,* 6
Varjo, 120
verification, education, regulation
 and, 165–171
Virtual Brand Group, 98, 99
virtual reality (VR), xxx, 1–2, 8–9,
 11–12, 32–33, 36,
 83–86, 112–113
virtual shopping assistants, 116
virtual travel agents, 116
virtual worlds, 67–73, 97
visualization, 121
Volvo Cars, 120
VR headsets, 113–114, 117
VRChat, 49, 159

W
walled gardens, 4–5, 12, 36, 38
Walt Disney, 93, 130

Wang, Tiffany Xingyu, 171
Warner Bros, 160
Warner Music Group, 90
wearable BCIs, 176–177
wearables, 55–61
Web 1.0, 1–7
Web 2.0, xi, xxviii–xxix, 5, 6
Web 3.0 technology, xi, 1–7, 26,
        37, 40, 41–44
Wendys, 95, 103
WhatsApp, 18, 40
Wilder World, 30
Wolf3D, 49
WordPress, 42–43, 73
work from anywhere mode, 109, 126
World Wide Web, 3

X
XR Safety Initiative, 157

Y
Yee, Nick, 52

Z
Zara, 60–61
Zepeto, 114–115
zero-knowledge proof (ZKP),
        167
Zirlin, Jeff, 149
Zoom, 15, 108–109, 110, 112
Zuckerberg, Mark, xii, 5, 8, 18, 117,
        147, 156, 180